"A delightful and enlightening journey into the woods...Lewis treads so softly, with wit and color, with care and passion, in an intimate exploration of how nature's magnificent expressions hold enormous capacity to inspire."

HARLEY RUSTAD, author of *Big Lonely Doug*

"A gorgeous manifesto for plotting a different course entirely. The timing of this book—with its wide roots and radical shoots—is just right."

KYO MACLEAR, author of *Birds Art Life*

"A thought-provoking and very funny tromp through the understory...Lewis writes with exquisite perceptiveness about living well in an age of superlative pursuits, about timeless joy discovered beneath some of the earth's last ancient canopies."

CHARLOTTE GILL, author of *Eating Dirt*

"Absolutely engrossing...Lewis is the perfect hiking companion!"

LYNDSIE BOURGON, author of *Tree Thieves*

"Generous, self-deprecating, and wise, this entertaining, informative, and inspiring book shows us that if a tree grows or falls in the forest, we need to listen."

GARY BARWIN, author of *Yiddish for Pirates*

"Lewis gets that good stories are like wild forests: impossible to classify, and awfully fun to get lost in."

ARNO KOPECKY, author of *The Environmentalist's Dilemma*

"I'd follow Lewis into the woods any day for more hilarious misadventures of a big-tree hunter...*Tracking Giants* left me enchanted, informed, and chuckling."

ADRIA VASIL, author of the Ecoholic series

"A book of arboreal delights, wisdoms, and many voices that reminds us of the value of slowing down and learning how to see the forest for the trees."

TRINA MOYLES, author of *Lookout*

"A towering forest-bath of a book, lush with insight, humor, and wisdom on living a happy, interconnected life. I loved this book!"

CAROL SHABEN, author of *Into the Abyss*

"Fresh, funny, and bursting with vivid detail...This is a quest that questions quests, a journey through forests of the land and mind—and one hell of a good time in the woods that we all depend on."

J. B. MACKINNON, author of *The Day the World Stops Shopping*

Tracking GIANTS

Big Trees, Tiny Triumphs, and Misadventures in the Forest

AMANDA LEWIS

FOREWORD BY **DR. DIANA BERESFORD-KROEGER**

GREYSTONE BOOKS
Vancouver/Berkeley/London

Greystone Books Ltd.
greystonebooks.com

Cataloguing data available from Library and Archives Canada
ISBN 978-1-77164-673-4 (pbk.)
ISBN 978-1-77164-674-1 (epub)

Editing by Paula Ayer
Copy editing by Crissy Calhoun
Proofreading by Alison Strobel
Cover design and composite by Belle Wuthrich
Cover and interior composite illustration credits (Shutterstock): Yuriy2012,
Les Perysty, Lex Sky, Chlorophyll, krusto, lestyan, Artem Musaev
Text design by Belle Wuthrich
All photographs courtesy of
Amanda Lewis except page 28 © Shaun Muc
Lyrics from "Ann the Word" © 2017 Beauty Pill,
used with permission of Chad Clark

Printed and bound in Canada on FSC® certified paper at Friesens.
The FSC® label means that materials used for the product
have been responsibly sourced.

MIX
Paper from
responsible sources
FSC
www.fsc.org   FSC® C016245

BRITISH COLUMBIA

BRITISH COLUMBIA
ARTS COUNCIL
An agency of the Province of British Columbia

Canada Council   Conseil des arts
for the Arts   du Canada

Greystone Books gratefully acknowledges the xʷməθkʷəy̓əm (Musqueam), Sḵwx̱wú7mesh (Squamish), and səlílwətaʔɬ (Tsleil-Waututh) peoples on whose land our Vancouver head office is located.

This book is a personal memoir of big-tree tracking. Searching for trees carries risk, as does any excursion into a remote or wooded area, even an urban forest. The author, publisher, and distributors accept no liability for any loss, damage, injury, or death arising from reading this book. Always check trail and weather conditions, and consult your own big-tree registry (if available) for coordinates, updates, and safety information before heading out.

For my family, large and small

You do one thing and then you do another
And you lay out the life you own.

BEAUTY PILL, "Ann the Word"

For the second time on the expedition I doubted
my own sanity. Rum Doodle was 40,000½ feet high.
Unless either my barometer or myself was mad,
we were at 35,000. What could have happened?

Then I saw. Over to the east a magnificent mountain stood
against the sky, its glittering summit 5,000 feet above me.

We had climbed the wrong mountain.

W. E. BOWMAN, *The Ascent of Rum Doodle*

Contents

Foreword

TREES AND THEIR COMMUNITIES, the global forests, set the limits for life on planet Earth—a delicate balance. They represent a unique form of vascular evolution, based on a simple switch of two base molecules. This process is not well understood in science, even today, yet its results are startling: a tree is born. Against all odds, some will survive to attain a terrific size. These ancient trees are true giants, seeming to preach from a different pulpit in the same manner as the great whales. The size and wisdom of these creatures can only be greeted by awe and absolute silence: the impossible *is* possible.

To seek out and catalog these giants is the starting point of Amanda Lewis's delightful book. Yet, as she soon discovers, trees are changing, living creatures with unexpected lessons to teach us. They defy simple checking off a list.

All trees are remarkable, big or small. A tree can run a bead of water uphill against the force of gravity to have safe, successful sex. A tree can exchange carbon "coinage" with a sibling tree and even to a stranger, a barter system that feeds the living soil. Trees and forests regulate the harmony of the food foundation of the oceans. They liberate plumes of aerosol molecules from glandular tissue to initiate the creation of weather patterns in the atmosphere. Every tree is an ace at quantum mechanics through a universal reaction called photosynthesis, of carbon capture and oxygen release. Trees farm the sun, feasting on photons as free energy. Leaves have the ability to listen with their gibbane "hearing aids." A tree's vertical carbon bulk alone can generate the communication of infrasound, or silent sound. Forests negate the albedo effect, stabilizing the northern jet stream.

Human encroachment and greed have taken their toll on our great forests. Yet the West Coast of Canada and the United States is still relatively rich in green giants—feral finds that remind us of the wonders of biodiversity. This is where Amanda captures the imagination. Her mission becomes not only to track these remaining giant trees but to meet them person to person: to stand before the green mirror of a tree and see what it reflects. In meeting these giants as individuals, she comes to understand them—and herself—as intricately entwined with their environment and with other living creatures.

Hidden within the folds of these trees is something unexpected. Giant trees, because of their age, carry very complex medicines, bled out from endogenous fungi that inhabit them. These medicinal molecules have the flexibility to shield the human body against disease as well as potentially hold the cures for many illnesses. This alone puts another kind of moral value on protecting these forest giants.

Nature, like poetry, needs constant creation from a new set of eyes. Amanda begins her endeavor as a novice tree tracker, learning about the West Coast forest. She is an ideal guide, bringing the reader along on her journey of discovery with warmth, wit, and curiosity. We are lucky that she has come out of her leafy glade to teach us all by tracking these giants. This is the real gift of nature for each generation: it opens a lifeline of learning, which in turn leads to connection and on to conservation. Out of conservation, protection arises like a phoenix from the ashes of our ignorance. And the delicate balance returns.

DR. DIANA BERESFORD-KROEGER

Author's Note

IN WHICH I GET AWAY WITH IT

THIS BOOK IS ABOUT searching for Champion trees, the largest known trees of their species. Finding Champion trees is like squeezing Jell-O. It seems that just when you locate a Champion, someone finds a bigger tree. Or the Champion dies or is reduced in size due to disease, wind, or fire, and you're left looking for the runner-up to take the crown. The Champions in this book reflect their status at the time I looked for them, and they might no longer be the record holders.

I have included the sizes of the trees when last measured, and as the BC Big Tree Registry uses the metric system, I have included their sizes in meters. (If you have trouble visualizing in meters, multiply by three to get a rough conversion to feet.) But as you will quickly find out, this book is less about quantifying and more about determining what we lose when we pursue bigness at the expense of small joys.

I am a settler and a guest in these lands, the unceded and traditional territories of numerous Indigenous Peoples who have distinct cultures and languages. As I looked for trees, I attempted to learn about their many uses by Indigenous Peoples and settlers alike. I've included some of that information here when it was readily available in guidebooks, rather than drawing on Traditional Knowledge without consent. I received permission from Dr. Luschiim Arvid Charlie and Dr. Nancy J. Turner to use material from *Luschiim's Plants*. I selected this guidebook as my main source on Indigenous uses of plants as it's wonderful and authoritative, and it contains information relevant to Cowichan Tribes, whose territory covers many of the places mentioned in this text.

The notion of trees being "found" or "discovered" is problematic, and I discuss the point in chapter 5, but for ease I have sometimes used the verbs in my accounts of looking for trees. I have also obscured some details about trees' precise locations out of cultural and ecological respect. Throughout the text, I have referred to lands under provincial jurisdiction as Crown lands.

This book is largely chronological, though I have occasionally taken liberties with the timeline, moving some tree trips so they better fit the narrative. I sometimes made repeat attempts on a tree over several months or returned to take measurements or GPS coordinates. I have condensed those visits to fit the narrative. I have also not included all the tree trips I took. You get the idea.

— 1 —

Norvan's Castle

WESTERN HEMLOCK

"An expedition that begins badly usually ends well."
STEVE O'SHEA

"THESE *FUCKING* TREES."

I spat the words as I turned slowly, peering into the brush around me. Salmonberry and sword ferns edged in on the narrow mountainside trail, crisscrossed with exposed roots. The trail had been slowly worn by hikers, deer, and larger creatures I hoped I wouldn't encounter. Douglas-fir and hemlock boughs draped above us, their dark green needles offering shade from the midday sun. The reflective tape on my bear spray holder, shoved in a water bottle compartment on the side of my red backpack, was a beacon in the low light. Sweat stuck my striped cotton T-shirt to my back and I wheezed like a poured kettle.

My boyfriend, Jason, and I had just climbed most of the way up Coliseum Mountain, a mound of granite in the North Shore range, a subrange of the Coast Mountains. Across the Burrard Inlet from Vancouver, the North Shore Mountains are a popular hiking, skiing, and biking destination. They're a beautiful vista, helping to drive up the cost of real estate in one of the

1

world's most expensive cities. But only a twenty-minute drive from downtown, these mountains are deceptively accessible and notoriously dangerous—easy to lose the path, slip on a rock or log, tumble off a ledge, or be caught unprepared for a rapid change in temperature. Hikers go missing every summer, the lucky ones rescued or wandering out themselves, the unlucky succumbing to the elements or their injuries.

We were in Lynn Headwaters Regional Park, usually referred to as Lynn Valley, on the unceded territories of the Tsleil-Waututh and Squamish Nations. The trail we were hiking on that August weekend was rated as difficult and usually closed from October to early summer. An emerald slice between mountains, Lynn Valley is packed on the weekend with hikers and trail runners, who usually follow Lynn Creek to Norvan Falls, a low waterfall cutting around boulders, but don't venture up Coliseum as it presents a full day of trekking. The Lynn Creek trail was beaten and wide, and logging remnants rested alongside it: rusted buckets, wagon wheels, metal cables. The nature of the trail itself indicated logging; in these temperate forests, when you're walking on a straight trail, rather than meandering around big trees or land features, you're generally on what was once a skid road, a corduroy path lined horizontally with greased logs to facilitate an ox or horse team pulling carts loaded with huge trees. Slender trees of a single species valuable to the timber industry, say Douglas-fir, growing tightly beside the path are also signs of logging and replanting.

After hiking for two hours along the creek-side trail, Jason and I had turned onto the path for Coliseum and climbed another hour up a dry slope strewn with boulders and huge stumps. Lower Lynn Valley is an exceptionally fertile site and used to be thick with majestic western red-cedars and Douglas-firs, some with a diameter of four to five meters, but many were cut down when the area was logged between 1920 and 1928. One, the Lynn Valley Tree, was the tallest known coastal Doug-fir in 1902; it measured more than 122 meters in length—after it had been cut down.

On our ascent, we slipped in the dense duff—rotting bark, needles, and twigs—grabbing hold of roots and logs to steady us. "Much up!" Jason said as we clung to the slope, catching our breath. Vertical advancement seemed to be a common theme of our pastimes: indoor bouldering, hiking. Jason was always up for what I was up for, and I was usually up for folly.

He had been in a foul mood when we set out that morning, upset about some work drama, and I hadn't slept much the night before, the plight of the anxious insomniac. But as we settled into our time on the trail, the exercise, fresh air, and the act of searching for something outside ourselves made us feel happier. It also might have been the aerosols from the trees, which have a healing effect on the mind and body, soothing us despite the climb. The trail up was dusty and laden with exposed rock, without much undergrowth, but where the path leveled out, the air became cooler and moister. We were met with a rich understory of salal, ferns, and thimbleberries. A mix of old-growth cedar, Doug-fir, and hemlock towered over us. I wondered if the logging had stopped here because it would have been too much work to haul trees any farther.

I stood akimbo and surveyed the forest, catching my breath. On one side of the trail, a steep slope, lined with rocky debris from an avalanche years earlier, led down to a tranquil blue-green pool fed by a stream and waterfall. Farther along the trail was an alpine meadow with wildflowers and, beyond that, the top of Coliseum. It was goddamn bucolic, but there was no time to stop for a dip in the mountain pool. I hadn't scrambled my way up here to find tranquility on the mountain. As Norman Maclean writes in *A River Runs Through It*, "You can't catch fish if you don't dare go where they are."

I was hunting big trees. My quarry, the Champion western hemlock in British Columbia, was supposed to be about fifty feet away from the trail on a gently sloping incline. This trip was my third time looking for this Champion, the largest known tree of its species in the province. Two previous times that year, I'd tried but had to turn around due to poor weather and trail conditions.

In theory, I couldn't miss the tree: it was last measured in 1999 at 45.7 meters tall with a diameter at breast height (DBH) of 3.05 meters. That's about the height of four telephone poles and the width of two pool cues, end to end. This western hemlock is the fourth biggest known anywhere, and it has the widest DBH ever recorded. I'd jotted down the measurements from the BC Big Tree Registry, an online database that records the sizes and locations of significant native trees. My notes indicated that the western hemlock's top had fallen off but that it had five or six new leaders (the thickest, uppermost branches) forming a candelabra shape at the top—imagine several flexed Popeye arms extending off the trunk. I hadn't found recent photos of the tree online, and it was anyone's guess whether it was still standing.

In this way, tree tracking is different from, say, mountaineering. One extreme mountaineering goal is to summit the fourteen peaks that are eight-thousand-plus-meters above sea level, all located in the Himalayan and Karakoram ranges. While climbing each eight-thousand-meter peak is exceedingly difficult and often deadly, at least it is possible to keep score of your successes and failures; the mountains remain largely intact for millennia, and there are no undiscovered eight-thousand-meter peaks to add to the list. But trees are mortal: they keep growing, and they are susceptible to fire, drought, wind, and insects. You can find a Champion only to have your achievement erased when that tree dies or is replaced by a larger specimen. Looking for Champion trees is like trying to count toddlers in a ball pit.

I'd been on the trail of Champion trees for over a year by this point and hadn't had anything to show for many months. I could measure a tree's circumference and its crown spread (if I had a buddy to hold the other end of the tape for me), but I was still sketchy on how to measure the height. I could tell trees apart—a cedar versus a Douglas-fir, for example—but I needed to look up other characteristics, such as the bark or seed cones, to determine if it was a yellow- or red-cedar. Western hemlock is the most common tree on the West Coast, but despite having grown up here, I had never paid it a moment's notice before now, preferring to gaze upon what I deemed the more beautiful trees: arbutus (called madrone or madrona in the U.S.), cedar, Doug-fir. From field guides and hasty internet searches, I had a fairly good idea of what western hemlocks looked like: lace-like branches, flat needles, and small seed cones. They were easy to pick out when looking at a tree line, as their flopsy leader usually drooped over whereas the similar-looking Doug-firs stood erect. But this far in the woods, all I could see was a wall of green as I looked for a single tree in a forest, the proverbial needle in a haystack.

We were standing near where the tree was supposed to be, still on the path lest we begin traipsing willy-nilly through the bushes. I spun in circles on the trail, staring into the forest then blankly at the GPS before handing it over to Jason, the Keeper of Gadgets. The term *bending the map* describes our bias toward trusting our own immediate perception rather than a representation, making us believe we're somewhere we're not. The map says a stream should be here, but rather than deducing we're in the wrong place, we assume the stream has dried up or naturally diverted itself. As adventurer Wade Ellett writes, people "look at the map and the world around them, and if these don't match, they start forcing them to agree." This form of confirmation bias, which often presents as not believing the map, GPS, or compass, is a surefire way to get lost.

I scrambled down the rock chute toward the pond to gain a better vantage of tall trees. "I know they said the tree is above the trail, but maybe they were wrong," I called up to Jason. "Maybe they're out to get me?"

"Everyone's arrayed against Amanda Lewis," he said, his bright blue eyes sparkling in the dappled light.

Jason preferred to work through problems methodically, while I bounced between hope and possibility. He reads IKEA instructions first; I glance at a recipe's ingredients and improvise as I go along. Allowing for an error of two hundred meters, Jason triangulated me to where he believed the Champion to be and called out to me to come back up. I ascended the chute and ventured into the dark forest alone while Jason remained on the path. The registry notes had indicated the tree was near the chute, so I used that sweep of rocks as a guide. A piece of weathered pink flagging tape on a roughly eye-level branch caught the light and drew me deeper off trail. "Thank you, tree-tracking stranger," I muttered.

The Champion didn't so much appear out of the forest as loom solidly in place, standing in a small clearing of its own making. Several smaller but no less impressive hemlocks grew nearby, surrounded by salmonberry and salal. Like a raccoon, I clambered along a mossy log toward the Champion, being careful not to step in its rotting cavities. Logs like this, as well as stumps, are prime places for hemlock seedlings to take hold above the forest floor. Once I was at the tree's base, I called

With Norvan's Castle, the Champion western hemlock in BC

back to Jason, who came in to take some photos for the registry. Christine Chourmouzis, the registrar, had asked me to take measurements and coordinates of all trees I visited; the registry encourages community scientists to gather directions, coordinates, photos, and measurements.

I stared into the tree's crown, its thick leaders jutting out, and placed my hand on its flaky reddish-brown bark. Ants ran along the furrows of bark draped with mint-green lichen and feathery moss. It took me about twelve seconds to carefully step around the tree's base, my boots angled on its duff skirt. From its immense size and its location up a mountain—where it is less likely to succumb to damage from wind or disease—I guessed this Champion was likely more than three hundred years old. Time stopped as the light filtered through its needles and captured dust motes in the air. I tried to imagine what legendary big-tree tracker Randy Stoltmann had thought when he'd found this tree in 1993. He'd nicknamed it Norvan's Castle, after the nickname for North Vancouver, and what big-tree tracker Robert Van Pelt called the tree's "multiple tops and overall very complex architecture."

"So... here you are!" I've always been great at introductions. After two false starts, I could finally access some of this huge tree's centuries-old wisdom, the intelligence that comes from staying in one place and committing oneself to nothing but growth. Hearing a vague humming, I pressed my ear to the bark, listening for the commotion of insects, even the sound of the tree itself. Then I noticed the passenger jet flying above me, its vibrations cutting through the canopy.

I wrote "tree" on the tattered flagging tape, in the hope it would aid other trackers, and we began our knee-knocking descent. With another Champion crossed off my list, even the long hike out didn't feel all that arduous, or the abrasions on our arms from protruding roots and pointed stumps too bothersome. Back at my car, I punched the air a few times in triumph and entered reflections on the day in my notebook, *Carpe Fucking Diem* sprawled across the cover in gold-foil cursive.

"Oh, I am delighted!" I said, as we drove out of the parking lot and down the tree-lined access road.

"You needed a win," Jason said.

"I can't wait to tell the registrar. She'll be so impressed." From what I could tell from online searches, no one had been up to visit the tree in years.

Jason and I celebrated with snacks at the bougie general store at the entrance to the park. He brushed needles from his chestnut hair, and we cheersed our ginger beer and kombucha. Once home, I showered and unpacked my tree-tracking kit, shaking out pieces of bark. Then I emailed Christine with my description of the tree and its coordinates, Jason's photos, and what I hoped were clearer directions.

That night, lying in bed in East Vancouver, I thought about the western hemlock on the mountain, growing taller and thicker in the dark, a quiet flourishing over centuries. The waterfall would be trickling into the cool pond, branches moving under starlit skies, animals shuffling through the undergrowth. The tree was a quiet image for me as I drifted off to sleep.

ABOUT FIVE WEEKS LATER, I heard back from Christine. "Can you please look under settings and tell me what datum the GPS is set to?" she replied. "It is actually quite important that we record this. The different systems can place trees *many* meters off. Anytime you determine lat and long, we need to record in the database the datum used when the co-ords were determined... Thanks for recording them, writing the access notes, and taking the photos!" Ira Sutherland, the chair of the BC Big Tree Committee, on cc, piped in to agree with Christine on the importance of the datum.

Huh? I consulted with Jason. Either the GPS coordinates were about two hundred meters off course in the first place, or our GPS was uncalibrated. As with a compass, you need to first calibrate your GPS so it knows where you are, but I didn't know how to use a compass or GPS, or that there was a datum let alone what it was.

"Did you remeasure this tree?" Christine wrote. "It hasn't been measured since 1999...that was a long time ago!!!!!"

My pride deflated. I generally measure trees when I find them, using diameter tape bought at a forestry supply store, but on this occasion I'd simply wanted to appreciate the tree, which had taken so long to find. I'd eyeballed the tree and satisfied myself with the measurement: *That tree looks pretty big.* Jason had coined my nonscientific way of measuring the Lewis Qualitative Assessment of Bigness. It's a binary assessment: this tree is big, that tree not so much. It also conveniently avoids miscalculating measurements; as every perfectionist knows, if you don't try, you can't fail. In his book *Show Your Work!*, artist Austin Kleon writes, "Amateurs know that contributing something is better than contributing nothing." That might be true, except when you're contributing data that might steer other big-tree hunters wrong. The registry is run by passionate, kind volunteers who love trees, but it lives and dies by its data. And data has never been my strong point.

"I didn't measure the tree," I wrote, wondering if my groan was coming across. "Long story. I'm planning to go up again in the fall/spring. I'll send you new measurements when I have them." It was my attempt to save face, though I didn't really have an excuse. Now that I could prove the health and location of the tree, perhaps a more competent tree tracker could return to take accurate measurements. Going back would mean I'd have to devote another weekend to a tree I'd already found, which would mean I'd need to delay finding another Champion on my long list.

The quiet tree began to softly laugh.

— 2 —

The Seed

SILVER MAPLE

"There is nothing that I may decently hope for that
I cannot reach by patience as well as by anxiety."
WENDELL BERRY, "A Native Hill"

I WAS GRATEFUL TO my friend Kate for not using the word *boring* to describe my original idea. In late May 2018, I texted her: "I'm thinking of starting a blog to commemorate one year living back in Vancouver. Maybe capture some of the hikes I'm making to local mountains and parks. Whaddya think?"

Kate responded swiftly: "Well, I just read a galley that mentions the BC Big Tree Registry. Why don't you visit all the Champion trees!"

Kate Harris, or, as her friends call her, Adventure Kate (AK for short), is an intrepid adventurer and author of the bestselling book *Lands of Lost Borders*, about cycling from Istanbul to India with her best friend, Mel Yule. We'd become friends through working on her book together; she had seen an article I'd written about environmental stewardship in a publishing magazine and knew I was destined to be her book editor. The galley (a copy of a soon-to-be-published book) Kate had read was Harley Rustad's *Big Lonely Doug*, about a 66-meter-tall Douglas-fir growing near Port Renfrew on Vancouver Island. Big Lonely Doug is the second-biggest Doug-fir in Canada. (The Red Creek Fir in San Juan Valley, near Port Renfrew, is the largest by volume.)

The BC Big Tree Registry was the brainchild of an activist and mountaineer named Randy Stoltmann. With his brother, Greg, he had long explored Lynn Valley and other significant forests of southwestern BC, keeping informal records of the big trees he saw. Stoltmann wrote three books about BC's wild areas, including two hiking guides for finding big trees, and his name is appropriately repeated in reverent tones by big-tree trackers to this day. Stoltmann was a member of the conservation group Western Canada Wilderness Committee (since rebranded as the Wilderness Committee), and he campaigned to save the ancient forests of the Carmanah Valley on the west coast of Vancouver Island, where he searched for big Sitka spruces in the 1980s. Motivated by the goal of conservation through documentation, he launched the registry in 1986 with the BC Forestry Association. The BC Big Tree Registry grew from a desire to know what was left on the southwest coast of Vancouver Island in the wake of industrial logging throughout the twentieth century. Beginning with the Meares Island protests in 1984 and the Lyell Island (Haida Gwaii) protests in 1985, in which seventy-two Haida were arrested, more national and international attention was being paid to the big trees of this temperate rainforest.

There are big-tree registries around the world, but the BC registry is significant in that it's a catalog of the standouts in a landscape already known for its amazing trees. The trees in BC's coastal rainforest regularly reach record-breaking heights and widths thanks to the combination of immense rainfall and a mild climate, and humans have had a long interaction with them.

First Nations have relied on forests throughout the province since time immemorial, for housing, clothing, canoes, and food. Trees are inseparable from Indigenous cultures on the coast,

with significance appointed to western red-cedar in particular;
First Nations harvest cedar for ceremonial masks, longhouses,
and commemorative poles. European colonizers saw the potential of the forests as revenue generators and immediately began
cutting them, using the wood for ship masts, as well as housing
and firewood in the new cities. Big trees literally paved the way
for settlers: Vancouver, Victoria, and other cities that developed
alongside the logging industry were originally paved in cut ends
of lumber soaked in creosote. Over time, selective hand-logging
gave way to large-scale industrial logging, characterized by
clear-cuts. Advancements in logging technology plus a demand
for timber and a belief that forests were an eternally renewable resource led to much of the old-growth forests in BC being
cleared throughout the twentieth century.

The BC government uses *old-growth* to refer to the age of
the trees, and the forest does not need to be "virgin" to qualify:
a site that was logged and replanted could still qualify if it's
old enough. To the casual observer of BC's forests, though, old-
growth goes beyond age to denote an ancient layered ecosystem
with a rich understory and canopy supporting diverse life-
forms—black bears denning in the bases of huge trees, screech
owls living in cavities, and pileated woodpeckers feeding on
insects under the bark. Second-growth forests lack the diversity
of old-growth forests and, when planted together closely to meet
stocking standards, don't allow a lot of light to filter through to
support the understory.

What most people think of when they think of original old-
growth—the largest trees, some over a thousand years old—is
now contained in small pockets of the province, such as valley
bottoms in the southwestern portion of Vancouver Island and
atop mountains like Coliseum in North Vancouver. But there
is old-growth all along the coast, in the inlets, as well as in the

Interior Wet Belt. Many of the biggest trees have already been registered, and historical records (and stumps) show many more have been logged. Stoltmann's registry was intended to capture the remaining big trees and record even bigger trees that might be out there.

Tragically, Stoltmann died in a mountaineering accident in May 1994 at age thirty-one. A grove in the newly formed Carmanah Walbran Provincial Park was named after him to honor his efforts in saving these trees; protecting land as a provincial park is one of the best legal and lasting ways to preserve big trees. After his death, the physical records, including photographs and maps, went missing, but a report he had made for the BC Conservation Data Centre, compiling a lot of the records, endured. The report, along with two bankers boxes of jumbled nomination sheets and photos, was handed between government agencies until 2010, when forest ecologist Andy MacKinnon brought the records to the University of British Columbia's Faculty of Forestry. There, professor Sally Aitken and the newly formed Big Tree Committee, in particular Christine Chourmouzis, sorted and digitized the records, launching the online registry in 2014. The committee now maintains the registry, supported by UBC Forestry.

The registry keeps lists of the largest deciduous trees, largest coniferous trees, and the Champion trees—the largest trees on both lists. Fred Besley, a state forester of Maryland, originated the idea of Champions in 1925, in response to big trees being logged out in his state. Champions are assessed using a score calculated by points assigned to crown, height, and circumference, which is used to find the diameter of the trunk at breast height. The registry can be sorted by total tree score, DBH, height, or crown—that way, you can search for the tallest Douglas-fir or the Douglas-fir with the biggest DBH. And while both would be big, it's possible that neither would be the Champion; Champions are based on total tree score. Not all Champion trees are giants; they are considered big compared to others in their species. A Champion bitter cherry would have nothing on a Champion Doug-fir. As the registry doesn't limit the number of nominations for each species, there are hundreds of trees listed in the online database. Sally Aitken, a forest geneticist, said, "There's no reason why we shouldn't be accumulating the twentieth biggest, the thirtieth biggest... It creates a bigger database to keep track of how these old trees are doing."

While I knew of and followed conservation groups that monitored clear-cuts and the overall health of forests in BC, I'd never before heard of the registry. But I have total confidence in Kate, trust honed while we were on a trip to celebrate her book going to copyedit. She'd navigated us away from several black bears we saw roadside while we were cycling from Whitehorse, Yukon, to her cabin in Atlin, on the BC-Alaska border. Kate told me I'm a bear magnet, as she'd never seen so many bears on one trip. (We'd also accidentally set off the ear-splitting wildlife deterrent horn in a pizzeria *twice*.) On the last day of that trip, I'd strained my right ACL so badly I had to hobble around her property with a ski pole for a week. Sure, I'd gone on that bike trip, but next to Kate who was holding the map and supplying the bear spray, or my archaeologist sister, Jenny, I wasn't a hardy explorer. In Pacific Northwest terms, I wanted to earn my fleece jacket and gaiters after nine years desk-bound in Toronto. I had a feeling I was playing it too safe in my life up to this point, running through the middle-class immigrant checklist—finish school, launch a career, buy a home—while trying to measure up to ever-shifting goal posts, winding up competing with only myself.

In that spirit of competition, I committed to the project on the spot. The next day, I launched a blog to capture these visits to the forty-three Champions. From a cursory glance at the registry, I knew that the Champions grew in all corners of the province, from urban lots to remote islands to Interior grasslands. Although I'd spent most of my life in BC, I'd barely been more than two hours away from Vancouver; this project gave me a reason to explore the province. I'd also learn more about trees; I didn't know most of the species on the list and was dazzled by the variety. Born in Ireland where the trees are small and raised in a suburb of Vancouver, I had a skewed idea of big trees. I'd grown up playing in and around the stumps left behind when the land was cleared for subdivisions, and my horizon was usually marked by mountains or tall trees. I assumed all the Champions would be roughly the same size: gigantic. I already knew how to identify the big 'uns of the coast: Douglas-fir (keeps its business up top; has "mice" in its cones), western red-cedar (looks like a hedge but bigger), arbutus (duh, it looks like an arbutus). I could barely tell a birch from a beech, but I figured it would be easy to learn how to identify the trees on the list. After all, I had a National Audubon guide to western trees, and I was a quick study.

Rather than grouping by species (say, Sitka spruce with Engelmann spruce), I mapped the location of all the Champion trees in a color-coded spreadsheet—green for close, indicating the numerous Champions growing within a short drive of my East Vancouver apartment; red for far; purple for Vancouver Island, the Gulf Islands, and Haida Gwaii; and yellow for everywhere I couldn't immediately locate.

Fort St. John... isn't that in Alberta? Where the heck is Clearwater?

But, really, how hard could it be? Surely the registry would provide clear locations and directions, or at least photos, and most of the trees seemed to be in the temperate rainforest of the southwest coast where I lived. That was for a few reasons:

this climate and terrain support the growth of big trees; these areas are more populated than the rest of the province, so big trees are noticed more readily; these forests had been thoroughly surveilled for logging, and it stood to reason that big trees grew near where other big trees had been cut down. I calculated that I could find one tree per week, and several in one day in urban locales. So, with time off for holidays, I vowed to find all forty-three Champion trees in a year. Lemon squeezy.

If Kate's idea was the seed, the maples outside my apartment window were the soil. I already had a practice of paying attention to nature, though on a surface level: springtime shoots in my balcony garden, cherry blossoms falling on city streets. But I'd seemed to have adopted these two maples, particularly the one closest to my window, and monitored them throughout my first year back on the coast. I studied the moss on the maple's grooved bark, how the leaves changed color gradually and then all at once, a flash of gold and red atop a silver underbelly. I watched northern flickers perch and peck, always in pairs, and juncos and chickadees beak through the moss and furrow for insects. Every Canadian knows the five-lobe maple leaf, but once I attached to the project, my curiosity was piqued about *which* maple they were. I used my guidebook to identify them as silver maples, and I named them Silver and Silas so I wouldn't forget. I realized I wanted to have a more intimate connection to individual trees, like these silver maples, instead of rushing past them on my way to work, the gym, a café. How did humans rely on them, and what were their growth patterns?

Perhaps I'd be lit by a feeling of transcendence in the presence of these trees, which would light up dimmer parts of my life. At the very least, the framework of the Champions meant I'd pay closer attention in a world that demanded one more scroll and swipe. I'd be daring through calculated risks.

And risk was inherent in this project. While I was proficient at day hikes, and I take safety and snacks to an extreme in all areas of life (I burn incense in the sink and maintain a cache of dark chocolate), I had never gone on a multiday hike. I imagined trekking through damp forests, jauntily scrambling over boulders, and crawling through hollow logs like Fred Penner. That a Canadian children's entertainer is my idea of an adventurer shows you my benchmark. The doggedness I'd cultivated as an acquisitions editor would serve me well, but I knew trees best through books, or *as* books—blocks of pulp on a shelf. I'd had a bit of a year, marked by burnout and a move across country, and I needed to regain my confidence by pursuing a different type of goal, one that would demonstrate my courage physically, as an outdoor adventurer. As Anaïs Nin writes, "Life shrinks or expands in proportion to one's courage," and I was willing to measure my personal scale against these big trees. I could square off against the bears I seemed to attract, tromp through swamps and along ridges with the wind in my hair and binoculars swinging from my neck, hit the open road with only my thoughts and a pack of Twizzlers.

I have always been drawn to completionist projects in which I could collect and sort all of a thing: Roald Dahl's books, provincial quarters, Pogs. I was generally successful at the indoor attempts, whether card-cataloging *National Geographic* with my sister one summer or sorting large bags of mixed buttons I'd buy at Dressew on Hastings Street in Vancouver. In my early teens, I saved up to buy each field guide in the National Audubon collection, dutifully checking off all the birds, spiders, and moths I identified through the window or in the back garden. One night, at the rustic cabin we rented each summer on Hornby Island in the Salish Sea, the moths crowding around the porchlight divebombed my face. I ran inside and gave up on the project to know and catalog them.

Many big-tree trackers have come before me. My story is not like theirs. I am a book editor, and I am here to manage your expectations.

- Camping skills: Average

- Ability to walk long distances: Above average

- Ability to dissect text: Excellent

- Ability to face down bears: Poor

- Fear of cougars: Healthy

- Ability to roll a decent joint: Dormant

- Superpower: Shortening back-cover copy

- Downfall: Anxiety-induced insomnia

- Ability to use GPS: Resistant

- Adherence to the scientific method: Nonpracticing believer

- Ability to parallel park: Developing

- Ability to identify trees: Middling

— 3 —

Hit It and Quit It

SCOULER'S WILLOW, BITTER CHERRY

"Give yourself permission to be a beginner.
By being willing to be a bad artist, you have a chance to
be an artist, and perhaps, over time, a very good one."
JULIA CAMERON, *The Artist's Way*

ALTHOUGH I FELT COMFORTABLE following trails in the forest, I knew better than to rush headlong into the bush looking for a big tree. Kids raised on the West Coast know to look up for cougars perched on wide limbs, to not go into the forest on windy days lest we be hit by a branch or worse, and to never venture into the forest alone without telling someone. Surveying the list of Champion trees, I selected a Scouler's willow as my first to find. It was growing near Jericho Beach, about a twenty-minute drive from my apartment, and seemed to be in a parklike setting. Vancouver has an overcast tendency until late spring, but the skies were unseasonably blue and clear that Saturday at the end of May. I packed a hat, sunscreen, and a tennis ball—in case I needed it for scale in a photo of the Champion.

Before I headed out, my phone rang. My friend and mentor, Diana Beresford-Kroeger, was on the line, as auspicious a beginning as you can get. Diana is an author and microbotanist and known as the tree whisperer. She was raised in the Druidic tradition of her Celtic ancestors and trained in the sciences by the bachelor uncle who took her in after she was orphaned at a young age. She continued her graduate studies in botany, organic chemistry, and biochemistry in her native Ireland and later Ottawa, where she met her husband and settled in the countryside. Diana is best known for her book *The Global Forest* and her bioplan, an ambitious but achievable project intended to reverse climate change through reforesting the planet. She is acclaimed internationally for her work propagating rare and endangered tree species, which she collects from around the world and raises in her extensive gardens and arboreta outside Ottawa. We met when I worked with Diana on her book *The Sweetness of a Simple Life*, and we connected over our shared Irish heritage, our mutual birthday, and our general openness to otherworldly experiences (spooky or switched on, you decide). It wasn't unusual for Diana to ring me out of the blue; she'd put out telepathic feelers to see if I was available, then get on the line to have a chinwag, which would be a lovely catch-up punctuated with info about her latest scientific paper on forests and the climate crisis, along with some gentle life coaching. "Listen, girlie..."

I explained my plan to visit all the Champion trees in BC, and Diana immediately understood the scope and purpose. She knew how difficult it had been for me to advocate for myself at my previous publishing job and in my last relationship in Toronto. I'd felt swallowed up by the expectations of others, as if I was losing track of what *I* wanted, which prompted my decision to leave everything behind and move back to the coast.

Diana has studied the chemical properties of trees and appreciates at a deep level how healing time in the forest can be. She advised me to meditate when standing in front of the giants. "Get very still with yourself," she said. "Center the focal point of your mind into the tree and then . . . tell me how it goes when I see you." She giggled, then continued in her singsong West Cork accent, "If you're still there." She cautioned me to take special care around the Pacific yew, which she described as "hypnotic."

"Oh, I don't know, Di," I said. "Let me see if I can even find it first." I knew that accessing the Champion yew would be difficult, as it was in a fenced-off watershed in North Vancouver. I'd try for that tree in a few months, once I had some easier Champions under my belt. But for now, a leisurely drive to the beach was on the agenda. I'd recently bought my first car, a Toyota Yaris that I'd nicknamed Trouble, so I could get in and out of it. I drove across the city and parked at the West Point Grey Community Centre, in a tony neighborhood of stone houses and manicured lawns ringed by hydrangeas and rhododendrons. The beach was a few blocks from the community center, and across the water were the gleaming downtown skyscrapers of what local artist and writer Douglas Coupland calls the City of Glass.

I ventured around back of the Tudor-style building, where couples intertwined or reading lay on a lush green lawn. I was looking for a Scouler's willow with a circumference of 2.16 meters and a height of 10.7 meters, last measured in 2006. Pictures online and in my guidebook showed that the Scouler's willow is similar to the more popular weeping willow, though its leaves appear shorter and its branches do not drape as low. I hadn't realized there are native willows in the Pacific Northwest. I was only familiar with weeping willows, my direct experience mostly limited to the one large willow that grew behind Royal Heights

Elementary in north Surrey. We'd grab hold of the tentacle-like branches and swing out off a cement wall, dropping down onto the gravel-strewn basketball court, until the incoming principal had all the branches trimmed short and kept them that way.

To ascertain the identity of my quarry, I combined the limited description in the registry with what I knew of willows:

- Grow in wet areas

- Common in children's literature
  (e.g., *The Wind in the Willows*)

- Branches can be woven to make baskets and chairs

- Roots, attracted to water, can be devastating
  to sewer systems

- Has healing properties, somehow linked to aspirin

- Fun playground equipment, not up to safety code

From my tree books, I learned that the Scouler's leaves are "velvety" and "oblong," and that the trunk could appear as a cluster of multiple stems. Up ahead I saw a row of three willows, twisting skyward. These willows definitely did not weep but stood proud, their furrowed gray-brown bark rippling like wet sand at Spanish Banks when the tide was out. Their branches were draped with long bright-green leaves, fractals upon fractals. Each tree had a single thick trunk, rather than multiple stems, but I figured they'd grown this way due to their immense size and age, befitting Champions. Anyway, I was used to willows having a single stem, so these matched my conception.

Birds sang and families strode past with beach gear while I surveyed, trying to stay inconspicuous. The two biggest trees seemed of similar size, so I guesstimated which one was larger.

I made a note to self to bring a tape measure next time, from my toolbox or sewing kit. The sunbathers didn't pay me a moment's notice as I stood mumbling in front of the two trees, eventually making a decision and placing a tennis ball at the base of what I thought was the larger one. Perspective is crucial when photographing trees, as even a large tree can appear like a shoebox-diorama prop unless there's a comparison like a car, person, or common piece of equipment to establish relative size.

This giant wasn't all that big. The leaves seemed right, but shouldn't it be a bit scraggier, matching the description in my books? I walked around the lawn looking for other likely trees, in case my original guess had been off, but felt too shy and intimidated to scan the larger area. This grove of likely willows was the closest I could find in this manicured landscape. I hoped I was looking at the Champion (I was in the right place, so shouldn't the tree be here?), because if I wasn't, I'd need to come out again for another investigation. Prioritizing truth could mean failing at my goal to find all these trees within a year. I shuddered despite the warm weather, realizing that I wouldn't be able to get by with my usual self-directed courses and late nights in a library carrel. I would need to seek help (drasted human condition) and ask stupid questions of experts. It had been a long time since I'd risked being wrong, but as rule two of the *Junior Woodchuck Guidebook* states, "All Junior Woodchucks must be open to the unknown in their quest for the truth."

I have been a casual student of Zen and meditation for years, and now I took partial comfort in the Buddhist idea of beginner's mind, or shoshin. The late Zenkei Blanche Hartman, a teacher and abbess at the San Francisco Zen Center, describes beginner's mind as "the mind that is innocent of preconceptions and expectations, judgments and prejudices." Beginner's mind allows us to embrace curiosity, ideally leading to more questions and learning. Meditation teacher and author Sebene Selassie demonstrates how beginner's mind can be of benefit to a new meditation practice, and the overlap with big-tree tracking is sizable. We might pick up meditation with the goal of reducing anxiety or stress (right here), but Selassie shows that the goal isn't the point. "We are not practicing to become good meditators," she writes in *You Belong*. "We are practicing to bring more awareness into our life."

Adopting a beginner's mind can be liberating, but without a spirit of playful curiosity, that supposed freedom of *not* knowing can be limiting to those who look for concrete answers and follow the line of reasoning "If it looks like a duck ..." I was already trying to impose my color-coded spreadsheet on the blank slate, to apply knowing to nothingness for the goal of a checkmark, and talk myself into truth. Standing on the green, I tried to silence my mind, ignore the cars trundling past, and meditate on what the Scouler's willow was telling me. There must be a lesson in its long leaves, a koan in its gnarled bark. These trees are *Champions*, for God's sake!

The tennis ball I included at the tree's base for scale in photos is really inadequate. Don't geologists use a rock hammer? But I'm not a geologist. I'm not a tree tracker either.

Oh man, I have to pee so bad.

When it came down to it, I was just a girl standing in front of a tree, asking it to change my life. I'd had similar anticlimactic experiences: finally shouldering up to the *Mona Lisa* and trying to feel transported while worrying I was holding up the line; making my Holy Sacrament of Confirmation and expecting to feel endowed with the Holy Spirit but instead feeling encumbered by the fulsome pleats of a red polyester robe. Bernadette McDonald, in her book *Winter 8000*, about mountaineering teams' efforts to summit eight-thousand-meter peaks in winter, writes, "Summit moments are private affairs. Some experience elation. Some feel gratitude. Almost all are overwhelmed with exhaustion and an innate reflex to descend. Quickly. The compulsion to survive takes over."

I briefly paid my respects to the giant, retrieved my tennis ball, and headed into the community center to find a washroom. Be still and know, then make a beeline for the bush or toilet. I hopped in my car, thinking about grabbing an ice cream cone on the way home. As I drove, I mentally drafted my Scouler's willow blog post and moved on to my next conquest. Hit it and quit it.

NOT LOSING ANY STEAM, I pulled out my copy of David Tracey's *Vancouver Tree Book* to look up my next target. This fully illustrated guide features over one hundred trees (native and imported) common in the Lower Mainland. I'd never heard of a bitter cherry before, but the guidebook told me that these trees have brown-gray bark with horizontal striations, and that the green leaves are serrated on the edges.

The day after finding the Scouler's willow, I drove across the Burrard Inlet and west of Highway 1 to Phibbs Exchange, a transit loop at the base of the North Shore Mountains. I parked at the A&W burger joint on Main Street and set out to explore the wooded lots just west of the transit hub. Buses belched as I found my bearings, facing two large patches of brush. The neighborhood reminded me of my stomping grounds in Surrey. Catwalks and rough trails skirted overgrown lots popping with Douglas-fir and alder, and ranchers and split-levels from the 1960s and '70s mixed with newer condos and McMansions. I blithely ignored a sign warning that herbicide had been sprayed two weeks earlier and entered the smaller of the two lots, abutting directly onto a backyard. The neighborhood hadn't yet woken up on this overcast, muggy Sunday, and I could hear the hum of Highway 1 cutting above me. Stepping gingerly through the dense underbrush, my feet crunching on dried leaves and chip bags, I approached large trees, attempting to match them to the images in my tree book. I couldn't spot a bitter cherry, though there were ornamental cherry trees in the lot—I could tell by their bark and the shape of their leaves.

I had good cell coverage and was able to look up the Champion's specs on the registry as I walked. The entry included a couple photos of the tree. Ralf Kelman, a big-tree tracker responsible for finding a lot of the trees in the registry, especially the smaller varieties, had nominated the bitter cherry in 2000. In one photo, he poses next to the tree, a foot propped up on its roots. His black tuque, blue wool sweater, and black rain jacket, along with the minimal tree cover in the background, suggest winter. The other photo shows the tree like a dancing windsock man, without leaves, next to the curb slick with rain. Shaun Muc, another big-tree tracker, from the Tri-Cities area (Coquitlam, Port Coquitlam, Port Moody), took the photos, likely when he and Kelman verified the tree as the Champion bitter cherry. When the tree was last measured, eighteen years earlier, it had a height of 18.9 meters (about as tall as a bowling lane is long), a DBH of 0.86, and a crown spread of 15.8. How much would it have grown? If it was still there . . . It was possible the residential area had crowded out the tree in the intervening years.

I moved toward the longer lot that ran between the transit exchange and a desire path, focusing on the trees growing on the lot's edges. By this point, I'd been on my slow-moving tree mission for about an hour, an eternity in bus loop time, and I hadn't seen anything that looked like the tree. I was about ready to pack it in when I decided to circle the lot from a new angle.

And then I spotted it: a huge bitter cherry growing right beside the curb. I had walked past it earlier, and when I compared the tree with the photo in the registry, I saw why. The shell of the winter tree in the photo had an added eighteen years of green.

At first I was skeptical that this was the Champion, as the tree was obscured by thick vines and ringed by garbage. I matched the layout of the limbs of the tree in front of me with the photo of the tree. Apart from two limbs on the left that were missing,

The Champion bitter cherry in fall/winter 2000

presumably fallen or removed in the eighteen-year interval, the tree I saw was identical. The bitter cherry's dancing shape was still apparent, its main branches spread wide and roughly symmetrical on the trunk, each ending in a splay of finger-like branches. A heavy crown of serrated green leaves hung over the ivy-covered trunk, and leafy branches from neighboring trees crowded in.

This Champion towered above the fifteen-meter average height of a bitter cherry. I was too early to see the flowers and

The Champion bitter cherry in late spring 2018

cherries that would form on this tree, enjoyed by birds but less often by humans, though we do consume the cherries as a thirst quencher. According to Cowichan Elder and botanical expert Dr. Luschiim Arvid Charlie, bitter cherry bark is traditionally used to decorate cedar baskets, and the wood can be used for walking sticks. I moved into the lot to take a closer look at the trunk and saw reddish bark covered in vines as wide as my wrist, growing into the canopy. The ribs on the bark ran horizontally, as befitting a bitter cherry, but the bark looked more weathered than the example photo in my *Vancouver Tree Book*.

In this partially cleared lot, with no other big trees around to crowd it, the Champion bitter cherry could surpass size and life span averages. However, with so much housing development going on around it, and vacant lots a hot commodity in Vancouver and North Vancouver's real estate game, there's a good chance its days are numbered. There are no automatic protections for Champion trees, unless they grow in an area that prohibits cutting—for example, a nature preserve, a provincial park, or a riparian (river) zone. Just listing the tree in the registry doesn't protect it, but the registry is an essential tool for letting people know these big trees exist. And as Sally Aitken of UBC Forestry says, "The first step to conserving something is knowing it's there."

The Champions growing in urban areas are challenged by pruning and clearing. Gerald B. Straley, author of *Trees of Vancouver*, puts it well: "Trees grow, die, are topped, pruned, clipped, limbed-up, mowed, run into and over, and are replaced with other trees, or too often, with buildings or parking lots." In viewing trees, especially big trees, we tend to think they've always been there, probably because this hint of stability offers consistency and comfort. "Humans are a species adapted to landscapes that stay stable through our lifetimes," David George

Haskell writes in *The Songs of Trees*. "Places that suggest permanence or durability—the thousand-year-old stone temple or ancient redwood tree—lift our spirits." Come at it from the opposite direction: consider how devastating it was when a significant tree in your life—a good climbing tree, the tree you ate under on your lunch break—was unceremoniously cut down.

The bitter cherry offered a lesson in big-tree tracking. I had a vision of how it would look, and when I got out there, the tree—a living being—was different. A missing branch. Extra growth. Or a Champion could be gone entirely. Real-life trees, subjected to winds, drought, snow, and pruning, don't often match the über-example in the guidebook. Dalia Nassar and Margaret M. Barbour, in their essay "Rooted," remind us that "trees are not only embodied recorders of their history, but also shapeshifters, whose structure transforms in relation to their environment." Knowing how to read the surroundings—not only the species growing with the tree but the effects of time, weather, and human activity—would be key to identifying each Champion. Or, as Walter Murch, the acclaimed film and sound editor behind classics including the *Godfather* trilogy and *Apocalypse Now*, put it: "If I go out to record a door-slam, I don't think I'm recording a door-slam. I think I am recording the space in which the door-slam happens."

I used my arms to measure the circumference of the bitter cherry, along the lines of "This tree is one hug and then half an arm to this freckle," and would measure that distance once I got home to my measuring tape, which I'd naturally neglected to bring again. My wingspan—almost six feet tip to tip—was only an affectionate approximation, but measuring physical dimensions with your body is not so unusual. Take the foot, for example. Or measuring a horse in hands, increments of four inches. cw&t, a design duo in Brooklyn, made a Personal Body

Unit Index poster to delineate the dimensions of our bodies, a way of sizing the world around us. "Instead of carrying around a tape measure, we use our bodies to measure stuff!" they declare in their Kickstarter campaign (result: backed). That way, you can tell if that side table you found on the street, five fists across, will actually fit your space.

Understanding relative bigness, as compared to our bodies or other trees, can help us clue in to the big trees all around us, even those that don't look that large—they might be giants. If we're noticing trees at all, we usually just note "big" or "small," not always the species. The fact is that many of us, particularly city dwellers, don't know what we're looking at when it comes to nature in general, trees in particular. The Champions in urban settings are unsung; often no one knows they're there. All these commuters at the Phibbs Exchange walked past a Champion twice daily, and locals didn't know a Champion grew in their midst in an otherwise underwhelming lot. Champions usually aren't identified with a sign; with their status changing as trees grow or die, the plaque would need to keep moving around the province. And with so many Champions in remote areas, who would see the plaque? In this way, they are different from heritage trees (culturally significant trees, usually in an urban setting) and Moon trees, which have a plaque noting their special status.

Stuart Roosa, an astronaut aboard *Apollo 14*, brought hundreds of tree seeds in his personal baggage on the 1971 lunar launch. These seeds, from Douglas-fir, loblolly pine, redwood, sweet gum, and sycamore, were in space for nine days. *Moon trees* is a bit of a misnomer, as they did not land on the moon but remained in orbit. Roosa manned the command and service module while his two fellow astronauts walked on the moon and gathered rock samples. Once back on Earth, the seeds were germinated and tended to by the United States Forest Service, where Roosa used to work as a smoke jumper. The USFS spread approximately 420 Moon seedlings around the country, as well as Brazil and Switzerland, and they were planted with fanfare in the U.S. The trees' status was often indicated with a plaque, and beginning in the 1990s, Moon tree enthusiasts set out to find and document their locations. "Some might have disappeared, felled by storms or saws, before someone could find them and feel curious enough to ask NASA about them," Marina Koren writes in *The Atlantic*, suggesting there are no automatic protections in place for Moon trees. NASA now maintains a database of about one hundred of the known Moon trees, living and dead.

I knew a bitter cherry this big was rare, and its presence should at the very least be known. Still, try as I might, I couldn't feel anything like transcendence when standing in front of it. It wasn't graceful like an arbutus or impressively large like a Doug-fir. By comparison, "At the base of a large baobab," Jori Lewis writes, about the wide trees that grow in Senegal where she lives, "I always feel such curiosity—about how many events it has witnessed, how much change it has withstood, how many generations of wanderers have touched or carved messages into its trunk." I was surprised what little credence I granted this bitter cherry as a sentinel. It seems I'd already allotted feelings of timeless awe toward the larger trees of my youth. Or perhaps the Champions I'd seen thus far hadn't turned my mind inside out precisely because they were so fathomable. I could touch the Scouler's willow and bitter cherry, wrap my arms around them. I could easily take in their height at a glance, without craning my neck into their crown.

I felt proud of connecting the dots that led me to this bitter cherry, but this was a low-stakes win. I knew I could have tried again with minimal investment if I hadn't found it the first time out—this tree was a hop across the inlet, fifteen minutes' drive from my home, and the area to search was relatively small. How could I best prepare myself for future treks to more remote trees where the chance of a repeat visit was slim? These forests would be away from highways and herbicide but pose other risks: falling branches, wasp nests, ticks, bears, cougars, holes in which I could turn an ankle. Whatever the dangers, it would be worth it to feel like this, more myself: wandering with a sense of both purpose and wild abandon, muttering vaguely, clutching a notebook. I hadn't felt this good since I was stomping around the sidewalks and abandoned lots of Surrey in my teens, nodding along to Beastie Boys on my Walkman, aware of when the batteries were dying by the slowed-down rhythm, scratching haiku on a coil-bound pad.

— 4 —

Like Shooting
Fish in a Barrel

BIGLEAF MAPLE, WESTERN
RED-CEDAR, RED ALDER

"In looking at a flower, you are doing the flower's job."
TIMOTHY MORTON, *Dark Ecology*

WHEN I WAS GROWING UP in Surrey, its slogan was City of
Parks. Some of the names of the suburb's eight-hundred-plus
parks denoted the creatures and forests there before clearing
and settling, like Bear Creek or Green Timbers. Stumps and
pockets of remaining old-growth were similar reminders of the
forest that had covered much of the landscape before colonizers
arrived.

At the foot of our street was a large park, ringed by cottonwoods that aggravated my allergies each year. Below the
slope of cottonwoods and blackberry bushes, accessed by a set
of steps or rough trails through the brush, was a small patch
of woods. The forest was a scary place to enter as a child, but
gradually I became more comfortable going in there alone, to
hunt for Easter eggs or later to smoke up as a teen. The woods
was called the Fitness because of the exercise equipment
scattered on its leaf-strewn paths: wooden hurdles, metal

monkey bars. There were a few old-growth western red-cedars and Douglas-firs down there, which I only knew then as big trees. From our house on the hill at the top of the street, looking down toward the park, I could see the Doug-firs, possibly fifty meters tall, towering above the maples and alders. Their extreme height was normal to me. In Surrey and elsewhere in the Lower Mainland, parks are still home to monstrous trees that until now I hadn't paid much notice.

As spring continued, now back to its usual soggy state, I headed to Vancouver's jewel, Stanley Park, to encounter notable giants. This city park is 1,001 acres of forest and beaches, just west of Vancouver's downtown core. From above, Stanley Park looks like a goose head, complete with Beaver Lake for an eye. Nina Shoroplova, in her book on the trees of Stanley Park, tells us that the park boasts 180,000 trees, both native and imported. Residents and approximately 8 million tourists every year come to traverse the quiet wooded paths and amble along the seawall, a paved pathway running shoreside. The park is a known cruising location, and underhoused people live within the forest. Vancouverites mark their evenings by the boom of the Nine O'Clock Gun, a cannon ignited with black powder, that sits on the seawall. Bordered on the southwest by English Bay and the northeast by Burrard Inlet, Stanley Park was officially named (after the Governor General, Lord Stanley) on September 27, 1888, just over two years after the incorporation of the City of Vancouver. The founding of the park, at that time a military reserve, was one of the first orders of business for the new city. Of course, the park's land wasn't unoccupied before then: the area had long been home to the Coast Salish Peoples, evidenced by trails, structures, and shellfish middens.

The tallest known tree in Vancouver, a 63.6-meter Douglas-fir, lives here in the Second Chance Grove, so named because these saplings continued growing after fires in the 1880s cleared the undergrowth and opened up more light in the canopy. Despite the fires, the park retains approximately 50 percent old-growth, a few of the conifers taller than the city's skyscrapers, and mixed in among them are some of the largest bigleaf maples in Canada. Prevalent in many varieties in this country, the maple is a national symbol: our flag is two bands of red framing a red maple leaf on white, Toronto's hockey team is the Maple Leafs, and I defy you to enter a grocery store in any small town and not find a box of maple-shaped cookies. The bigleaf maple, also called the broadleaf maple, is common on the West Coast.

The telltale sign of a bigleaf maple is its dinner-plate-sized leaves (from eight to twelve inches), which offer shade in the summer and glow yellow in fall, their litter useful as mulch in compost. The tree is easy to spot in winter, too, with its knobby trunk and wide branches. Some Indigenous groups use the lightweight maple wood for canoe paddles, and the grain is also prized for musical instruments and fine furniture. Bigleaf maples can be tapped for sap to make syrup, and the flower buds that emerge in spring are edible. These temperate forests near sea level are so damp that the orienting measure of "moss grows thickest on the north side of a tree" doesn't really hold—moss grows fairly solid the whole way around. Their trunks and branches are often covered with pads of thick green moss (bryophytes) and draped with lighter green moss that looks like an old man's beard, giving the Pacific Northwest forest the feeling of a Louisianan swamp. Bigleaf maples can generate their own soil on those mossy branches to support epiphytes—plants that don't grow on the ground—like slender licorice ferns, which are drawn to the tree's thin calcium-rich bark.

It was a short-enough bike ride from my apartment to Stanley Park, but I'd driven because the rain was torrential, much needed after an exceptionally dry May. I'd come to the park to find two Champions. Starting out from Third Beach near Siwash Rock, I flagged down a park ranger passing in his white truck. Unbeknownst to me until then, Stanley Park has rangers, a dream job up there with fire tower lookout or lighthouse keeper, only this way you can grab a cappuccino on your lunch break. I asked him where I could find the Hollow Tree—near that landmark, the second-largest bigleaf maple in Canada grew alongside the trail, and that runner-up would point me toward the Champion. The ranger motioned toward an intersection of trails and handed me a map, with a directive to "Try to stay dry, ya?"

The Hollow Tree is a regular stop for tours, positioned as it is in a keyhole of Stanley Park Drive, the peripheral route. This fifteen-meter-high western red-cedar stump is the widest tree in the park at just under 5.5 meters in diameter. It's possible to guess a tree's age based on species, diameter, and height, but rings are the best determinant of age, and you don't need to cut down a tree to count its rings; you can use an increment borer, which drills into the tree for a small sample. But the Hollow Tree, into which you can easily walk, is a shell without rings, so best guesses put it at eight hundred to one thousand years old. A chimney tree (hollowed out by fire, perhaps by a lightning strike), it's similar to the Shrine Drive-Thru and the Chandelier Tree, both redwoods in California, which have openings at ground level made wide enough that cars can drive through. The Hollow Tree became a popular spot for photographs, with tourists driving their horses, buggies, and cars directly into the opening. Historical photos show a bar set up for refreshments in the tree, and even an elephant backed into it.

But western red-cedar's importance to peoples on the West Coast goes much deeper than a tourist novelty or even its status as the official tree of British Columbia. Indigenous Peoples rely on the Tree of Life for everything from longhouses to dugout canoes, bentwood boxes, and masks. I appreciate this description of the lifelong role of western red-cedar, or xpey' in Hul'q'umi'num', shared by Dr. Luschiim Arvid Charlie: "when we were first born, we were wrapped [in cedar-bark blankets], our diapers were pounded red-cedar bark... And when we died, in the past we were put in a cedar coffin. So right from birth, everything in between, to death, cedar was important to us." Harvested cedar lasts for years, making it valuable for shingles, fence posts, and other building materials. The bark is relatively smooth, with vertical lines looking like frequent but inexpert cuts in cardboard, and it can be stripped in one long vertical piece to be woven into baskets, hats, and clothing. Cedar trees have the remarkable ability to heal themselves from damage by growing over pulled strips or the rectangular holes made by pileated woodpeckers. Stripped-bark trees, called culturally modified trees (CMTs), are evidence of Indigenous Peoples' interaction with the forest and are automatically protected by BC's Heritage Conservation Act if the modification dates to before 1846 (pre-contact) and the tree grows on provincial land. Western red-cedars rot from the inside out, losing their heartwood as the outer layers live and the tree continues to grow, making them popular locations for black bear dens.

As a kid, I spent a lot of time playing in and around rotted stumps in the ravine, a slip of green running through Royal Heights, our neighborhood in north Surrey. I was amazed that anything grew along the ravine's steep sides, let alone old-growth cedars and Douglas-firs that remained mostly as huge stumps. The sunlight didn't so much dapple into the under-story as blob, falling in liquid blotches on the ferns and mud. Mosquitoes floated and hummed in the cool air, moving from still pond to sweaty skin. We measured the serpentine ravine in distance from home and hours of play before the call of dinner. The ravine drove perceptibly down, alongside the rushing cars of Scott Road hill and toward the flats surrounding the Fraser River, its creek moving alongside homes, banks, and auto-repair shops, continuing beneath a wreckers yard, a motorcycle club headquarters, and various fenced-off lots before meeting the muddy river. A railroad track ran along the top edge of the ravine, and my best friend, Caleigh, and I would lay pennies on the rails, then search for the flattened copper shields after the train had passed. We dreamed of hopping a graffitied boxcar and riding somewhere exotic, like Saskatchewan.

There were two options for entering the ravine, sometimes called the gully. You could take the stairs, one hundred steps and landings plunging in Jacob's ladder fashion down each side and meeting in a walkway over the creek. From the momentum you'd built running down the stairs, your footfalls would pound and echo on the wooden bridge, laid with stainless steel hatching to prevent slipping. Or you could take your chances and barrel down the side of the ravine, building up mounds of dirt and leaves as you slid, grasping at roots and vines, taking care not to collide with innumerable tires, shopping carts, and other crap that had been dumped there over the years. I'd gingerly sidestep my way down the ravine sides, rarely letting loose and sliding unless I could see a place to level out ahead. Braver souls than I would swing out over the ravine on a rope swing suspended from a maple branch.

We'd hop between slick rocks in the creek, lose our balance on log seesaws, play hide-and-seek in rotted-out stumps. When I sat inside a cedar stump, the buttressed roots created a proscenium onto the expanse of the ravine. Spiderwebs constellated with dust and beads of water hung in the opening and lined the flaking wood around me. Most of the tentacle-like roots plunged directly into the soil, plug in socket, but cavities formed as a gap between the soil and wood or a deep opening in the rotted root. There's something captivating about stepping inside or even through a tree—your body made miniature, an intimate acquainting, a portal. At the same time I was bombing around the ravine, one of my favorite books was *My Side of the Mountain* by Jean Craighead George, about Sam Gribley, a twelve-year-old boy who leaves the city to live in a hollowed-out hemlock in the Catskills. This novel captured me with its sense of adventure and self-sufficiency, so between that fictional hemlock and the raw cedar stumps around my home it's no wonder I missed the memo about the significance of the Hollow Tree. In all my years living in and around Vancouver, I had never visited the stump, but I suppose the novelty of experiencing a famous tree can't be underestimated. I stepped inside the Hollow Tree, grabbed onto a metal support for balance, and gazed upward, rain falling through the chimney opening onto my face.

When a December 2006 windstorm leveled thousands of trees throughout Stanley Park, the Hollow Tree was left listing. The tree had previously been braced on the inside after it was damaged by Typhoon Freda in 1962. After the 2006 storm, the Vancouver Park Board and arborists assessed the damage and determined that another storm could knock it over. In early 2008, the Park Board debated whether to preserve the Hollow Tree or allow it to continue its natural demise. But a committed band of activists, engineers, historians, arborists, and one big-tree tracker—Ralf Kelman, who nominated the bitter cherry—formed the Hollow Tree Conservation Society and received permission from the Park Board to temporarily support the stump with struts, cables, and buried cement blocks. After the stump was supported more permanently with an internal metal tripod, an arborist trimmed the top and a welder manufactured a custom steel cap, like a crown for a molar, impeding rot and preventing other species, mainly hemlock, from taking hold in the top.

The Hollow Tree, altered as it was by humans, is also a CMT—or, as Kelman calls it, a CMMT: culturally modified monument tree. The now-supported Hollow Tree is a marker of how we dictate a tree's life cycle for our pleasure. In controlling trees, we tend to focus on the biggest or the smallest, like bonsai, overlooking the majority in the middle. The Hollow Tree stands out less for its size and more because it only resembles a tree. Douglas Coupland's tribute to the Hollow Tree is an appropriate simulacrum, removed from the forest and positioned in a business district at sw Marine Drive and Cambie in south Vancouver. Called the *Golden Tree*, the public art installation is an exact replica of the Hollow Tree, constructed of steel, fiberglass, and resin and coated in artificial gold. The showiness of the *Golden Tree*, and its location between the international airport and downtown Vancouver, make it an ideal subject for performative pilgrimage and selfies.

It's appropriate that in a city known for its trees, Vancouver's prominent public art comments on our extractive relationship to nature. Consider two other instances of stump-inspired art within Vancouver: *Trans Am Totem* by Marcus Bowcott and *Your Kingdom to Command* by Marina Roy. *Trans Am Totem*, created for the 2014–2016 Vancouver Biennale and until August 2021 installed at the corner of Quebec Street and Milross Avenue, is a 33-foot-high, 25,000-pound public art piece—a vertical steel-reinforced 150-year-old cedar stump stacked with five scrap cars, ranging from the smallest Civic at the bottom to the largest Trans Am at the top. The stump has a bear claw carved into it by Xwalacktun (Rick Harry). The artwork pays homage to Indigenous poles of the Pacific Northwest as well as to BC's logging history, while condemning our car-centric consumerist culture. *Your Kingdom to Command* is an installation in the financial district between the Paradox Hotel (formerly the Trump Tower) and the Shangri-La Hotel. In front of a mural featuring a large tar and bitumen triangle are two stumps: one is plain and appears dead, and the other is covered in growth, its root ball and moss skirt intact. The nurse stump is atop a fountain, which "pisses" on the bare stump. Roy sourced the naked stump from Spanish Banks; it's one of the deciduous trees that blew over in a windstorm in August 2015. She found the nurse stump at the UBC Malcolm Knapp Research Forest in Maple Ridge, about thirty miles from the installation. In her artist's statement, Roy highlights the capitalist nature of the artwork: the haves pissing on the have-nots, accentuated by the installation's situation in the center of capital in Vancouver, one of the most expensive cities in the world.

Roy opted not to preserve either stump, preferring that they decay naturally, unlike the Hollow Tree. Wondering why, in a park full of living trees, the propped-up dead one is the attraction, I turned my attention to the real thing, leaving behind the supported stump and continuing down the fern-lined Rawlings Trail to find the runner-up maple. Draped in ferns and moss, with a height of 29.5 meters and a crown of 17 meters, this maple is remarkable, but I paid it hardly a second glance as I hustled past toward the Champion, located about thirty feet into the forest and ringed by slender trees. I learned another lesson: large trees tend to clump together under ideal growing conditions. Bigness is only one metric for appreciating trees, but by seeking out the Champion and focusing on it as the largest, at the expense of the runners-up, I conferred and confirmed its status.

When Randy Stoltmann verified the Champion bigleaf maple in 1992, the circumference was 10.71 meters (DBH 3.41).

The tree is likely two hundred to three hundred years old, and its massive crown of 20 meters spread out 29 meters above me, dotting the sky with green. Even if I had brought my measuring tape, I didn't see a need to measure this tree when it was already so well documented, appearing in tourist guides to the park. At first glance, this Champion looks like three smaller trees growing at opposing angles from a nurse stump, obscured with moss, ferns, short branches, and leaves. But it's all one tree, resembling a green helmet with devil horns snaking into the canopy. Lady ferns and deer ferns grow at the tree's base amid a thick mulch of decaying leaves. Once I stepped closer, I could see that the "helmet" was not as intact as it appeared, with the limbs meeting more at ground level, almost on a landing pad between the three trunks. Looking at the tree, I had the sense that I had never really seen a maple before, though I had grown up hiding my face behind their huge leaves, searching for the biggest leaf on outings with friends, and ironing them between wax paper in arts and crafts. I didn't know there could be such variety in their trunk shape.

HAVING TAKEN IN this marker of greatness, I was ready for another. From the Champion bigleaf maple, it's a short wander to the province's Champion red alder, located near the concession stand on Third Beach, a popular sunbathing site. The beach, its sand and driftwood wet from the rain, was mostly deserted save for the occasional dog walker. Stoltmann also nominated this Champion, in 1980, and the tree was last measured in 2016. Alder typically blends in, as the tree is common in the Pacific Northwest, but I couldn't miss this specimen due to both its considerable size and the notes and helpful photo in the registry. The photo shows Shaun Muc leaning against the red alder in his suit and overcoat. He works as a financial advisor when not tramping through the forest, and he had dropped by the tree in between appointments. It's possible to do that with a tree this accessible, a Champion right in the city. I spotted the alder almost as if a neon sign were hanging from its upper branches, declaiming "It's me!" *Could it really be that easy?* I thought. It was like shooting fish in a barrel. Comparing its current appearance to an earlier photo and stepping away to peer at the crown showed me where some of the uppermost branches had been lopped off, perhaps after being damaged in a wind- or snowstorm. That would make sense, given its exposed setting right on the seawall. A trail cut to one side of the alder, next to a western red-cedar of approximately the same height.

The red alder is a deciduous tree with serrated toothed leaves that curl downward at the edges and stay green when they drop in autumn. Male catkins are brownish and pollen-filled "tassels," while females resemble small seed cones; both male and female can grow on the same tree. The male catkins are edible, and they drop in late winter or early spring, breaking apart underfoot and spreading pollen, while the female cones endure throughout the year. Red alder has medicinal properties and is a nitrogen-fixer, meaning it adds nitrogen to soil. It is also opportunistic, growing in sites of recent clearing, say after a fire. Though red alder's thin outer bark is gray and marked with white lichen, the tree is so named because of its orange-red wood and inner bark, which is edible and valued as a dye.

This alder was 24.6 meters tall, its crown spread 15 meters; it grew so large partially due to its location, unobstructed between the beach and an open field. Alders are fast growing but short lived, and this Champion was likely forty to sixty years old, thus nearing the end of its life cycle. A similarly sized alder in Haida Gwaii could move into the Champion position, and while I wanted to wrap up my project on schedule,

I would welcome any excuse to travel to that beautiful part of the province. I was thrilled to land two Champions in one day (✔, ✔), though staring at the alder, its thick base the color and shape of an elephant foot, I felt a bit underwhelmed. I preferred the showiness of the bigleaf maple with its moss and ferns, or the larger cedars and Doug-firs that grew all around me.

IN THOSE FIRST WEEKS, everything felt possible. The early wins sparked my confidence, and I felt the familiar high of working toward a huge goal. I was proud of myself for picking these trees out of the forest, and for starting to become more familiar with the differences between species, just as I'd intended. Setting out on a trip, starting a new job or relationship, planning a big project, you feel so hopeful. You're the top scene in Norman Rockwell's before-and-after vacation diptych, *Going and Coming*, of an excited family leaving on summer holiday, and then in the bottom painting, returning worn out from the experience. I wasn't yet up against my deadline of a year to find all the trees, and any big tree I saw had the potential to be *the* tree. I just had to run toward it.

— 5 —
Here Comes Trouble!

CASCARA, YELLOW-CEDAR, BLACK COTTONWOOD, DOUGLAS MAPLE, SUBALPINE FIR

"Everything is photographable."

ALEC SOTH

FROM AN EARLY AGE, I was well versed in cutblocks and replanted forests and could point out the marks of springboard logging in stumps around Surrey and Vancouver. Loggers would insert these steel-tipped planks in small cuts on the trunk so they could stand higher up on the tree, out of the dense undergrowth where the trunk was straighter and less flared. The two men (or even a team of men, if the tree was especially huge) would then use axes or later a crosscut handsaw to cut down the tree. I was familiar with log booms—rafts of tree trunks—drifting down the Fraser River, and with heavy trucks loaded with raw logs or pallets of timber, some of them processed at the mill on River Road ten minutes' drive from our house. On summer holidays in the Interior or on Vancouver Island, the cabbage smell of a pulp and paper mill was never that far away. On road trips, if I spotted patches of brown on mountainsides, I knew they were lodgepole pines killed by the mountain pine beetle infestation in the early 2000s.

The nine years I spent in Toronto had distanced me from the big trees of my youth but also from the obvious interaction between the local economy and the forest industry. On the coast, trees didn't just mean beauty: they meant jobs. In Toronto, trees were valued for their canopy offering shade, their leaves clearing the smoggy air, and their stately presence providing a slower footing in a city that never stopped rushing. I made friends with a large Norway maple in my front yard, leaning against her in summer. In springtime, I'd visit the rows of cherry blossoms in front of the brutalist Robarts Library at the University of Toronto, dreaming of the cherry and plum blossoms back home. I overlaid a mental map of trees on the city: my landlord's Saskatoon berry in our shared backyard connected me to a larger Saskatoon berry growing at the corner of Spadina and Harbord in the Annex, where I would forage for purple berries on hot summer afternoons, their splotches staining the sidewalk.

I'd been gone so long that I felt compelled to reconnect to trees and their myriad uses, and the province with all its varied geography, not just the coast where I felt most comfortable. British Columbia is unique in that it has fourteen distinct biogeoclimatic zones, a result of its mountain ranges and coastal climate, which lead to markedly different vegetation from zone to zone. I'd started my tree-tracking project just before setting out on a road trip around BC. This three-week trip was meant to reacquaint me with my home province and break in Trouble, a compact car with low clearance that is more comfortable handling city streets than potholed logging roads. Or, let's face it, I was more comfortable handling Trouble in those controlled environs. I hadn't yet figured out my trip plans (in typical fashion, my plans extended as far as "up and around"), so now I overlaid my route with Champions, using the holiday as an opportunity to reach these more remote trees. It looked like I could cross a lot of trees off my list that summer, and I plotted out their locations like a detective tracking a serial killer. My set list of over a dozen trees seemed easy to reach on a map, but I didn't take into account whether these trees would be easy to access.

I love traveling alone to cities but had never taken a solo road trip like this, willingly putting myself in remote locations. I reasoned that's what adventurers do. I'd resisted getting my driver's license for years, citing a reluctance to contribute to emissions yet still opting to ride shotgun in my sister's silver vw Golf named Gwen, vanilla air freshener hanging from the rearview. As a teen, I'd perfected the role of copilot, handing Jenny her water bottle with the cap off, puff-puff-pass, mixing our selections on the six-disc changer: Pantera, Black Sabbath, Primus, and Metallica (hers); NOFX, Propagandhi, Sublime, and Pennywise (mine); and always Beastie Boys (ours). Our favorite destination was the Java Hut, a café-shed in the parking lot of a Chevron in Whalley, the neighborhood of Surrey where we lived. We'd order hot chocolate with a thick mound of chocolate whipped cream, hotbox Gwen, then flip a coin for who would ask the attendant to fill the half-empty cups with more whip. Since then, I'd spent most of my intervening years in cities as a cyclist and pedestrian. A solo drive would be challenge enough, but it stung that the main way to reach these far-off giants would be through driving. Automobile emissions are contributing to the climate crisis, which is threatening trees through drought, flooding, and wildfire.

My first stop was Cathedral Grove, a sliver of old-growth on both sides of the highway between Parksville and Port Alberni on Vancouver Island. This stand of towering Doug-firs, western red-cedars, hemlocks, and grand firs is located within

MacMillan Provincial Park, but most visitors rarely leave sight of their vehicle. H. R. MacMillan was the chief forester of the BC Forest Service and responsible for developing much of the province's forestry program. His name is dotted around the province, from an arboretum near the Harmac pulp and paper mill in Nanaimo to the planetarium in Vancouver. (The conservatory in Vancouver is the Bloedel, named in honor of the son of another logging titan.) There aren't any Champions in Cathedral Grove, but it's a famous site for trees, so I couldn't help visiting. A wide path lined with split-rail cedar fences took me on a rather tame walk around big trees, most between three hundred and eight hundred years old. The pathway and fencing are intended to prevent the public from trampling delicate root systems and eroding the soil around the bases of the trees. We don't just want to gaze upon trees: we need to touch, hug, and step inside them if possible. Stoltmann noted in 1987 that a number of these Doug-firs were weakened in their heartwood by a fungus, making them more susceptible to falling in windstorms, and a lot of the forest has since blown down. Many tourists stop here on their way to the surf towns of Tofino and Ucluelet on the west coast of Vancouver Island, and now in early summer parked cars lined the road. Though this old-growth forest is accessible to most, one of its main selling features, I wasn't content with such a small showcase. This fringe seemed inadequate recompense for the clearing that MacMillan and other loggers had done throughout the twentieth century. *Fenced paths and boardwalks are fine for tourists*, I thought, *but not big-tree trackers.*

I headed to my first overnight, Jenny's house in Bowser, a village about one hour north of Nanaimo, on the east coast of the island. Jenny lives with her husband and two young sons above a pebble beach, in sight of twisted firs and in earshot of sea lions barking during the spring herring run. She lives for The

Roots, twenty-minute workouts, and chocolate squares dipped in decaf. Jenny is a professional finder; an archaeologist with many years' experience in the bush, she's stared down bears and middle-aged mining execs. I bet that, with child care, she could find all these Champions in six months.

"So, what's your trip plan?" she asked the next morning, as she filled a Ziploc bag with gorp for me. Instead of the usual trail mix of "good ol' raisins and peanuts" (I can't stand raisins and I'm not a big fan of peanuts either), it was mostly beef jerky, chocolate chips, coconut clusters, and walnuts—with pocket cheese on the side. (Costco, feel free to sponsor me.) She told me that when she was in the bush, she'd forgo a sit-down lunch in favor of a large snack bag in her pocket so she could keep moving. I outlined my plan for the next few weeks, mentioning the logging roads that would bring me to the Champions.

"Pro tip if you want to get on with forestry types," she said, now making me an Americano in my travel cup. "Don't call them logging roads. Call them FSRs." Forest service roads. "And stop calling them loggers. They're foresters."

She talked me through the equipment I'd need in the forest each day. Then, in a classic big-sister move, she gave me an old Weber barbecue for my apartment balcony. It wasn't the ideal time to take a used BBQ, but it was too good an offer. It took up my whole trunk and made the car smell like grease, but I reasoned I could use it at a campsite. I laid out all my supplies on the back seat, including the safety equipment I'd purchased at Mountain Equipment Co-op the previous week. I'd carefully wrapped my bear spray and wildlife deterrent horn in old underwear (itself a deterrent) and tucked it inside a shoebox so I wouldn't inadvertently let off either spray or horn. When I had posted about my project on social media, the chair of the BC Big Tree Committee, Ira Sutherland, had reached out to praise my initiative and asked me to contribute measurements and photos from the road. I wasn't working on behalf of the registry in seeing these trees, but with this added interest, I felt I needed to up my game.

I took a deep breath. This tree-tracking road trip would be my most ambitious yet—stringing together Champions day after day, far from home, with the trees growing in dense forests rather than city parks, some of them not seen in years. I felt like I couldn't let the committee down, and I had given myself a rare opportunity to see a lot of these trees, their statuses unknown. Would they still be standing? Would I, by the end of the three weeks?

Adventure, I thought, starting Trouble.

DAILY PACKING LIST:

- bear spray
- wildlife deterrent horn (aka bear horn)
- hiking boots
- extra socks
- chocolate
- water
- glow stick
- tree guidebooks
- notebook and pens
- bug spray
- whistle
- knife
- headlamp
- rainshell
- matches and lighter
- sweater
- first-aid kit
- emergency blanket
- tiny wooden robot

THE FIRST CHAMPION on my road trip list was a cascara in Comox, near Courtenay, thirty minutes north of Bowser. Courtenay is a picturesque city with a charming main street, microbreweries, boutiques, and a great washroom in the library (ask me how I know). I started with the basics: What the heck does a cascara look like? Internet sleuthing and my guidebooks gave me a general idea, but you can glean only so much from a written description and Google Images. You have to see, feel, even smell to really identify a tree.

I was looking for a cascara with a 1.09-meter circumference (DBH 0.35 m) and 12.4-meter crown, standing at 17.8 meters (about the distance between the pitcher's mound and home plate). Cascaras are smallish trees with scaly thin brown or gray bark, green leaves, naked buds, and flowers that yield a small fruit. Their trunks can have a single or multiple stems. Cascaras aren't valuable as timber, but their bark is a powerful tonic and laxative, and it was in demand as a pharmaceutical source until the invention of synthetic laxatives in the 1960s, a moving story altogether. I'd never heard of the tree before, an obvious oversight when this tree is so common in this part of the, ahem, woods.

The notes on the location of the cascara Champion in the registry didn't fill me with confidence: "When nominated, the tree was located in the Lannan Forest. Current tree and land-ownership status is unknown." The Lannan Forest is about forty acres of second-growth maple, cascara, and Douglas-fir abutting a residential area. In 2004, the province sold a parcel of the forest to a housing developer, Silverado Land Corporation, which cleared part of the forest in 2010. Residents have resisted the sale of these public lands for years and have led conservation efforts, including the restoration of the forest's Brooklyn Creek. If the land was rezoned as a park, then the area couldn't be developed and trees couldn't be cut. According to the registry, the Lannan Forest is also home to a big trembling aspen and a Pacific crab apple, neither tree a Champion but certainly meaningful to those who nominated them, as well as significant to the critters who live in and around them.

I entered the cascara Champion's coordinates into Google Maps, which sent me to a residential street on the Comox peninsula. The street was quiet at 12:30 PM on a Monday. I parked at the last house on the left, a tidy home with flower baskets on the porch. From the street, I could see tall trees in the backyard. Could the cascara actually be on this property? I didn't know then that if a tree is on private property, the registry indicates that and asks tree trackers to view it from a respectful distance. I would later learn that the registry obscures the directions and coordinates for trees that are on private property, sacred to an Indigenous People, or nearing the end of their life cycle and thus sensitive to boots tromping around their roots.

I knocked on the front door, ready to introduce myself as your regular tree fanatic and could I look in your yard please? The reply was a dog barking. A trail led from the dead end into the woods, so I decided to take my chances. Despite some dumping of organic materials at the trailhead and a few overgrown areas along the path, the trail appeared to be well used. Between November and April, the forest must become wonderfully damp, with Brooklyn Creek winding around and across the paths. On this cloudless day, it was soothing to walk along mulched paths and plank bridges, protected from the sun and listening to birdsong. The small parcel of forest, still dense in places, reminded me of the verges at the top of the ravine or at the bottom of Scott Road hill, on the flats near the Fraser. We knew we could play in those woods without fear while experiencing a frisson because we weren't supposed to be there.

Using the BC *Tree Book*, a government guide to popular species in the province, I looked around and guessed at cascara. Now that I knew how to identify it, the tree seemed to be growing everywhere, mixed among tall conifers and maples. I found a grove of cascara, but none of the trees was the approximate size I was seeking. I tromped around the paths, looking up and around, the "So What'cha Want" video looping in my head.

On my way back to my car, I spied a large cascara off the path. It grew straight into the canopy, and I estimated it surpassed seventeen meters in height. I pushed through shrubby limbs to take a closer look. A sparse layer of dried moss clung to the bottom half of the tree's gray trunk, slightly lined with horizontal cracks and marked with knots. "Are you my mother?" I whispered, laying a hand on its broad trunk. The tree was not forthcoming with its Champion status. I made a quick estimate of its diameter using my arms and vowed to shell out for diameter tape once I found a forestry supply store up north. Judging from the bark, leaves, and size, it could very well have been the tree I was seeking. Then again, it might not have even been a cascara. Still, it was the largest most-likely-to-be-cascara I had come across, and that was good enough for now. I still had time in the year to return if I needed to verify this Champion. Back at my car, I brushed myself down and checked for ticks, then ate a couple of salad rolls. There's posh.

LEAVING COMOX, I DROVE two hours north to the village of Sayward, passing loaded logging trucks on the way. The highway was lined with a dense wall of dark green: fir, cedar, hemlock. Ravens on the shoulder panted with their beaks open, and snakes sunned themselves on the asphalt. This seaside community used to be accessible only by boat and developed through the logging industry; logging still occurs around the town, but the area now markets itself as the gateway to north-island ecotourism. As I needed to pass by the road to Sayward to make my ferry connection in Port Hardy the next morning,

I'd decided to make a quick detour to search for the Champion yellow-cedar just outside town.

This Champion, charmingly nicknamed Sir Daniel Samson, stands 46.4 meters high and has a crown of 12.2 meters and a DBH of 3.69 meters. (The diameter is almost the length of a Volkswagen Beetle.) It is also the largest known yellow-cedar in the world; five of the six largest yellow-cedars grow on Vancouver Island, and the sixth is in Washington State. Sir Daniel Samson grows in an area under a tree farm licence, a tract of Crown land leased to a timber company, and is surrounded by a buffer of about 2.8 hectares.

I hadn't known it when I nicknamed Silver and Silas, the maples outside my apartment window, but I was already engaged in a tradition of big-tree tracking. The person who nominates an individual tree is given the honor of naming it. Committee member Sally Aitken says naming is "an interesting incentive for people because that ability to name a tree is something that people can connect with"—I imagine in the same way we can "own" a patch of the universe by having a star named after a loved one or "adopt" a polar bear in a conservation campaign. Indeed, this practice is well used in the forest conservation movement. In the late 1980s, as part of its campaign to preserve the Carmanah Valley, the Western Canada Wilderness Committee used this adopt-and-name approach. "Thousands around [Canada] mailed in twenty-five dollars with a chosen name and received a certificate in return," Harley Rustad writes.

A name personalizes the tree, but I wondered if it tokenized it too much or brought unnecessary symbolism to an already weighty forest. Jordan Kisner, author of *Thin Places*, writes, "For some reason, it's difficult to be impassive about trees, difficult to see them clearly... We've turned them into oracles, goddesses, ancestors, external souls, sympathetic witnesses of our sorrow, absorbers of our illness, living temples, axes mundi that hold up the cosmos and connect heaven and earth." Add to the fact that tree trackers are generally dudes, giving powerful bro names to large trees thrusting skyward. For instance, it's a quirk of big-tree tracking that trees are often given military names. Big-tree tracker Robert Van Pelt explains the practice in his book *Forest Giants of the Pacific Coast*: "Giant sequoias were discovered right before the Civil War and their native range was extensively explored during and after the war, hence the preponderance of Civil War heroes in the naming of these trees (at least three trees were named after Robert E. Lee)." Another giant sequoia, General Grant, was named after Ulysses S. Grant, former Union Army general and U.S. president from 1869 to 1877. General Grant grows in Kings Canyon National Park in California and is the second-largest known sequoia, after General Sherman. General Sherman is named after Civil War general William Tecumseh Sherman and is the largest tree by volume in the world.

British Columbian tree trackers simply carried on the tradition, assigning a naval flair in the case of Admiral Broeren, the runner-up yellow-cedar, also located in the Sayward Valley. BC Big Tree Committee member Bill Beese, an ecologist at what was then MacMillan Bloedel (MacBlo), used the company's cruising records for the area to find huge yellow-cedars. Forester Ally Gibson tracked down General Buxton after a phone call from Beese. General Buxton is a 3.32-meter-DBH yellow-cedar that was growing in a designated cutblock in Kelsey Bay on Vancouver Island, and it was saved just hours before it was due to be cut. The recognition of General Buxton prompted other foresters to look for big trees. Another yellow-cedar, Sergeant RandAlly, was named after the two road engineers who measured it: Randall Dayton and Ally Gibson. At 61 meters high, it was once the tallest known yellow-cedar, until it fell naturally in 2003 or 2004.

Tree names also take on mythical overtones, like the King Arthur sequoia in Garfield Grove, California, which was the ninth largest sequoia by volume before it burned in the Castle Fire of 2020. *The Lord of the Rings* figures prominently in tree-naming practices, such as Treebeard, a cedar in the Ancient Forest/Chun T'oh Whudujut Provincial Park and Protected Area east of Prince George, and the Tolkien Giant and Hobbit Tree in the Seymour River Valley in North Vancouver. All of which proves that big-tree trackers are big nerds. Naming big trees does give them more personality and highlight them in the news cycle, increasing the chances of conserving them. After all, we're more likely to empathize with Big Lonely Doug than, say, CDF66. (I made that up. Catchy, no?) On the topic of assigning nicknames like Gaston, inspired by the ripped cad in Disney's *Beauty and the Beast*, Ken Wu says, "We don't have the luxury to be boring... It's just a fun way to draw attention—in a viral way, hopefully."

Ken Wu is the cofounder of the Ancient Forest Alliance and the executive director of the Endangered Ecosystems Alliance. Raised in the Prairies, he fell in love with big trees from photos he saw in a book as a kid, which drew him out west to attend UBC and become involved with local conservation groups. He's one of the minds behind naming Avatar Grove, which big-tree tracker TJ Watt first cataloged in 2009, after the James Cameron film that had just come out. The Pacheedaht First Nation's name for the area that contains the grove is T'l'oqwxwat, which means "wide bluff overlooking the river." It was their fishing camp in the summer.

The trees in the old-growth forest were marked for clearing by Teal-Jones, a Surrey-based timber harvesting and milling company. Once Watt and Wu had their name in place, they launched AFA and the campaign to save the grove. It's much easier for the public to connect to Avatar Grove than TFL 46, the name of the tree farm licence that contained the cutblock. The Ancient Forest Alliance reached out to the Pacheedaht but, when they didn't hear back initially, ran with the Avatar Grove campaign because the trees were slated to be logged. The AFA met with the First Nation in 2012 and added the name T'l'oqwxwat to the sign for the grove.

When Avatar Grove was protected in 2012 after a public campaign, the provincial government decided to set off one cutblock (fifty-nine hectares, or 145 acres) of the old-growth cedar forest as an Old-Growth Management Area (OGMA) and to give Teal-Jones the right to harvest nine cutblocks of old-growth, and older Douglas-firs in second-growth patches, in OGMAS on the island. That's the problem with OGMAS: they don't guarantee protection, and the BC government can renegotiate their borders and status. Though Teal-Jones had marked some areas and trees to clear in Avatar Grove, the company didn't regard it as a high-value timber site, so it wasn't a huge ask. In 2013, with the participation of the Pacheedaht, Avatar Grove was declared a recreation site, and boardwalks were built to safely bring tourists to the trees without damaging roots and undergrowth.

Some of the next generation of big-tree trackers are not carrying on the tradition of naming trees. When I asked big-tree tracker Sean O'Rourke, in his early thirties, if he engages in the practice, he said, "I used to name them, usually based on whatever impression they gave me, but I no longer do this. It feels weird to name something, like it implies ownership... I don't have any issues with other people naming things; I just don't want to be the person who decides what something is called. That's not the type of relationship I have with the places I visit. I spend my time out along the Fraser, which people have

lived along continuously for at least nine thousand years, so it's
unlikely I am ever the first to see a tree anyways." Finding and
naming the tree raises the issue of "discovery," a colonial mindset. Such a large tree would likely already be known, its growth
monitored over generations, and it might be regarded as sacred
to a community. Consider that Kiidk'yaas, for example, had
a name and origin story before it was known to populations
beyond the Haida as the Golden Spruce. If a name is not known
for a tree, big-tree trackers could adopt the decolonizing practice of asking the Indigenous Peoples of the area to suggest one,
or otherwise leave it unnamed. "Things are what you call them,"
says legendary musician Ahmir "Questlove" Thompson, "but
they're also not what you don't call them."

I wasn't looking for the glory of nomination, just seeking
those trees that had already been declared notable. It was getting on four in the afternoon by the time I pulled into Sayward.
I'd jotted down some details from the registry before leaving
Courtenay, not knowing if I'd have cell coverage up island. The
directions indicated the tree was "Between White R. and Adam
R., north of Tlowils Lake; south of Sayward." That's a huge
region to cover, but thankfully the entry includes coordinates.
I, however, hadn't thought to write those down, and now I was
without a signal or a clue. Some big-tree trackers prefer this old-
school method of tree tracking, in which you use "clues" to earn
the tree, rather than "cheating" with coordinates and a GPS. But
I figured that asking for directions would test me enough to earn
the tree. I stopped at the gas station for some water and directions, anticipating that everyone in town must know the location
of the biggest yellow-cedar in the world. Thankfully, the attendant knew this area well and didn't seem all that puzzled by
my request. "People are always coming in here looking for big
trees." She said the yellow-cedar was in White River Provincial

Park, the "Cathedral Grove of the North Island." This beautiful ecosystem, sister grove of the forest I'd visited the day before, supports huge trees and numerous species, from coho salmon and steelhead trout to black bears and Roosevelt elk.

From the gas station, I drove until the road became a gravel FSR, inclining up the hillside. It was Trouble's first FSR, so we took it easy, watching out for potholes and kicking up a steady cloud of dust. I passed dense forest, then clear-cuts, looking for a sign for the park. "There's a little brown sign that says 'Now entering sanctuary,'" the station attendant had said. "They should make the sign bigger." I drove past the twelve-kilometer marker and stopped at a clearing to survey. It was a Saturday so there could have been active logging on the road, but I had seen no one. I got out of Trouble and shielded my eyes with one hand. Sun beat down as I stared at the debris of rocks and brush lining both sides of the FSR. Jagged gray stumps, piles of slash (branches), and slender stripped logs rolled out ahead of me. I could see fully across the exposed cutblock to the stands of second-growth on the hills in the background, the darker green up top suggesting older trees, the uniformity marking monoculture. There were no large cedars anywhere in sight.

Yellow-cedars are some of the oldest trees in these temperate rainforests, living between one and two thousand years, and of particular value to the forest industry. Also called a yellow cypress, its watertight, rot-resistant wood is useful for boat-building and paddles. It looks similar to a western red-cedar, but its wood is yellow, its bark gray and "shaggy," and its foliage more of a dark green-blue. Yellow-cedar has lacy branches and small round seed cones, while western red-cedar has pointed cones. Another difference between the two cedars is that it's possible to pull western red-cedar's bark vertically, in strips; yellow-cedar's bark doesn't peel the same way, but the inner bark is used for clothing and baskets. Also, yellow-cedar's foliage can only be stroked smoothly in one direction; western red-cedar's is smooth in both directions.

A dusty, banged-up roadside sign shouted in red on white: LIMITED VISIBILITY. I didn't know then to radio ahead and tell the forestry company I'd be there in my little car; besides, I didn't have a walkie-talkie. My skin prickled in the silence, and I suddenly felt very alone. I hadn't found the park sign; I had no indication of how much farther I'd need to drive; and I was wary of being out there on my own so late in the day. I turned around. I knew from photos on the registry that Sir Daniel Samson has purplish-gray bark and a large buttressed trunk coated in thick green moss, and I'd need to be content with the photos until I could return with appropriate wayfinding equipment or, even better, someone who could bring me to the tree. Still, I felt deflated for failing as an adventurer so early in the trip. Maybe I had been close, the grove around the next bend, or maybe the yellow-cedar was hours ahead of me on that FSR. I didn't know when I'd be back to Sayward, and since it was such a significant tree—a perfect BC Champion—I couldn't complete my project without it.

On my way north to Port Hardy, I took a quick detour to Telegraph Cove and saw a black bear cub running along the road, followed by the mama with two more playful, skinny cubs. The lobby in the Port Hardy hotel smelled like cigarette smoke, the elevator like tomato soup, and my room like packaged Hotel Smell, comfortingly decorated like a financial advisor's office. After a fitful sleep, I was up at four to catch the ferry. I drove through the dark to the terminal at Bear Cove, following a smear of taillights. A young elk ran beside my car, keeping time. Its tawny fur shone blue-black, starlight and velvet, the eye I could see catching the sheen of my headlights.

The MV *Northern Expedition* is a souped-up version of the ferries I'm used to, large vessels that ply the waters between the Lower Mainland and Vancouver Island, and smaller ferries for hopping between the Gulf Islands. The journey up the Inside Passage, a sheltered inland shipping route, is sixteen hours, so I paid extra for an oceanside cabin, a BC Ferries version of a cruise. I laid my stuff on one of the twin beds and napped three times in the other while listening to the *Savage Lovecast* archives. Staring through my porthole or standing on deck, I saw three orcas and a migrating humpback whale. My tree whisperer friend Diana once told me it's auspicious to dream of large mammals, especially whales, and these real sightings boded well for my trip north.

AFTER A NIGHT AT MY FRIENDS' PLACE in Prince Rupert, I started out slow and low with a coffee from Cowpuccino's, then drove alongside the Skeena River to Terrace, where I was bunking at a pal's house for a couple nights. He'd forgotten I was coming, opting for a last-minute mountain-biking trip, but he told me where to find the key, every introvert's dream. In a thrift store, I picked up a hardcover from 1969 called *What Wood Is That? A Manual of Wood Identification*, complete with forty "actual wood samples" slipped into a sleeve at the front, and as if that wasn't enough, part one was titled "The Wood from the Trees," chapter one "Man Masters Timber." Now feeling altogether rugged, I walked into an outfitting store and finally invested in diameter tape. This long measuring tape is used by timber cruisers, arborists, and archaeologists to measure the diameter of trees. The thin metal tape has a hook on one end for securing to bark when wrapping the tape around the tree.

The next morning, I drove about sixty miles toward the Nisga'a village Gitlaxt'aamiks, formerly New Aiyansh, in the Nass Valley. I would be searching for the Champion black cottonwood, which grows in Nisga'a territory. The Nisga'a are self-governed and have been free of the confines of the Indian Act since they won back their territory in a landmark agreement in 1999. The Indian Act, created in 1876, is a racist piece of legislation that still dominates the lives of Indigenous Peoples in numerous ways, such as restricting self-government and reinforcing the reserve system. The Nisga'a Treaty came into effect in May 2000 and is the first modern-day treaty in BC. (The previous one was in 1854.) The treaty recognizes that the Nisga'a have always lived on these lands and have sole title to them. From a forestry perspective, it means that the Nisga'a can do what they want with their trees. It's not Crown land, so it differs from a First Nations–managed woodlot, in which the Nation would control how the trees are harvested but couldn't license out clearing work to a timber company.

The day was hot and windy, and along the way to the tree, I stopped at Gitwangak (also called Kitwanga), meaning People of the Place of Rabbits. The Gitwangak are a member of the Gitxsan Nation. The village of Gitwangak has a large collection of poles, honoring the different clans who lived here. I toured Battle Hill, a national historic site dating from the mideighteenth and early nineteenth century, near the village. This formerly fortified fort sits atop a steep green mound, from the top of which defenders would release spiked logs that would roll down and crush invaders. I also visited Ts'itksim Aks/Vetter Falls, where I saw freshly pulled bark on western red-cedars, new CMTs. I then headed through Anhluut'ukwsim Laxmihl Angwinga'asanskwhl Nisga'a/Nisga'a Memorial Lava Bed Park, a haunting lunarscape of hardened brown lava from a volcanic eruption in the 1700s that killed approximately two thousand people. All these landmarks—the poles, Battle Hill, the CMTs, the lava bed memorial—were reminders that I was moving through a place occupied by people reliant on these forests and the larger landscape of mountain, river, and nearby coast. I felt indebted to be a visitor on these lands, searching for one example of bigness among a living legacy of greatness.

I turned from the Nisga'a Highway toward Gitlaxt'aamiks. The registry indicated that the Champion black cottonwood, 47.5 meters in height with a 27.5-meter crown, would be just before the bridge over Ksi Sii Aks/Tseax River. Black cottonwood is one of the fastest growing trees. The world's largest poplar, it can obtain a massive size in its relatively short lifetime of about two to three hundred years. There were dozens of big cottonwoods listed in the registry, and it was possible that the Champion would soon be replaced due to the species' short life cycle and tendency toward damage. Full of water, the tree is susceptible to breakage due to freezing or stormy weather. Black cottonwoods grow in a straight thick column, branching out at the top, making them popular roosting trees. Their bark is gray and ropey, and as their wood is inclined to rot, they are common wildlife trees for birds, insects, and small burrowing mammals. Wildlife trees are sometimes called standing snags or simply snags, and appear dead but have a lot of value for birds and other critters. Trees that are declared wildlife trees and marked with a yellow blazon, or that grow in Wildlife Management Areas, are protected.

Cottonwood is often used as a pulp source and has a lasting legacy as a tree of many uses for Indigenous Peoples, from face cream and shampoo to salve. Of black cottonwood seedlings, David George Haskell writes, "Only those that start life high on the riverbank, on the ebb of a flood, grow into mature trees."

I was in the right place beside this flowing green water. I parked in a gravel lot and stepped out of Trouble into a swirling mass of fluffy seeds. Alders, Doug-fir, and black cottonwoods ringed the parking lot. The cottonwoods were in full leaf, deep green triangular leaves with silver undersides. I approached the largest of the cottonwoods and whipped out my new d-tape, fumbling as I tried to find purchase for hook in bark. I measured the tree at 9.75 meters around—large, certainly, but not the 10.68-meter circumference (3.4 m DBH) cottonwood I was seeking. I headed a bit farther along the bank into a small stand of trees. Scrambling around dried leaves and catkins, taking care not to slip into the river, I measured another cottonwood at 6.5 meters around, watching for the recoil as the hook whipped back around the tree. I wasn't yet confident in my ability to eyeball the size of a tree, so I was measuring anything vaguely large to get used to the practice.

I emerged from the woods for a scratch and a think on the dendro-koan I was here to crack: the registry had indicated that this Champion cottonwood "appears to be a large grove visible from the highway, yet it is just one giant tree." I looked across the water, past a screen of alders to the tree towering behind. On an island in the river was a large tree that was either several trees or one tree with multiple stems. I couldn't see another big tree this close to the highway so I reasoned it must be the Champion. I was content to come close, without thousands of balloons dropping on me. Just seeing the tree felt like a win.

I brushed the white cotton off my car and drove through the lava fields, intent on soaking in the Hlgu Isgwit hot springs as reward for my tree-seeking efforts.

Up to this point, I'd seen four bears along the road, the mama and her cubs near Telegraph Cove. I figured the hot springs would be busy and not too far into the forest, so I brought my bear horn but left my bear spray in the car.

Don't get ahead of me.

I walked for about five minutes through the forest and marshland, the smell of sulfur becoming stronger, overpowering even
the skunk cabbage next to the trail. Two wooden tubs steamed
with water piped in from the hot springs. Swiftly changing, less
for modesty as there was no one around and more because of the
swarms of mosquitoes, I opted for the smaller tub.

I soaked. And I sighed. And I got all Shel Silverstein up in
that hot spring.

On my way back through the forest, I rounded a corner and
surprised a large black bear foraging in the marsh, not ten feet
from me. I froze and gasped, almost dropping my wet bundle.
The bear turned and crashed through the forest. I proceeded
to clap, sing, and shake as I headed back to the car, stealing
glances over my shoulder. That's when I noticed the scat on
the highway at the entrance to Hlgu Isgwit. Had it been there
when I'd driven in?

As I drove back to my friend's for another night, I had to
conclude that by undertaking this tree-tracking trip, I was
seeing gorgeous landscapes and incredible trees, yes; I was
soaking in glorious hot springs, sure; but by wandering in bear
and cougar territory and driving along FSRs during the loaded
season, I was also willingly engaging in risk. I took risks in
the city, some calculated and others stupid: biking in downtown Toronto at rush hour (and getting doored), buying acid
as a teen at Surrey Central Station where it's unwise to walk
alone during the day (and getting jumped immediately after
in an alley). But in the woods, I could mostly plan for haz-
ards—watch for signs advising of rock fall hazard, look for
scat or claw marks on trees, avoid tromping in berry patches
or marshland when the berries were juiciest and the skunk
cabbage smelliest.

I felt the larger risk was that I'd get home and this whole trip would have been for naught. I wouldn't have found the Champions, wouldn't have learned about the trees firsthand, wouldn't have proven myself. Making dinner that night in Terrace, I realized I had miscalculated the scale of the adventure, wrongly believed myself still capable of the ambition that had driven me this far in life.

I HAD ALLOTTED A TREE PER DAY on this road trip and was increasingly aware that rushing between Champions was not an ideal way to learn about each species in the intimate way I'd intended at the start of my project. Searching for the Champions, individual standouts, is a lesson in fragments. The registry presents an artificial forest where trees grow alphabetically, alongside those they might not pair with in real life, like a virtual arboretum. I was partial to some of the Champions over others—the biggest trees, the spruces, firs, and cedars—but in surveying all the Champions in an equal light in my spreadsheet, they became a democratic forest, to borrow a phrase from photographer William Eggleston.

In his photobook *The Democratic Forest*, Eggleston and his editor Mark Holborn consider over one thousand photos, taken in the 1980s, of a range of subjects. His photos capture his travels around the U.S., particularly in the South, and to Berlin. Everything becomes heightened first through his lens and then our gaze. Holborn pairs landscape photos with still life, what critic Sean Sheehan calls "the ordinary furniture of daily life— parking meters, cars, brick walls, signage, leftover food on a plate, trash, an empty road." Rather than always opting for an easy pairing of photos on a spread, say a diptych of two pipes, Holborn will combine unlike objects, reinforcing the "democratic" nature of Eggleston's project. Eggleston demonstrates that when you open your eyes to look for an item of interest, you generally find it. And crucially, what's of interest might not be the biggest or even the most objectively interesting. Case in point: my next quarry, a rather small Douglas maple notable only by looking for it and pairing it in the registry with more impressive larger trees.

In eager pursuit of that Douglas maple with a height of 18 meters, I headed to Lakelse Lake Provincial Park, about seventeen minutes' drive from downtown Terrace. The Douglas maple seemed an unassuming tree in this 875-acre park with old-growth cedar, Sitka spruce, and hemlock. This park is located between the Skeena and Kitimat Rivers on the unceded traditional territories of the Kitselas, "People of the Canyon," part of the Tsimshian Nation. The waters of these territories have long been harvested—*Lakelse* (from Tsimshian *Lax Gyels*) means "fresh water mussel"—and before the area became a provincial park in 1956, it was home to a federally operated sockeye salmon hatchery.

The registry listed the Douglas maple as "near" campsite 21 in the park. After cruising around the campsites and not noticing a number system, I asked a camper for directions. She was there with her kids and looked at me askance.

"This site is booked for a Scout gathering," she said. "You want the campsite down the highway."

Just like me to crash a Scout outing. Now at the right campground, I saw campsite 20, 22, 23 . . . I entered the nearby visitors' center, a modern-style cedar-clad building with a black metal roof. The building sat in a fresh gravel area ringed by cedars and Doug-firs and brightened with clumps of fern and green maple leaves on stems twisting into the canopy. Approaching the blond, tattooed parks employee behind the desk, I said, "Excuse me, where is campsite 21?"

"You're standing in it," she said.

I blinked. "What do you mean?"

"It was a very quick decision to build this visitors' center last November," she said brightly, gesturing with her hands to the cement floor that had been recently poured. "We haven't had a chance to update the camp signs."

"So you're telling me we're standing in campsite 21?"

She nodded.

I stared at her for a beat, then explained my project. "Have you seen any large Douglas maples around here?"

Blank look. "I think there are some around back?"

David Douglas was a Scottish botanist who made his mark all over BC and Hawaii, spraying his surname on streets and trees like a territorial dog. The Douglas-fir is a well-known example of the flora he marked, easily recognizable for its tall straight trunk and crown of dark green boughs. The Douglas maple, my target in Lakelse, is a relatively small variety of maple. It's important to recognize that size does not equate to age in the tree world. Small trees, such as larches, bristlecone pines, or Pacific yews, may be older than other bigger trees. Related to smaller maples like the vine maple, bigtooth maple, and box elder, Douglas maples are the dominant variety of Rocky Mountain maple on the coast, west of the Continental Divide. They have three- to five-lobed leaves, and their wood is very hard; Indigenous Peoples of the islands and coastal mainland use it for bows, clubs, paddles, and snowshoes. These trees grow in a clump of narrow stems, adding to my understanding of maples. I'd long thought of maples as a single broccoli-like stem wearing a Beaker-like wig of leaves.

The Lakelse Lake Provincial Park employee I spoke with was interested enough in the registry that she wrote down the name and said she'd check it out. Not that I expect all provincial park employees to know about the registry, but if there was no widespread awareness of the Champion within the park, how could I be guaranteed that it wasn't cleared during construction? Trees are protected if they grow in a municipal, provincial, regional, or federal park, but I wondered if the park could apply for exemption if building something essential, like a visitors' center. Another form of protection is voluntary retention, practiced by the forest industry and based on tree size— a minimum DBH and sometimes a minimum height. For example, in 2017, BC Timber Sales set up the Coastal Legacy Tree Program, which manages four species based on DBH (coastal Douglas-fir, Sitka spruce, western red-cedar, and yellow-cedar) in four coastal areas. BC Timber Sales, or BCTS, is a governmental organization that manages 20 percent of Crown land in BC and sets the price for stumpage—the cost of harvesting timber on Crown land, based on the prices BCTS receives when it puts blocks up for auction. The Coastal Legacy Tree Program's purpose is to show that BCTS values the multiple roles of big trees, beyond a timber source. BCTS voluntarily retains the tree if it meets a minimum DBH and strives for a one-hectare buffer around it too.

I told the park employee that I'd be trotting around, looking for a large Douglas maple. In the dense undergrowth between campsites, I found mostly coniferous trees, mosquitoes, and ferns growing along a small creek. Maples were mixed in around the campsites, their spindly reddish stems shagging with moss. I was not a mindful tree tracker, balancing phone and guidebook while responding to texts from Jason, who was cheering me on in my hapless quest.

Circling my way toward the visitors' center, dodging low maple branches and sidestepping roots, I cut around back of the building and saw a number of small maples coated in moss.

I measured the DBH of the largest maple as 0.87 meters, which, if this were my tree, would have been a significant increase for a tree that was entered into the registry with a DBH of 0.36 meters. The tree was nominated and verified in 2001, and I doubted it would have grown so much in seventeen years. More likely, I didn't yet know how to measure multistemmed trees, or the tree I was looking for was gone. Whether it was the Champion or not, I had found *something*, measured it, and studied it, which elevated its interest in my eye. I had ventured into the forest expecting to find something of note, à la Eggleston's democratic forest, and failing that, a confirmation of absence.

The loss of a tree can be a microcosm of greater losses, and in a way more tangible. An individual tree being cut is a way to consider an entire landscape being cleared; one death a means of comprehending thousands killed after a volcanic eruption— it's grief on a more manageable scale. When a houseplant or pet dies, we can feel these "small" losses so much more than the bigger ones because they're more personal and on a scale we can grasp. My responsibility in this project was to pay attention, even to what I could not see; to mourn what might have been lost. In his memoir *Horizon*, the late acclaimed travel writer Barry Lopez describes his responsibility of viewing through a trip to Galápagos. "My regular routine here in the morning is inquiry," he writes. "Every day I consider how fortunate I am to be free to wander in Galápagos. Not everyone gets to come. Pay attention to small things I tell myself. Look closely at what are clearly *not* the answers to some of your questions." I was lucky indeed to be wandering a safe campsite with no agenda but to look at trees, including other species not on my list and certainly deserving a closer glance.

ON MY WAY BACK TO TERRACE, after checking out a big Sitka spruce (not a Champion) near Stewart on the U.S.-Canada border, I pulled off the Stewart-Cassiar Highway near Meziadin Junction. Coordinates from the registry told me the Champion subalpine fir (aka Rocky Mountain fir) was growing in the forest adjacent to the highway. These tall dark-green spires look like skinny Christmas trees, with short branches jutting out along the length of their trunk and purple seed cones that sit upright at the crown. This Champion was last measured in 1987 at 50.3 meters high and with a DBH of 0.81.

I stared into that dense block of forest for a few minutes, black pillars against an overcast sky, alert to the possibility of being surprised by an animal or, perhaps more dangerously, another human. I had seen an additional four bears on the road that morning (nine bears so far, dear reader), but more likely I would catch my foot in a hole and go down, with no one around to know where I was. I psyched myself up to step over the line, leaving the highway shoulder, walking over the gravel embankment, blundering straight into the woods. It seemed a dangerous undertaking for a tree that hadn't been seen in more than thirty years. No cars passed for long stretches, and the silence weighed on me. That's why you often see empty cars on the side of the highway, I reminded myself—people wander away for a piss or to check on something real quick, and they sometimes don't make it back. Still, I had the coordinates and the red marker on Google Maps. The tree was perhaps just thirty minutes' walk out, but there was little way of knowing the conditions as the satellite image showed a mass of trees. I worried I wasn't pushing myself far enough and texted Jenny for advice. She wrote back immediately: "Put a pin in it." She used to spend a lot of time alone in the bush, searching for archaeological sites, and insists on strict safety protocols, buddies, and check-ins. Her text was the permission I needed to shut down this quest for the moment, despite feeling the pull of the tree.

Adventuring, I was learning, doesn't look like fists raised in triumph on a mountaintop. Adventuring is instead made up of preparation and practice, safety checkers and guidebooks, and the "power of the gut": having the guts to do it and listening to your gut (or your sister's) when it's time to pack it in and try another time. Sometimes adventure looks like stillness and sounds like silence. The sandwich board outside the Two Sisters café in Smithers spelled it out for me the next morning: "'If only I had checked myself.' —Guy who wrecked himself"

I WAS STARTING TO GET SICK OF the "one tree a day" pace I'd been pulling on my road trip. I'd leave a day or two as a shoulder between trees, but I was now letting their locations dictate my travel, bypassing scenic outlooks in favor of remote FSRs and deserted towns. I was spending long hours in Trouble, grabbing drive-through meals, not having the relaxing holiday I'd planned before starting this project. I was reminded of the Intensity in Ten Cities trip I'd taken with my sister in Europe before starting my master's. Stay up all night packing and fly to Istanbul, overnight ferry to Greece, Eiffel Tower ✔, carry a bag of groceries onto the train in case we couldn't find snacks in, you know, *Europe*. How was my rush to see all these Champions in a compressed time frame any different? Was the point to fly in and fly out, seeing only the best, biggest, brightest? It felt like visiting the West Coast to go on a whale tour but missing the sun rising over a quiet kelp forest or watching dew bead on moss. In trying to see so many trees in hard-to-reach places, I was burning out on the project intended to bring me back from exhaustion.

At this point in my project, I had seen the Scouler's willow, bitter cherry, bigleaf maple, and red alder. I'd possibly found the cascara, was pretty sure I had seen the black cottonwood, and didn't know about the Douglas maple. I had cut short an hours-long drive down an active FSR outside Vanderhoof to see a tamarack, James Brown's greatest hits on repeat and my Google Maps spinning me in circles, and I had missed out on the yellow-cedar and subalpine fir. Perfectionist tendencies die hard, and the trees I had missed loomed larger than my successes. I felt, all things considered, I was making a decent start, but I was mostly blundering through guesswork. I wasn't taking accurate measurements to be an asset to the registry, and I didn't know to plot my coordinates like real big-tree trackers—arborists, ecologists, and forestry technologists—do.

I decided to cut the trip short a few days so I could enjoy the last bit of my holiday in Jason's company. We'd been dating for only a few weeks, about as long as I'd been a big-tree tracker, and I wanted to revel in that new relationship energy. I made an eight-hour beeline from Quesnel in the center of the province to Vancouver. On the radio, I heard reports of wildfires, closing roads in some areas near my route. I wondered if these fires would burn any of the trees remaining on my list. As author and activist Naomi Klein, writing about the widespread wildfires in the summer of 2017, reminded us, "You are not breathing pollution from power plants or exhaust from cars," which presents as smog, "but rather trees that were very recently alive. You are breathing in forest."

Driving down the Coquihalla Highway, looking for a park with hoodoos where I could take a break, I took a wrong turn and found myself below the highway in ranching country. I drove across metal cattle grids and stopped to absorb an emerald hill, ringed by trails from cattle traversing the slope. The green mound against the blue sky was a reminder that beauty existed just off the highway. Once settled at home, I headed into the second-growth forest of lower Lynn Canyon in North Vancouver to remind myself why I was searching for these trees: not for the photo op or the checkmark but for immersion. I was starting to recall that the forest is the place I feel most myself, squarely in my body, butting up against my biggest dreams and fears.

— 6 —

Attention Grows

WEEPING BIRCH, DAWN REDWOOD, LABURNUM, NORWAY SPRUCE

"What we pay attention to grows."
ADRIENNE MAREE BROWN

NOW IT WAS SUMMER, a frustratingly fallow season for my project. After returning from my road trip around the province, I felt it was unwise to travel farther afield, with roads closed due to wildfire and the skies too smoky for comfort. My eyes started watering when I returned to the Lower Mainland and didn't stop for six months. The wildfires each summer create an annual mourning in the Pacific Northwest, the grief only intensifying with smoke becoming more common from fires in the Interior or south of us, in Washington, Oregon, and California.

Another virtual obstacle lay in my path: throughout the rest of the year and into 2019, while I was trying to find the western hemlock Norvan's Castle as well as other trees, the registry site continually crashed, sometimes for months at a time. When it would go up again, I'd hastily download an updated spreadsheet of the trees' measurements, descriptions, and locations (there weren't many updates in my first year on the case).

When I'd started this project, I had a clear picture of what Amanda the Adventurer would look like when given the space to spread her wings. I would take six months off work and drive around BC in a little blue pickup and camper, looking for trees and playing my ukulele, with a dog named Johnnycake by my side, of course. Call it the overlapping influence of growing up on the coast in awe of self-supporting tugboat operators, the myth of tree planters, and the #VanLife of social media. But I had books to edit, a life in the city, and I was attempting to reform my habit of taking on too much at once. I reminded myself it's absolutely okay to take breaks, that I had just returned from almost three weeks looking for big trees, that driving my small car way down FSRs among loaded logging trucks wasn't all that wise. The time away from looking for the trees, sitting on my deck on the weekend with a beer in one hand and a celebrity biography in the other, allowed me to take stock. Sure, the main registry was down, but I did have a spreadsheet, and I bet I could reach out to other big-tree trackers for help. I was already in touch with legendary big-tree hunters like Shaun Muc, who'd searched through forests with Ralf Kelman, and Ken Wu, who was seeking big trees with photographer and tree tracker TJ Watt with the goal of saving them from being cut. Shaun and Ken kept encouraging me to get out there, find bigger trees.

> *Go up to Davis Lake, Logan Lake, and Hornet Lake!*
> *Get up to Lundbom Lake to check out the ponderosa pines!*
> *Get over to the island!*
> *Go see the ponderosa pines out in the East Kootenays!*
> *So many lodgepole pines have died from the mountain pine beetle... We need a new Champion.*

I wondered if there was some novelty about me being a woman hunting these giants, but it was more likely that such tendencies to go farther, longer, bigger are common among tree trackers. In a short film called *Giant Tree Hunters*, TJ Watt, who located Big Lonely Doug and a pile of other big trees, says, "I think about trees all the time. I don't really feel like I have a choice in my interests. I read about trees, I take pictures of trees, I dream about trees. I would be the happiest person ever if I found the biggest tree in the country." What is it about trees that sends some into rapture? And did I lack the gene? I felt I must be doing something wrong since I was not feeling the same obsession as the other trackers. I had been obsessive as a youth—after-school cartoons, the 1920s film star Louise Brooks, Richard Linklater films, Edgar Allan Poe's life and work—but I'd grown skeptical of overzealous commitment to a topic after a deep dive in grad school broke my brain.

I knew that Shaun and Ken were sharing their passion as much as encouraging me to nominate my own Champions, to make my mark. But didn't these big-tree trackers realize that to reach this point, I'd already pushed myself? I wasn't out to break records or find the next biggest tree, wasn't poring over forestry maps and Google Earth to find sections of old-growth that hadn't been logged (evident from a "scruffier" appearance, darker green with shadows, compared to lighter green second-growth tree plantations), and wasn't using lidar (light detection and ranging, a form of remote sensing) to find the tallest trees. Longtime big-tree trackers know exactly where to look, then go into the bush to ground-truth the image, using measuring tapes, drones, even climbing into the tree and dropping a plumb bob to determine height. As TJ said, "I have a bit of a GPS in my head from staring at these maps for so many bloody hours." I was happy going where others had gone, but the scope of my project had killed the passion of looking. I now shrank from big trees, mumbled responses to friends' supportive questions about the locations of the biggest, and wasn't enthused by the smaller Champions. In her book of poetic essays, *Bluets*, Maggie Nelson writes, "I must admit that not all blues thrill me. I am not overly interested in the matte stone of turquoise, for example, and a tepid, faded indigo usually leaves me cold. Sometimes I worry that if I am not moved by a blue thing, I may be completely despaired, or dead." In my smaller moments, I regarded other big-tree hunters who were bowled over as naive, awed by single trees while whole forests—continents!—burned.

I didn't overly mind the hiatus brought on by real and virtual conditions, as it gave me an out from spinning in the forest. Even easy gets like the Hollyburn Giant, a cedar on nearby Cypress Mountain, where I often hiked, eluded me. The weekend-warrior project had become a grind, an addition to my week's labor rather than a break. Oliver Burkeman, in his brilliant book *Four Thousand Weeks*, a realist's take on what we can actually achieve in our rather limited life spans, writes of this tendency to make our leisure time "productive"—missing out on the joys of a walk, say, by focusing on taking a certain number of steps per day. I had been thinking of the project as something productive: complete my goal, learn more about trees, and transform myself in the process. If I reframed the project as something creative, it felt lighter, more doable. Aldous Huxley wrote, "It's dark because you're trying too hard... 'Lightly, child, lightly.'" And whereas I was out of my depth reading maps, as an editor I was a pro at recognizing the ups and downs of the creative process: initial excitement, followed by a dawning realization that the project would be harder than anticipated, and a final recalibration into something more manageable—an ending, but perhaps not the one I'd envisioned. As a creative undertaking then, it was natural for my Champions project to have assumed a slower pace, as my enthusiasm lessened and the size of the task set in.

I reevaluated my goal: all the Champions but over a longer period. I could take a cue from my subject, with the trees on their own longer time frames. The trees didn't care whether I came with a feeling of ardor or obsession, whether I dreamed about them; they didn't care if I visited at all. I realized that being around something growing for itself, without measurement, could offer welcome relief. Here my skills in qualitative assessment could really shine. After all, Western science has overemphasized quantitative data at the expense of other useful information, and it has long situated plants as singular, growing alone, rather than in an interconnected way. As Gina Rae La Cerva writes in *Feasting Wild*, during the seventeenth and eighteenth centuries, "Botanists painstakingly described, cataloged, and renamed wild plants that had previously been so commonplace and ordinary that they weren't mentioned in cookbooks or herbals. Exotic specimens were drawn on blank backgrounds, without the context of the landscapes where they grew."

Gradually, it became less important to me to see the Champions than to experience seeing these trees amid their settings, which felt more respectful and even decolonizing. In *How to Do Nothing*, artist and educator Jenny Odell writes, "If we think about what it means to 'concentrate' or 'pay attention' at an individual level, it implies alignment: different parts of the mind and even the body acting in concert and oriented toward the same thing." Being in the forest made me feel alert and effervescent, confronting the real risks of injuring myself or becoming lost. I felt that all my cells were firing with the same purpose: *Keep moving. Keep breathing. Keep paying attention.* Odell began birding in a rose garden near her apartment in Oakland. She found that once she started looking for (or, more often, listening for) a certain type of bird, she detected a larger context. "After birds, there were trees," she writes, "then different kinds of trees, then the bugs that lived in them. I began to notice animal communities, plant communities, animal-plant communities; mountain ranges, fault lines, watersheds." Odell later realizes she's experiencing bioregionalism, which she defines as "observation and recognition of what grows where, as well as an appreciation for the complex web of relationships among those actors."

I had been looking at trees as individuals. Now by virtue of staying mostly in place, in and around the Lower Mainland, I was seeing the whole ecosystem. I began training my eye on multiple scales: smaller trees and larger context, using the early lessons from the pruned red alder in Stanley Park and the overgrown bitter cherry in a residential lot to understand how trees live with us. Tree identification makes the world a friendlier place. I said hello to Pacific yews while hiking the Larsen Trail on Grouse Mountain. I focused beyond learning how to identify only native Champions and came to know all the trees in my neighborhood, nodding to the weeping birch on the hill between my house and the grocery store each week, noticing the subtle changes in its leaves over the seasons.

After finally finding Norvan's Castle on Coliseum Mountain, that fucking western hemlock, I realized I didn't need to push so hard on the weekends. Burkeman writes, "We might seek to incorporate into our daily lives more things we do for their own sake alone." In other words, we can make them hobbies. In doing so, ironically, we can find more success. In her article "An Elite Athlete's Real-Life Training Plan," Katie Arnold, winner of the 2018 Leadville Trail 100, writes about how she was able to meet her everyday commitments and train for a hundred-mile race. "Frankly," she writes, "the entire endeavor seemed improbable, delusional even. I had two young daughters at home, a book to finish writing, and a metal plate the size of a spatula in my knee from breaking my leg two years earlier in a white water rafting accident... Did I mention I was in my mid-40s?" Without a coach or any spare time, she realized the secret was to make training an ordinary part of her life. "The most important metric in training for a hundred-mile race isn't pace or mileage but time on your feet," she writes. She snuck short runs around her everyday life: after dinner with her family, while coaching her daughters' lacrosse team. "I let the rhythm of our family life dictate my training schedule, not the other way around."

I learned to do the same thing while tree tracking, rather than planning another ambitious multiweek road trip. Visiting friends and their newborn outside Victoria? I could pick off the Champion shore pine, easily accessible in the front yard of an apartment complex. A trip to Kelowna to visit an author? I could sneak in a few trips to see trees on my spreadsheet. Going to the doctor's? I could take an extra twenty minutes to check out the big vine maple I knew grew in a nearby residential area and see if it was bigger than the current Champion growing in Burnaby's Central Park.

I already went for long walks each afternoon or evening, a habit I'd developed in my teens. "Area woman hangs on to summer," I headlined my jaunts around my neighborhood with the air of Harriet the Spy, jotting down details about trees in my notebook, drawing connections between species.

That horizontally striated bark looks like a cherry tree...
Ah yes, there are the leaves to back up that hypothesis.
I'm sure that's a cedar but the bark is not reddish...
Ah, I see the round cones now. It's a yellow-cedar.
Those long narrow leaves mean this tree must be related to willow, just as cottonwood is. And elm?

*Not all peeling trees are arbutus; this one is surely a Japanese
paper maple.*

*Some trees have maple leaves but are not maples, like London
plane.*

Instead of ignoring interesting-looking trees on my way to
Champions, I made a point to stop and look them up in my guidebook. That's how I learned about dawn redwood, a deciduous
conifer with a braided red trunk and delicate needles that fall
each autumn. I realized there was an avenue full of these rare trees,
originally from China, within walking distance of my apartment,
near the Pacific National Exhibition on East Hastings Street. I
recalled that the PNE grounds had a sanctuary forest and pond, as
well as a Japanese garden, and I started steering my walks there.
Standing in front of a mystery tree, I'd say to Jason, "I'm just
going to do a little research," pulling out my phone to look up a
tree, or I'd lightly compare across species, see which trees grew
with which, or search for clues that might lead to identification—
fungi that grow with a certain type of conifer, for example. I didn't
go too deep, though—quickly looking something up, the way a
copy editor might check the height of the Statue of Liberty (it's
305 feet, FYI). Also valuable to me was knowing who to consult,
and I took to Instagram to ask local arborists, "What tree is this?"

As a daydreamer prone to rumination, I welcomed the mindfulness my curious focus gave to these rambles. Dr. Kaeli Swift,
who writes the *Corvid Research* blog, says, "There's something
about going out in nature, looking for something, and finding it
that feels unworldly [and] gratifying to me... By and large, to
succeed consistently, you can't *just* get lucky. You need to pay
attention. To learn the signs of what you're looking for." Tree
tracking is like playing Eye Spy, like looking for certain letters or numbers in an urban environment. When I'd be running
errands, I'd give myself a task.

*Today I'm looking for cedars. I'm comparing western red-cedar
with yellow-cedar.*

*I'm examining how trees grow to different heights on the same
street, or reflect light differently.*

I'm seeing which trees the crows like and which they avoid, if any.

I didn't need to pressure myself to see a pile o' trees in the
summer. After all, spring is a great time to look for big trees in
BC, as the budding flowers and fresh greenery can aid in identification. Fall is another sweet time to look for trees: it's cooler,
the valleys (where trees can grow the biggest) are drier, and the
West Coast's Novembruary rains haven't settled in yet. Winter
is certainly possible: it tests identification skills for broadleaf
trees, but it's easier to see conifers when the understory demands
less bushwhacking. I learned that September is an ideal time to
identify trees, as they still have their leaves plus their fruits, like
the long seedpods of the Chinese wingnut, which look like an
origami chain. I hadn't realized there was one growing around
the corner from my apartment until an arborist on Instagram
helped me out.

I was learning that sometimes the best way to find trees of
any size or variety is not just to look up but to look *through* the
landscape immediately in front of you: trees rise above, but they
also layer in place. That's how I noticed cherry blossoms puffing
along a city block, laburnum glowing golden up ahead, and yes,
a larger trunk in a forest while seeking a Champion. I looked
for the interactions between the city and its trees, beyond the
roots bulging the sidewalk. Walking through the city as the
rain falls, one looks instinctively for shelter. You can tell where
the urban canopy extends over the sidewalk by the lighter gray
half-moons of dry concrete. If you need to check something on
your phone or write something in your small journal, you can
wait until you enter a half-moon.

This leisurely looking helped me recall that such fixation on trees was not new for me. I had buried my dendrophilia in the years of focusing on school and career, but even in my work-obsessed years in Toronto, I had allowed myself to be pulled to urban trees. I recently hauled a box out of my parents' basement, where they'd been storing books and photo albums for me while I moved between Vancouver and Toronto. A flood some years ago had damaged the boxes, soaked into the old term papers and yearbooks. Ignoring the musty odor, I opened a water-warped photo album emblazoned with a green leaf and red ladybird, the pictures protected under plastic film. Alongside photos of field trips and birthday parties, I found evidence of my first experiments in photography. I was fixated on the Doug-firs at the bottom of our street and the maple at the corner of our driveway, enraptured by the Japanese maple, cherry blossoms, and cedar hedges. I knew that trees featured in my childhood memories, but now that I had proof I'd revered them, I wanted to deepen that relationship through understanding. The poet Mary Oliver writes, "Attention is the beginning of devotion," and Burkeman makes the case even stronger: "Attention... just *is* life: your experience of being alive consists of nothing other than the sum of everything to which you pay attention."

Sure, I didn't have the field skills that would give me a leg up in tree tracking, but maybe being an Everywoman Tree Tracker skilled in literary arts gave me a different kind of advantage. Walter Murch, the revered film and sound editor, says, "What you do as an editor is search for patterns, at both the superficial and ever deeper levels—as deep as you can go." Editors detect patterns in an author's prose or ideas, like a repeated thought or word, or a tendency to hold back on emotional subjects. Of course, assigning patterns to life is in no way unique to editors; we all do it, whether to explain coincidence, normalize the uncanny, or prove our horoscopes. I began "reading" trees as I read text, learning their particular languages, noting the patterns that are unique to a species or a section of forest, depending on whether it's coastal or Interior, old-growth or replanted. The editor asks questions about the text, on behalf of the eventual reader, and I began to ask questions beyond "Are you the Champion?":

- What types of cones do you have, and do they grow straight up or droop down?

- Are your needles soft, poky, round?

- Is your bark smooth or coarse, thick or thin, and does it peel easily?

- Are your leaves growing alone or in clusters?

- Do you grow flowers in springtime? Are those "flowers" actually bracts—leaves that look like flowers?

- If you're a conifer in winter, are you evergreen or have you dropped your needles?

When you're revering all the trees, it doesn't matter if they're Champions. To put it from the perspective of filmmaker Kirsten Johnson, A roll and B roll footage both count. "Even the terminology 'B roll' I'm over because it implies that it's not important," she said in a conversation with Michael Moore about her autobiographical film *Cameraperson*. "It's A roll. It's like everything that you're shooting for your film matters for your film. So think of it all as a whole."

WHILE THE REGISTRY WAS LESS AVAILABLE, I decided to explore the arboreta around Vancouver. The city's mild climate makes it an ideal habitat for these collections of native and imported trees, and we have at least three significant botanical gardens that include arboreta. On a blustery fall day, my friend Hiromi Goto and I grabbed hot chocolates and headed to Shaughnessy Park, a 3.5-acre circular park more commonly called the Crescent, in one of Canada's wealthiest areas. Canadian Pacific Railway, the major landholder in Vancouver in the late nineteenth and early twentieth centuries after the federal government transferred the company six thousand acres, designed Shaughnessy to be an elite neighborhood. One way CP Rail ensured an upper-crust population was requiring that single-family houses, on larger lots, cost six times as much as they did elsewhere in the city. This housing development enticed the wealthy from the already elite neighborhoods of the West End, Fairview, and Kitsilano. Vancouver continues to be a city of marked wealth disparity, and Shaughnessy is an insultingly short drive away from the Downtown Eastside, often called the poorest postal code in Canada. CP Rail hired engineer L. E. Davick and prominent landscape architect Frederick Gage Todd, who had apprenticed with Frederick Law Olmsted (co-designer of New York City's Central Park). Todd considered hundreds of tree species from around the world, planting approximately forty-seven ornamentals and conifers over a century ago, and many remain in the Crescent today.

I'd learned about the Crescent in Gerald B. Straley's *Trees of Vancouver*, a guidebook published in 1992, and invited Hiromi to come explore. Hiromi is a writer, editor, and teacher. We became friends after I moved back to Vancouver; I wrote her a letter of appreciation for her short-story collection *Hopeful Monsters*. I'd read the book in undergrad and its collision of the domestic and the monstrous had stayed with me. Sipping our hot drinks and using the numbered map to the trees in Straley's guidebook, we wandered from number to number, sometimes finding an immense tree, and sometimes nothing—the tree either fallen or removed in the intervening years. A Norway spruce had recently fallen in a windstorm and lay battered near the edge of the circle. I thanked it for existing and took one of its long cones to place on my dash.

Like they do in a park, trees can grow larger in an arboretum than they might in the forest, as they have an open canopy, fewer competing species, and less undergrowth. Arboreta are a great place to learn about tree species, as the trees often appear with an identifying sign. VanDusen Botanical Garden, near the Crescent, is an especially educational site as most of its trees have signage. While arboreta used to be grown for practical purposes, such as establishing a woodlot or food source, today they are often kept for scientific, conservation, therapeutic, or aesthetic reasons. Arboreta date back to the pharaohs of ancient Egypt, and Kublai Khan of the thirteenth-century Mongol Empire, and were commonly constructed in England and Europe throughout the nineteenth century, the practice then spreading to North America, Australia, and New Zealand. I was tempted to turn the parkette near my apartment into an arboretum, labeling the yellow-cedar and western red-cedar that I'd studied in order to tell them apart. Actually, this would be a pinetum, an arboretum of conifers.

Hiromi is engaged in her own practice of looking at and learning from the nature around her, finding "a little beauty, every day," through her photo and writing project of the same name. By example, she was slowly helping me see the landscape not as a place full of big things to catalog, but as a place full of trees, animals, mosses, and insects who are other living beings to know. While I tried to align a tree in front of me with the number on the map, Hiromi simply gazed up at the tree and asked, "Whose child are you?"

Fellow writer Kyo Maclear, author of *Birds Art Life*, a memoir of a year spent learning to bird in Toronto, went for a walk with Hiromi in Pacific Spirit Regional Park, a 1,900-acre seaside forest west of Vancouver's urban core, in 2017. Maclear found Hiromi opened her eyes to what was below her feet, not just in the skies and trees above. Maclear calls Hiromi's kinship with the forest and trees a "'peopling' of the forest... Hers is a world-view simultaneously informed by a commitment to Indigenous teachings, queer ecocentric ethics, Japanese-inflected animistic thought, and efforts to decenter the human." Robin Wall Kimmerer, a professor of environmental biology and enrolled member of the Citizen Potawatomi Nation, speaks about deepening our relationship to plants and animals through the pronouns we use. In her book *Braiding Sweetgrass*, she notes that using *it* for a living being, such as our grandmother, "robs a person of selfhood and kinship, reducing a person to a mere thing." When we objectify the world around us, we make it something we can own, a land of things for the taking and abusing. By using pronouns other than *it* for trees, we recognize their intelligence and identity as living beings, with kin relationships. As she writes, "If a maple is an *it*, we can take up the chain saw. If a maple is a *her*, we think twice."

In my previous forest outings, I'd been limiting my understanding of the tree to "here it is" and the binary label of Champion or not-Champion, big or small. To simply say, "Hello, here you are" or "Who are you?" brought me a sense of spaciousness and curiosity. I had been dutifully learning the names for trees, but some of them, like Douglas maple, were tied to the colonizer who'd appended a name to them, rather than an older language and naming. Nicknames were personal to the tree tracker who nominated the tree and could be descriptive, particularly of size (Big, Giant), but often those names don't capture the way cedars swirl or how beings grow, flow, or age. "Can we unlearn the language of objectification and throw off colonized thought?" Kimmerer asks. "Can we make a new world with new words?" Kimmerer noticed that when her students in field school "put more energy into memorizing Latin names, they spend less time looking at the beings themselves." By focusing on quantitative criteria (DBH, crown, height), I missed out on so much of the tree: the sound of its leaves moving in the hot breeze, the coolness the green water suggested as it flowed around the island where the tree grew. By seeing each tree as a being, I could come to know each Champion as a true individual growing in community, rather than a representative species or an entry to check off in an Excel sheet. I could know them as they lived and as they died.

THE CURIOUS THING ABOUT hunting for living beings is that sometimes what was gone grows back. Such was the case with the Champion Sitka alder in the Old Arboretum at UBC. On a sunnier day, I met Ira Sutherland at the Forestry building. Ira grew up in Dunbar in Vancouver, and before returning to grad school for his PhD, he worked as an arborist. He has an easy air about him, and I was instantly at ease, though this was my first time looking for trees with someone so experienced, who was taking formal measurements. We set out to find this small forest, established when UBC's Point Grey campus was under construction. The oldest trees in this arboretum were moved here in 1916 from their former home at Riverview Hospital in Coquitlam near the Pitt River, about a fifty-minute drive from Point Grey. The first provincial botanist of BC, John Davidson, established the arboretum at Riverview, then called Essondale, in 1911 for therapeutic purposes, and patients were involved in the planting. Riverview closed in 2012 and is now a popular filming location for TV and movies. The only way for the public to access the grounds is on a tree tour hosted by the Riverview Horticultural Centre Society. The Kwikwetlem First Nation's name for the area, səmiqʷəʔelə, or the "Place of the Great Blue Heron," is supplanting "Riverview," and the Nation is playing an active role in the site's redevelopment. There are about 1,800 trees in the arboretum, including a few that are rare in Vancouver, like a princess tree and a female gingko with its fruits that smell like a cross between semen and pus. (For this reason, males are commonly planted around Vancouver.)

After World War II, imported trees were planted in UBC's Old Arboretum, some unique within Vancouver. Straley's map showed eighty-eight trees, but we couldn't count on that many remaining decades later. Over time, the university constructed more buildings in green spaces around campus, denuding the canopy and leaving the Old Arboretum a bit forgotten. UBC has experienced a lot of construction in the intervening years, and some of the buildings and parking lots crossed into the arboretum zone, causing the removal of some trees. Using a PDF map Ira found online, we set out to find the remaining trees, their identifying plaques intact.

Randy Stoltmann nominated and verified the Sitka alder as a Champion in 1992, two years before his death. When last measured, the tree was 8.5 meters tall with a diameter of 0.52 meters. Straley noted of the Sitka alder in the same year: "There is a large, very typical tree with many trunks in the Old Arboretum at UBC. It is larger than is usually seen in the wild because it is growing out in the open with no competition." The Sitka alder was growing in good company with red alder and hemlocks, but it was much reduced over the years. Ira looked into the shrubby tree to find where the central stem had been cut, maybe twelve years ago. Such is the nature of the registry that this tree remains the Champion, simply because it's the only Sitka alder on record. A few saw-toothed leaves grew around the periphery of the cut stump, the other stems of the trunk growing in closely around that.

Ira showed me how to measure a multibranched tree like this, focusing on the largest stem. Each taking opposite ends of the d-tape, we measured the crown, taking the average of two cross-points. Ira used a laser rangefinder to take the height, and we determined this Champion to now be 4 meters tall with a crown spread of 5.5 meters and a diameter of 0.085 meters. In watching Ira, I realized I could learn how to take these measurements, too, and that it wasn't all that complicated—like most things, a matter of practice. Easy's what you know how to do.

Sitka alder commonly grows in avalanche chutes and is generally considered a shrub compared to the red alder, but when given the space to grow, it can reach the status of a little tree. What do we mean by *tree* anyway? Dictionary compiler Samuel Johnson defined a tree as "a large vegetable rising, with one woody stem, to a considerable height," which Jessica Francis Kane's narrator in *Rules for Visiting* calls "a dreadful description from an otherwise great writer." Before becoming a big-tree tracker, I determined any shrub that had surpassed four feet to be a tree, for no other reason except that I had heard the four-foot designation along the way. *Merriam-Webster* defines a tree as "a woody perennial plant having a single usually elongate main stem generally with few or no branches on its lower part," and the *Oxford Canadian Dictionary* offers a similar definition. But tell that to a bushy western red-cedar, its boughs almost at ground level, or a multistemmed black cottonwood. Straley writes, "There is no problem saying that big trees with single trunks are definitely trees, while small, bushy plants with several trunks and limbs down to the ground are shrubs, but where does one stop and the other start?" He concludes, "A tree is not always a definite entity, but rather a combination of genetic make-up, size, form, and age." A tree is what we make of it.

— 7 —
Three the Hard Way

VINE MAPLE,
PACIFIC CRAB APPLE,
BLACK HAWTHORN

"If you must begin, then go all the way, because if you
begin and quit, the unfinished business you have left
behind begins to haunt you all the time."
CHÖGYAM TRUNGPA, *The Myth of Freedom
and the Way of Meditation*

"I LOOKED FOR YOUR PROJECT," my friend Jan told me, "but it
seems to have died off."

I was still looking for trees each weekend, when registry
availability allowed it, but since I wasn't posting about it online,
my project was invisible to other people. I was reminded of how
performative accomplishment can be in this era of likes. By not
posting on social media or my blog about the "failures" I'd had
over the summer and fall—the misidentifications, the days spent
trolling the same patch of forest with nothing to show for it except
a walk in the woods—I felt that I was protecting the integrity of
my project, preserving it for those days when I bagged a tree. I
had embraced the creative approach and longer timeline, and I

still wanted to complete the project, but perfectionism dies slowly, by a thousand precisely placed paper cuts. A deeper part of me wished I could just meander around parks, appreciating trees.

In an episode of his marketing and culture podcast, *Akimbo*, Seth Godin focuses on the sunk cost fallacy. You're likely familiar with this cognitive bias: the concert you go to, though you're not in the mood and know you won't enjoy it, because you already bought the ticket; the degree you finish even after you realize you're no longer interested in the subject, because of the time and money you've already spent. Or, to put it in a less capital-intense, more theatrical and murderous way, Macbeth decides to keep killing because "I am in blood / Stepped in so far, that, should I wade no more, / Returning were as tedious as go o'er." Godin points out that there's always a dip in a project, "that moment of pain when we feel like quitting." So when we're trying to move from first draft to second draft and think *What's the point?*, that's the dip in action, and a lot of people quit at this point. That you've invested time and money in the project isn't reason enough to keep going: you have to be motivated by a larger goal that's still worth pursuing. Crucially, Godin says that "if you know the dip is coming, then you can sign up for it; you can be delighted when it arrives. 'Oh good! It's here. That means I can get through it now.'" We can double down on our efforts and push on through. And sometimes doubling down can mean doubling up: on big trees and attempts to find them.

On a hot day in July, when I was still hoping for each outing to end with a Champion, I headed out in search of a vine maple with a 0.44-meter DBH, 11-meter crown spread, and 11.9-meter height. Central Park, 220 acres located in the heart of Burnaby, outside Vancouver, is ringed by condo towers and adjacent to the SkyTrain—what my friend Kate charmingly referred to as the "AirRail"—and that behemoth of consumerism, Metropolis at Metrotown. The park was created in 1891 and named after New York's Central Park, and its western red-cedar, hemlock, and Douglas-fir stands continued to be logged throughout that decade. Remnants of springboard logging can still be seen in the park's stately stumps, many of which have become nurse stumps, with young trees taking hold in the nutrient-rich wood. So straight and dense are the trees here that in the 1860s the area was the reserve of the Royal Navy, supplying logs for masts.

Central Park today is mostly second-growth forest, a mixed area of conifers and deciduous trees, including another new-to-me variety of maple. The vine maple is native to southwestern BC, including small parts of Vancouver Island. This variety of maple has a particularly beautiful leaf, with a wide circular "palm" and seven to nine short lobes. When the light shines through its thin leaves, they glow with a brilliant green in spring and summer, and a yellow or red intensity in autumn. The *vine* designation likely originates from the appearance of its multistemmed trunk, which the National Audubon field guide describes "as turning and twisting from [its] base, *often vine-like* and leaning or sprawling." Its bark is typically smooth and ranges from greenish gray to reddish brown. The vine maple reproduces by both touching down its branches to the ground and sending up new shoots and roots, a process called layering, and by sending out seeds in samaras (also called helicopters).

The registry indicated that the Champion vine maple was "south of tennis courts in Central Park, Burnaby." Ralf Kelman nominated and verified it in 2006, and there were no coordinates or photos for the tree. I cursed such obscure directions. On my way to the tennis courts on Patterson Avenue, a woman in slacks and a blazer called out to me. "Excuse me! Where is the party?" A fair question, since I was tree hunting in a long skirt and crop top. I shrugged and kept walking. I dutifully combed the forest alongside the tennis courts, sidestepping old clothing, tennis balls, and used condoms. I found large firs and cedars, measuring one Douglas-fir's DBH at 1.68 meters. Once I'd swept the southern perimeter of the tennis courts, I wove through the rest of the local forest. I saw many vine maples, beautiful but none large enough to write home about. Though the park was filled with walkers and fitness enthusiasts, and police bike patrols after the recent murder of a thirteen-year-old girl, I was wary of going too far off the main trail, perhaps even warier in this city park than I might have been in a more remote forest. After spending two hours in the park, I packed it in for the day.

That night I dreamed my archenemy invited me to be part of a three-piece band, me on cello, her on violin, a fellow on a horn. I don't know how to play cello, so I busied myself sucking the five reeds that were around its neck. Then, dressed up for the performance and bow poised, I never emitted a sound. At the end of the concert, a man called out, "She doesn't even know how to play!" and I wondered, *Why would my enemy want to humiliate me in this way?*

Failure was following me into sleep, but like the cello I had dreamed into existence with reeds instead of strings, I recognized my acts of looking for trees as creative. Failure often looks like not doing work, but the act of trying increases the odds of success. Journalist Marni Jackson draws the similarity between fishing and writing in her essay "What I Learned From a Summer of Not Catching a Single Fish": "You put your line in the water, your pen to paper, but there's no guarantee anything will take the hook. The ratio of failure to success is staggering. And yet, people persist . . . So fishing is mostly a matter of not fishing. At that, I excelled." Big-tree tracking would be about tossing out the line again and again, more tracking than trees.

In late August, after realizing that my project would take longer and involve numerous attempts on each tree, and with a strong desire to see vine maples flaming on their way toward autumn, I headed back to Central Park. With my direction pointed squarely south of the tennis courts, I decided to go farther afield than last time. I hopped a split-rail fence and found myself in a golf course, still within the park grounds. The tightly mowed lawn was spongy, and the course smelled like sewage and salt water. Dodging the balls of pitch-and-putters, I wandered the groomed course, travel mug of mint tea in hand, with no yellow flags or numbers to mark my way. I headed toward every tall shock of yellow and red I saw throughout the course. Golfers looked at me askance as I passed them for the third or fourth time; there are, after all, better places to walk. I combed the course—many a maple, but no vine maples—and then hopped another low cedar fence to head back into the forest between golf course and trail. There were two large vine maples in a grove, but not near the size I was seeking. One was tall, and the other had a vast crown. The afternoon sunshine filtered through their ochre leaves, and their trunks gracefully twisted upward and outward. The twigs and dried leaves littering the forest floor crunched as I stepped over moss-covered logs. The air smelled less of sewage and more of fir, and the strident voice in my head quieted for a moment.

That night, as I posted on my blog about my multiple attempts to see this Champion, I started to make peace with not finding the vine maple, and perhaps not seeing all the Champion trees. When journalist John Zada set out to search for Sasquatch in the Great Bear Rainforest, on the north and central coast of BC, he realized early on, "I have set myself on an impossible mission, a fool's quest." At least I knew the trees existed, or at least had once existed, but my desire to see many was reducing my chances of finding one. I might not check off every tree on my checklist, and maybe that was okay.

In *The Snow Leopard*, Peter Matthiessen goes looking for the elusive title animal on a rough pilgrimage in the Himalayas, and he gradually comes to terms with not seeing it. "I would like to see a snow leopard," he writes, "but if I do not, that is all right, too." In the grove of vine maples, I had been willing to set aside the quest for the beauty of the moment. If this tree wanted to be known, it would have revealed itself, whether I had earned it or not. "That the snow leopard *is*, that it is here, that its frosty eyes watch us from the mountain—that is enough."

"SO, THIS TREE HERE is about the size of the Pacific crab apple we're looking for." I unhooked the d-tape from the tree's scaly bark and let the tape reel back. "I don't know what type of tree this is, but let's find a crab apple about this diameter."

Jason and I were standing on a leg of the Shell Road Trail in Richmond, near the Vancouver International Airport, surrounded by patches of farmland scattered over the Fraser delta. He'd bought me a waffle iron for my birthday, so that morning we'd dined on waffles and the high culture of Mike Oldfield's *Tubular Bells*, one of the sounds of my youth along with Gregorian chants, Vivaldi's *Four Seasons*, and *The Rocky Horror Picture Show* soundtrack.

Jason and I had driven out to the delta in the hopes of landing two trees: a Pacific crab apple and a black hawthorn. He and I had been dating for a few months by this point and spending a lot of time together, but this was my first tree-tracking trip with him. I was wary of letting him in on something that was uniquely "mine" since we already shared so many activities—bouldering, reading in cafés, eating chocolate for breakfast—but I needed someone to help me measure the trees, and it was finally time for him to see me in all my wandering, tie-dyed-sock glory.

Nominator Ralf Kelman had positioned both trees at the "south end of Shell Rd., Richmond." Shell Road is about two miles long, running from River Road at the Fraser River near Mitchell Island to Westminster Highway. We parked at Richmond Nature Park and then walked north along the Shell Road Trail, a recreational trail that runs ramrod-straight between Shell Road and a CN railroad track. We walked up the trail along one side of Shell Road and then along the grass on the other side, which was marked as private property. Signs alerted us to the risk of wildfire, and peering through the chain-link fence, we could see that a section of the forest had recently burned. We scoured the woods, spotting fly agaric mushrooms and plenty of alder, but no crab apples and no hawthorns. Numerous runners, walkers, and cyclists passed us while we drifted with a measured pace and wide-ranging eyes.

"Thanks for taking the tape from me when I was trying to measure the circumference of that big tree," I said. Doing so alone usually means fumbling the pass to yourself.

"Amanda," he said, "I will take the tape from you any day."

We bounced identification ideas off each other as we examined unknown species, dividing up my stock of guidebooks and comparing leaves and bark.

"Doesn't this feel like an episode of *Sherlock*?" I said, my voice a mixture of skepticism and excitement. My then favorite show was the BBC-produced update of Sherlock Holmes starring Benedict Cumberbatch.

"No," Jason said.

"What if we found a body?"

"Then it would be more like *Sherlock*, yes."

After wandering for two hours south along the trail, we headed north on Shell Road for one last look.

"You know," I said, "I think that tree we saw at the start, the one we measured for reference, is the biggest one around here."

The windfall crab apples around the tree's base should have been a dead giveaway. We'd missed them when we measured the sample tree, believing crab apples to be, oh, I don't know, more like orchard apples? These yellow crab apples were so small, under an inch in diameter, they resembled berries or beads. Pacific crab apples are the only native apple tree in the Pacific Northwest, and their fruit, which grows in clusters, preserves well, growing sweeter with time. Coast Salish Peoples have long eaten the sour fruit, used the tree bark for medicine, and made the very hard wood into tools. As is common with big trees growing under ideal conditions, this huge Pacific crab apple was next to another of similar proportions. And once we'd found the biggest, we started to identify smaller crab apple trees all along the trail.

Jason rolled along with the excitement of finding the Champion, but it was a facepalm moment for me. Wasn't I supposed to be a tree expert by this point? I decided to distract him with my usual deep questioning.

"Are you deciduous or coniferous?" I asked.

"I'm definitely deciduous," he said. "I have moments of growth and rebirth, and also moments when all my leaves fall off and I get all mopey and droopy."

"Am I deciduous or coniferous?" I asked him, thinking *I'm obviously coniferous.*

"You're neither," he said. "You're not a tree. You're something slow-growing that grows over and through, establishes its roots more each year, flowers."

"Like ivy? Scotch broom? I'm an invasive species?"

"Exactly!"

Now that we'd bagged one Champion, we set out to find the black hawthorn in the same area. Ignoring CN's signs to stay off the train tracks (all railroads are private property in Canada), we walked down the railroad in case we could spot a black hawthorn from that side. The hawthorn is another native fruit tree in the Pacific Northwest, bearing small deep-red-to-black fruits eaten by birds. Like the Pacific crab apple, it's referred to as both a shrub and a tree. I'm getting around that lack of distinction here by referring to it as a small shrubby tree, but the registry considers both species native trees. In its size and the appearance of its leaves, fruits, and blossoms, black hawthorn is similar to Pacific crab apple, but it also has long thorns on its branches, which First Nations of the coast and Interior used as needles to pierce ears and lance boils, and as fish hooks. The wood is hard and useful for tool handles and implements for digging and fishing, and the Cowichan use the charcoal in face paint. Its Latin name, *Crataegus douglasii*, marks another David Douglas "discovery," and *haw*, meaning "hedge" in Anglo-Saxon, denotes its ancient use.

After tromping over the same ground, our grumbling stomachs declared our hunt over for that day. Upon reinspecting Google Maps at home after the trip, I saw that the Shell Road Trail that runs south of Westminster Highway connects to two other branches of Shell Road. We were at the southern end of the most northerly branch of Shell Road. Perhaps the black hawthorn in question was at the south end of the other Shell Road, the "southest."

WE HAVE A FEW BREAKOUT AREAS in our publishing office on Main Street in Vancouver. One is a couch by the front door. It's great—I mean, it's a couch—but if you sit there, it means you're in charge of answering the door. Anyone can show up: staff members' kids, delivery people, authors.

I was editing on the couch when someone tried the door handle, found it locked, and then gently knocked. Setting aside my laptop, unplugged earbuds still dangling from my ears, I opened the door. In the hall was a man who looked to be in his late sixties, wearing baggy black pants, an oversized camp jacket, and an army surplus green wool tuque. His gray hair was pulled back in a low ponytail, and he was carrying an artist portfolio.

"Oh, I think you're the one I'm looking for," he said, a smile slowly spreading. "You're Amanda."

Was he an illustrator looking for work? While I was deciding whether to welcome him in or bolt the door, he said, "I'm Ralf Kelman."

"Oh! My goodness! Come on in," I said, stepping aside.

Along with Randy Stoltmann in the late 1980s and '90s, Ralf Kelman recorded some of the biggest trees on the coast. He'd campaigned with the Western Canada Wilderness Committee to save Seymour Valley on the North Shore from logging. (The area is now protected as a regional park, the Lower Seymour Conservation Reserve, and the watershed is restricted—no public access.) He built trails in the '90s with the WCWC to some of the area's sensational old-growth. I'd been following in his footsteps, in that he'd verified a lot of the smaller Champions I'd been looking for, and I'd hiked the Temple of Time trail, which Ralf helped build.

"I've been trying to reach you," I said.

"I got your emails," he said, "but I hate email. I have this thousand-dollar smartphone," he said, pulling a pristine phone out of his front pocket, "and I don't want to use it." He lived in the Downtown Eastside, where he has a magnificent view of

Mount Baker "between two buildings, and, man, those buildings are creeping in. Who knows how much longer I'll have
that view." He'd been reading my blog and told me he admired
the spirit of my writing and what I was trying to do with
the project.

I protested, "I'm only a learner."

"Nah, it's great," he said. "But I think you were wrong about
that Pacific crab apple. Maybe the Scouler's willow too."

"Really? Well, shit. Where is the crab apple, then?"

"It's by the warehouses," he said.

Of course. What warehouses?

Trying to keep our voices down so as not to disturb my
colleagues in the open-concept space, Ralf and I connected on
not caring overmuch about data like measurements and GPS
coordinates. I know this is rich, given that I could have used
some coordinates when looking for that vine maple behind the
tennis courts.

"In the old days, it used to be about the trees!" he said. "Not
this GPS coordinates, data crap. You'd just draw a map! This
committee, let me tell you, they're all interested in the data. It's
all political." I assumed he meant the BC Big Tree Committee's
focus on having precise measurements and coordinates for scientific reasons, so conservationists could use that info when
working with governments and First Nations. "Have they invited
you on the field trip to Campbell River to see the big Doug-fir?"

"No," I said. "What field trip?"

"With the logging company!" he said. "Well, you can be my
personal guest. When they start talking science, you can go get
a falafel."

I warmed to him immediately. "Can I take you for lunch—
we can talk trees, look at maps? We could go out to Richmond
and find the crab apple and the hawthorn." He readily agreed. I

gave him my number, and he promised to call that weekend so we could head out.

"Oh! I have something for you." He carefully unzipped his portfolio and took out a large print. It was his drawing of the Hollow Tree in Stanley Park as he imagined it before it died. Straight leaders shoot up from a thick trunk, and a woman wearing Victorian clothes stands at the base of the tree for scale. Keep in mind that people were smaller back then.

"I want you to have this. Don't tell the committee I gave this to you." He inscribed the print to me on the back, titling and signing the drawing with a flourish. He demonstrated immense skill in draftsmanship and offered other prints if I wanted them. I felt an affinity with this artist who had taken a shine to big trees, and maybe to me as a fellow qualitative assessor.

I WAS UP AT UBC, working as a guest editor in the MFA summer residency. On breaks, I wandered the avenue of catalpas flowering next to the brutalist Buchanan block. These trees have heart-shaped leaves, long bean pods, and delicate white flowers with pink centers and a brushing of yellow. Tellingly, I hadn't noticed them in four years of hustling from lecture hall to library, my single-pointed focus on gaining an off-the-charts GPA. Gradually, in pursuit of that goal, I had set aside most social activities, even the swing dancing I loved so much, in order to study into the night. Apart from yoga and long solo walks, I essentially forgot I had a body, at least the pleasure of it.

After my duties wrapped one sunny day, I headed to the Forestry building to meet Christine Chourmouzis, the registrar, for the first time. I'd been corresponding with her over email since the start of my project. I read into her somewhat terse replies that she was irritated I was not taking measurements properly, not including the GPS or the tree ID, which is the number assigned to each individual tree. *Why did I need the ID?* I initially wondered. There's only one Champion for each species. But there are hundreds of trees in the database, and the Champion title can change swiftly.

I knocked tentatively at Christine's office door. She spun around and stared at me, eyes wide behind her glasses. Her dark brown hair, threaded with silver, was pulled back in a ponytail.

"Hi, Christine," I said, introducing myself. "Is it still a good time?"

"Oh! Amanda! Come on in!" She'd thought our meeting was on a different day. She cleared space on her desk, and I wheeled a chair up to her computer. We'd arranged to go over some of the photos and descriptions I'd gathered of Champions in the Lower Mainland and from my road trip on Vancouver Island and up north. Christine was warm and welcoming, incredibly knowl-edgeable about these forests and enthusiastic about every detail. She's a forest ecologist, working on forest conservation genetic projects at UBC, and grows seedlings as a horticulture technician. Since 2013, she has managed the registry off the side of her desk, and I got the sense that time was at a premium for her, so I was extra grateful to her for walking me through my findings.

"What's that?" Christine asked, as she opened my email attachment.

"That's the Champion black cottonwood, in Nisga'a terri-tory," I said.

"No, it's not," she said. Christine showed me a photo of the Champion black cottonwood growing on the banks of Ksi Sii Aks on the way in to Gitlax̱t'aamiks but closer to the lava field. Had I even seen this photo before? I wondered if it had been recently uploaded, or if I'd simply missed it. The two trees' shapes looked similar, but the Champion was covered in moss in the photo, perhaps taken in a wetter season. An arborist from

Terrace nominated the tree and even climbed it to take photos, including one of a large eagle's nest in the upper branches.

"Oh, damn," I said, my face reddening. I truly was so close that time, possibly just a zig this way or a zag that way.

Like Ralf, she wasn't sure about the Scouler's willow. She encouraged me to bring Ralf to the tree, as he was familiar with more of these lesser-known species and could help me with the measurements. I told her that Ralf had come to my office.

"He'll want to give you a picture," she said. "Did he give you a picture?"

"Yes," I said, feeling bummed that he didn't bestow the Hollow Tree print solely on me.

She volunteered to go out with us to see the trees in Richmond and was exasperated that Ralf doesn't record coordinates, favoring sketches. "I'd take a hand-drawn map!" she said. We stepped outside so she could have a cigarette.

"How long have you worked here?" I asked.

"*Years*," she exhaled. "So, tell me how the measuring is going."

I explained that I was fairly confident in figuring out DBH and crown, but as we got into it, I wondered if I'd been mixing up DBH and circumference with my measurements of the earlier trees. I had leapt so quickly into the project that I hadn't factored pi into my circumference measurements to calculate the diameter. Memories of failing Math 10 brought on a flop sweat. I admitted I didn't have a clue how to measure height. When I'd looked at various methods online, I became a bit queasy. Essentially, you need to know the distance between yourself and the tree, and then use a ruler or even a stick or pencil to calculate the height. But this scale hypsometer technique, used since ancient times, involved too much trigonometry for me. And there were variables to work around if the tree was obscured by brush or the ground slanted. I knew I'd been slacking in this area, but I figured my poetic glimmers about trees on my blog might reach new heights. Charm will get you far, all the way to the top.

Thankfully for you, dear reader, there was an easier way. Christine showed me how to use a laser rangefinder, a hand-held device that aims a beam at the base of the tree and at the top, and then calculates the height for you. Ira had used this device when measuring the height of the Sitka alder. You need to be at least the height of the tree away from it, and the measurement becomes more accurate the farther you are from the tree. Together, we practiced measuring the heights of trees and buildings. "Don't move, don't crouch, stand straight," she said, as I lined up the tree in the viewing panel. She showed me how to hold a reflector, in this case a small mirror, against the tree to capture the beam of the laser, important when measuring in dense forest when there might be bushes in front of the tree or branches obscuring the trunk. In high foliage situations, you may need to use a foliage filter in addition to the mirror.

She also showed me how to spot a tree in a forest when I was trying to measure its height but couldn't determine the top of the tree due to multiple treetops (this method works best with a buddy). "Wiggle it! Wiggle the tree." She braced both hands against a trunk and pushed back and forth, and sure enough the top of the tree waved back and forth. "It's really incredible!" she said.

Christine loaned me a GPS and a laser measure, which she called "the laser measuring thing-a-ma-jig." Between Ira, Ralf, and Christine, I felt new camaraderie with these experts in the woods, who possessed the tree-tracking skills I currently lacked but could certainly learn. Up to this point, the technical details just weren't my thing, and I was worried I'd make a false move. I also believed that focusing on the measurements would take away from knowing the other elements of the tree; I was barely keeping up with the skills demanded of accurate identification. But after seeing Ira and Christine balance skill in the field with unbridled enthusiasm for the tree as a being, and witnessing Ralf using his artist's eye as a strength, I realized I could mistakenly identify a Champion and recover. I could step into a new path, balancing technique with experience for its own sake.

— 8 —

Yew
Complete Me

PACIFIC YEW

"The pose begins when you want to leave it."

B. K. S. IYENGAR

"HIKING CAPILANO RIVER PARK with Stephen Hui and heading into the Cap watershed to find large Pacific yew. Safety," I texted my Official Safety Checker early one morning.

"Safety," Jenny texted back.

I met Stephen at East Café, on the corner of Nanaimo and Hastings in East Van (good jazz, great sausage rolls). I'd invited him over Twitter after reading his book *105 Hikes In and Around Southwestern British Columbia*, a follow-up to David and Mary Macaree's classic hiking guide. I figured at least he'd know where he was going, in relation to this tree. (Spoiler: he didn't.) I drove us to Capilano River Regional Park in North Van and parked at the salmon hatchery. After checking out the spawning chinook and the Cleveland Dam, which contains the water from the Capilano watershed that supplies Vancouver with fresh drinking water, we headed into the woods, Stephen's orange backpack leading the way.

The registry lists the Champion Pacific yew as 23.5 meters in height (about the height of a seven-story building) with a 0.91-meter DBH and 10.4-meter crown—huge for a yew, indicating a great age for this usually small and slow-growing tree. Yews generally reach a height of ten to fifteen meters but can grow taller when left undisturbed in sheltered areas, like gullies, and in protected areas, like closed watersheds. Pacific yew (or Western yew) generally grows in the shelter of Douglas-firs, hemlocks, and cedars, its long, somewhat spindly branches sweeping the ground and seeming to nod compared to the surrounding upright conifers. Yews tend to lose their heartwood and cease growing as they reach old age; they reproduce through seed dispersal and layering, as western red-cedar and vine maple do. The cones hold one seed each, and they don't look like typical conifer cones: each seed is surrounded by a red aril, similar to a berry and open on one end. I love this description in *Tree* by Matthew Battles: "The flesh of the yew's aril is moist, sticky, and sickly sweet, and there is at the bottom a tiny porthole where a bullet-shaped seed not much larger than a pencil eraser peers out." The aril is edible for birds and rodents, who eat it whole and spread the seeds in their droppings, but the seed and the other parts of the tree are poisonous.

The Pacific yew's needles grow in a flattened spiral, and the outer bark is scaly and thin, red or purple, with a rosy inner bark. The vascular cambium and bark used to be harvested for paclitaxel, but drug manufacturers now use a semisynthetic version of cultivated Pacific yew bark to make the chemotherapy drug Taxol. The forest ecologist Suzanne Simard recounts in her memoir, *Finding the Mother Tree*, that Indigenous Peoples had long known of the medicinal quality of the yew. "When the anticancer qualities of the yew were brought to the attention of the modern pharmaceutical industry," Simard writes, "there was a bounty on the trees. I'd find the small yews—their branches as long as their stems—stripped naked of their bark, looking like crosses, specters of maltreatment." Indigenous Peoples also have multiple uses for the Pacific yew's strong wood, from paddles to digging sticks to bows; it's similar to the English yew, which was used to make longbows. Yews are regarded as sacred in numerous cultures and are common in churchyards in Ireland and England. Jim Robbins, author of *The Man Who Planted Trees*—about David Milarch, who cofounded the Archangel Ancient Tree Archive—argues that their purpose was for conversion: "Churches and monasteries throughout Ireland were often built on sites sacred to the pagans, so that people who came to visit the sacred yew might also visit the church and be converted." The true reason, however, might have been more economical: planting a toxic yew was a less expensive proposition for the church than building a fence to keep sheep out.

I turned to Randy Stoltmann's hiking guide for more information on the old-growth trees in the Capilano River area, including a map of where to find them.

"What is that, a library book?" Stephen scoffed. "Just buy the thing."

Stephen and I set the GPS with the coordinates for the Pacific yew and headed into the woods. We soon emerged in the swanky residential area of the British Properties in West Van and hiked uphill on the roads for about fifteen minutes, passing multimillion-dollar homes. We're all down on industrial logging, but Vancouver real estate, now that's the real crime in the woods.

"Have you checked out the Capilano Suspension Bridge yet?" Stephen asked. This long swinging bridge is suspended 230 feet above the Capilano River, and the surrounding park has lots of old-growth.

"No! That's a good idea," I said. "I haven't been there since I was a kid."

"You should go," he said. "It's like Disneyland for trees."

The irony of looking for a Pacific yew is that yews tend to pop up when you're not looking for them. These short slender trees blend in and thrive in the shade of bigger trees but sometimes give themselves away with a flash of blue-red bark. We looped back into the forest, coming to a water tower. The Champion Pacific yew is in the Capilano watershed, one of the few closed watersheds in North America, and entirely off-limits to the public. But we figured it wouldn't hurt anyone if we walked, pure of heart and with responsible faces, for half a mile in the watershed to see a tree, right? We didn't plan on the barbed-wire fence enclosing it. After skirting a section of the perimeter, we found a way to get in but decided it wasn't worth being "prosecuted" for trying to find the yew. While trespassing is sometimes worth the risk, it could also result in official charges that I didn't want shadowing me on this big-tree journey.

Not wanting to waste the sunny day, we set out on a section of the Baden Powell Trail, a long connector route along lower Hollyburn Mountain, which Stephen hadn't hiked yet. Near the Brothers Creek forestry road, we saw the Candelabra Fir described in Stoltmann's first hiking guide: a dead Douglas-fir more than sixty meters tall, so named because of the candelabra-shaped leaders at its top. This area was logged in the 1920s, and some old-growth firs were left because their tops were gnarly, which can indicate rot, or because they had twisted trunks, like the Candelabra Fir. Along the trail, we found rusted buckets and spikes from the logging railway. Logging outfits would first make skid roads and then miniature railways to transport logs out of the woods. Another way to move lumber was through flumes, long troughs with rushing water that would carry logs, shingles, even daring loggers who wanted a quick ride into town on a Friday night. These flumes inspired the Flume at Playland at the PNE, in which passengers sit in a log-shaped car and splash down in a trough of water at the bottom of a gentle roller coaster; it had been my favorite ride as a kid, when it was called the Log Ride (most locals still call it that). While we hiked, we contributed to the numerous "faces" hikers had left in buttressed cedar trunks, adding white and gray rocks to the springboard cut marks for eyes.

Back at the parking lot, we followed Stoltmann's map to find three Pacific yews near the garbage cans. You know what they say: location, location, location. The largest of these three yews, leaning at a rakish angle above the path, is possibly more than two hundred years old; it is growing needles on just its top half, which speaks to its age. I adhered to Diana Beresford-Kroeger's advice to not stand too long in front of the yew, lest I be hypnotized. I found the bright peeling bark beautiful, but there wasn't anything particularly mesmerizing about it. Still, since we couldn't visit our quarry, and there were no photos of it on the registry, I used these present examples to imagine the Champion yew, growing at an angle on a rocky hillside in the watershed. In my mind's eye, I saw dirt loosely packed around the yew and moss clinging to the bark that hadn't flaked away to reveal the surprisingly smooth inner bark. Bright red arils glistened like ornaments amid the green needles, and birds flitted in to eat the pulp, leaving the delicate branches to sway when they alighted. The forest was not silent.

We headed back across the Burrard Inlet, and I dropped Stephen off, making plans for a future hike. I hoped we could return to see the Hollyburn Fir, a 1,100-year-old Doug-fir just a bit west from where we'd been hiking. A tree for another day.

"Back in East Van," I texted Jenny.

"Safety," she texted back.

LATER ON, I WROTE TO Metro Vancouver to ask if I could go on a private tour of the watershed, expressly to see the Champion Pacific yew. They wrote back, "Unfortunately our closed watershed policy does not allow us to grant permission for access into the watersheds outside of established educational tours with designated routes." So on a rainy Saturday, I joined a public watershed tour and hoped it would bring me near the yew.

We met on the berm of the Cleveland Dam (built in 1954), about twenty participants and two enthusiastic tour guides, Judith and Dana. I was initially surprised there was so much interest in learning about the source of our drinking water, and I came to regard this public watershed tour as a hidden treasure. The Capilano reservoir is 3.7 miles long and holds a third of the drinking water for all twenty-one municipalities in Metro Vancouver (Coquitlam and Seymour reservoirs hold the rest of the drinking water). The Capilano watershed was created in response to water crises in the late 1800s. The watersheds were located in the North Shore Mountains because water is heavy to pump upstream, water was already gathered in the valley, and most of the population was located below the watersheds. The area was logged extensively in the 1800s, so it's mostly second-growth here, but there's some old-growth higher up and in the canyon.

We piled onto a school bus and passed through a steel gate, and our guides checked us in at the security office. Our bus traveled up the east side of Capilano Lake below Grouse Mountain, the driver radioing ahead his position on the narrow road. I knew that the tree was on the west side of the lake, and when I realized that I wouldn't have a chance of seeing it on this tour, I settled back to learn about the forests and the watershed maintenance. We passed hydro crews brushing under the power lines so there wouldn't be any fires that summer from the hot lines arcing down and touching the dried grass. The watershed has a dedicated forest firefighting crew and is self-maintained— for instance, staff use wood debris and gravel from the site to repair slopes after landslides. We passed dry streambeds and tall foxgloves, and we visited the original water infrastructure for the city, a system of aqueducts that used to filter the water before it flowed straight to Vancouver. We also learned how fish are managed in the reservoir—coho and steelhead are caught in a rotary screw trap and transported below the dam so they can continue their life cycle.

There's no hunting in the watershed, so it's a natural wildlife preserve, and you can see black bear, deer, cougars, and elk here. Mammals and birds roam freely about the watershed, as they might in a demilitarized zone. Kate Harris (yes, that Kate) visited the DMZ between North and South Korea after attending a conference in Seoul. She'd researched the DMZ as part of her master's research at Oxford on scientific peacekeeping. As she describes in her travel memoir *Lands of Lost Borders*, this 2.5-mile-wide area, sealed off from entry since 1953, was "the most fiercely guarded wildlife sanctuary on the planet." She paid to look through a viewfinder at the wetlands and forest that have reclaimed farmers' fields, where animals now wander without threat. "To my shock," she writes, "I saw wilderness staring back at me down the barrel of a cocked and loaded border."

I was furiously taking notes at the edge of the aqueduct pond while rain dampened my page. When we were parked deep in the watershed, walking near the foundations of the former caretaker's home, Judith sidled up next to me.

"You're taking a lot of notes," she said, smiling.

"Yeah," I whispered.

"Whatcha writing about?"

"A project about trees," I murmured, then gathered my courage and described my quest. "There's a big Pacific yew in the watershed, but it's on the other side of the reservoir and I can't get to it."

Though I felt I was close, and I still wanted to see the yew—I'd come to love this slightly scrappy tree that emerged trailside on hikes in the North Shore Mountains, each rare spotting a delight—by that point I was questioning my completionist tendency. It's certainly the case that being able to say you saw or visited all of something can be motivation in itself. For example, Jessica J. Lee, a British-Canadian-Taiwanese nature writer, spent a year swimming fifty-two lakes around her home in Berlin, which she recounted in her memoir *Turning*. She was getting over the heartbreak of a divorce and the loneliness of being in a new city, and she craved a break from working on her PhD. "I was completely swallowed up by writing my dissertation," she said, "and needed something to take my mind and body away from the text. So I started swimming, and gave myself the structure of visiting a new lake each week, as a way to cope with how isolating the writing process can be." Swimming in these lakes, even in the winter, brought her to a fuller experience that seemed less about the structure of the project and the accomplishment therein. "It forced me not to be in my head; it forced me to be in my body and to be in the place I was, exactly in the middle of the landscape when I'm swimming in the water."

Others have set out to visit constructed elements of a cityscape. In 2015, Jake Tobin Garrett, writer, illustrator, and then manager of policy and planning at Park People, a "friends of parks" group in Toronto, wanted to see more of the fifteen-hundred-plus parks in his city, so he set out to see at least one park in each of the forty-four wards, ultimately visiting almost one hundred. When I asked him about what drives our completionist mindset, he said, "I think, as humans, we're obsessed with categorization and patterns. We see them everywhere, and we get a lot of pleasure from 'completing' things, whether it's a set of to-dos for the day or a larger project. Part of doing a large project is using that inherent human drive and harnessing it as a way to motivate yourself. It also helps to put brackets on something so you know when you're done."

I could definitely relate to the impulse to categorize and find patterns, but in my project there was no way to put "brackets" on trees that were dying or difficult to reach, being cut down, or replaced in the ranking. I started to accept that this project would be a series of em dashes and semicolons, and I realized too late I was setting myself up for a lifetime of eyeballing tree size. Maybe I could take a cue from Davis Vilums's mindset of happiness in the moment. Bored with his regular twenty-five-minute bike commute, he decided to take a new route every day by setting out to cycle all the streets of London. As he recounted on his site, "That was an enjoyable waste of time, and I liked every bit of it." Or Arlin ffrench, who cycled every street in Vancouver over three years, adding some variety by using the Strava exercise tracking app to map out shapes, like a penis formed by twenty-two miles of city streets.

Some people embark on projects knowing from the beginning that they're destined to be incomplete, and perhaps that acceptance can be a goal in itself. The late Jason Polan, for example, attempted to draw all the people in New York. He knew his goal was impossible to achieve—the purpose was in the doing. "Any way he approached it," Gideon Jacobs wrote in a profile of Polan's art project in 2014, "there would be countless tiny gaps in a portrait of the city, holes that would render the thing fatally incomplete." As with Lee's lake swimming, Polan's goal provided structure and motivation; the real benefits weren't in its completion. I was wary of my big-tree quest turning into something potentially devastating—another burnout or the system shutdown I'd experienced during my master's. I took a lesson from the cautionary tale of Dr. Steve O'Shea, marine biologist and giant squid hunter. In 2004, David Grann published a *New Yorker* article about oceanographers' decades-long hunt to find a giant squid. "How could something so big and powerful remain unseen for so long—or be less understood than dinosaurs, which died out millions of years ago?" Grann writes. "The search for a living specimen has inspired a fevered competition." Grann concentrated on the quest of O'Shea, who was looking for a baby giant squid, or paralarva. O'Shea had been on this quest for years, using private funding and his own savings to aid his hunt in the Pacific.

O'Shea spent ostensibly every waking hour he could on his mission, to the chagrin of his family. "I don't want him to stop," his wife, Shoba, said. "I just wish he could temper it a little bit and see that there are other things out there." When at last O'Shea pulled in a paralarva among krill, he lost it when transferring it to a container. His prize was so close, within his reach, and then slipped out of his grasp. After all that—nothing. "It's a fucking catastrophe," said O'Shea.

I'd see a big yew sometime, maybe just not the Chosen One in the watershed. Altering the ambition of my quest made the list of trees feel less like the list of top songs from *High Fidelity*, or BuzzFeed for trees. Why not be content with one or two visits to local Champions? Why did I need to claim *all* of the trees on the list? I'd thought I was embarking on an adventure in forest ecology, and I'd realized it was a creative project. I was going further by simply sticking with it, catching glimmers of beauty along the way. And once I knew I would fail at my quest to see all the Champion trees, I could finally focus on the experience, which would keep the project a source of enjoyment rather than a chore, a hobby rather than an obsession.

— 9 —

Heir and a Spare

COASTAL DOUGLAS-FIR, INTERIOR DOUGLAS-FIR, PONDEROSA PINE

"It really takes so much time to become a writer and you
have to be able to roll in time itself, that was my experience,
it seems to me, like a dog likes to roll in dead fish at the beach."
EILEEN MYLES, "Copying & Lying"

"SO, I HAVE MY BACKPACK, rain jacket... But I don't have any cocks."

Jenny raised an eyebrow.

"You know, the boots that foresters wear, with the spiky soles," I said. "C-a-u-l-k-s."

"You don't call them *cocks*," she said, shaking her head while hooking her thumbs in her overalls straps. "You call them *corks*. Call them cocks and the foresters will laugh you out of there." This from the woman who'd convinced me, just before I entered the graduate seminar room to lead a lecture on psychoanalysis in literature, that Carl Jung pronounced his last name with a hard *J*.

In August 2019, I took up Ralf Kelman's invitation and joined a field trip as a guest of the BC Big Tree Committee and

Western Forest Products (wfp) to see a big Doug-fir that wfp
had found on Vancouver Island. (Ralf didn't come.) They had
run a company-wide competition to see who could find the tallest tree, and this tree was standing at a shocking 94 meters tall
(that's about twenty-eight stories) just outside the village of Sayward. Western Forest Products was nominating this Doug-fir for
the registry, along with some other big trees. The committee
hadn't worked with a forestry company in this way before, so
a bunch of the members showed up to learn more about wfp's
intentions and see if this standard was more than a pr move.

These big trees fell within the voluntary retention limits wfp
had set, so they wouldn't be harvested. wfp's big trees standard
is driven by sustainability and recognizes the ecological value
of big trees and rare ecosystems; such a standard is novel for
forestry companies, and the program predated the provincial
government's old-growth strategic review by three years. While
wfp wasn't pressured into creating this standard, it's worth
putting its formation into some historical context. Beginning
in the 1980s, voices were rising against the industrial logging
of old-growth, which didn't economically benefit Indigenous
communities. There was increasing pressure from the public,
mainstream media, First Nations, and ngos for forestry companies to make sustainable changes. The Clayoquot protests in
the 1990s in particular emphasized the multiple values of trees,
not just as a timber source, and that was a message the forestry
companies couldn't ignore if they wanted to retain social license.

Ira Sutherland, the chair of the committee, had told us that
we'd have a walk, "less than 1 km, moderate bushwhacking with
some uphill." I knew I could handle that, but Jenny was priming
me on how not to embarrass myself in front of the foresters and
ecologists. She said if they gave me a cruiser vest, don't wear
it *and* my backpack, since "the big back pocket is essentially a

backpack." We were meeting in Campbell River at 8:00 AM, about ninety minutes north of Nanaimo, so I'd opted to stay at her place in Bowser. I had a fitful sleep on a plastic-lined sheet in the bottom bunk of my nephew Jasper's bunk bed, consoling myself with glow-in-the-dark stars on its underside. Any grumps I had fell away when I saw his sweet face excitedly peering down at me the next morning, and I scooped him up and carried him down for breakfast.

Just before I rolled out, Jenny suggested I pop into a gas station to buy some "rubber gloves, lined, about seven dollars. Used for fishing. They'll save you in the bush." I nodded over my shoulder and hopped in Trouble, cruising up island past clumps of red alder growing beside the highway. I stopped in a gas station just before our meeting point, peed in the station washroom, bought the gloves, and hurried back to my car. I'd made sure to bring all my bushwhacking gear in my big red backpack. When I showed up at the meeting place, a Starbucks in Campbell River, I saw that most committee members had just a purse or day bag, so I kicked my backpack under the table.

I'd spent time with Ira before, when looking for the Sitka alder, and now met Sally Aitken, Shaun Muc and his wife, Sara, and Bill Beese. Shaun is a longtime big-tree tracker, and it was Sara's first time looking for trees. Bill had been the company ecologist for MacMillan Bloedel, a major Vancouver-based forestry company in the 1990s before it was bought by Weyerhaeuser in 1999. Bill is now retired from teaching forest ecology at Vancouver Island University. When he worked at MacBlo, Bill pushed the company to adopt a big-tree standard, but one was never put in place.

We sipped our coffees and swapped big-tree stories of the good ol' days and of the big trees that could become giants if given the chance. I was reminded of "It was *this* big" fishing stories, of the trees that got away. I joined in, told them about some of the trips I'd taken, the trees I'd almost seen. "I felt like I just missed it!" I said, referring to, well, any number of Champions I'd searched for up to this point.

"This is big-tree hunting 101," said Shaun. "Prepare for disappointment."

After about forty-five minutes of chatting about the state of the forest industry, which companies were logging where on the coast and in the Interior, we headed upstairs to the WFP office. There we met Jonathan Armstrong, VP of fiber supply, and Shannon Janzen, VP of partnerships and sustainability and chief forester. I noticed two paintings by Judith Currelly, a painter and pilot based in Atlin and Salt Spring whom I'd had the immense pleasure of befriending through Kate, hanging in the hallway, their northern landscapes brightening the otherwise empty office on this weekend morning. We positioned ourselves around the long oak table in the boardroom, checking out the forestry maps on the walls. Any tension in the room was shot through with Canadian civility. Sally thanked WFP for being proactive in finding and conserving these big trees. Jonathan and Shannon were respectful of the registry's mandate, and it was clear they love the forests they help manage. I kept my head down, making notes.

Western Forest Products put a formal big-tree standard in place in 2016, which protects five tree species (western red-cedar, yellow-cedar, coastal Douglas-fir, Sitka spruce, western white pine) based on height and diameter (over 80 m and/or with varying DBH per species; the height inclusion came about in 2019, before which it was just based on DBH). WFP's public standard is distinct among forestry companies in BC, and it sets the precedent for nominating big trees to a greater extent than BC Timber Sales' Coastal Legacy Tree Program does (BCTS's program came after WFP's). WFP's retention strategy applies to big trees on public (Crown) and private lands (which can be owned by a forestry company). And WFP retains single trees as well as groves, with a buffer around the tree or the grove.

But what the criteria miss is that trees within the acceptable limits to cut are still big; given more time to grow, they might be spared. Sally used the example of trees in the protected region of Carmanah Walbran Provincial Park that are currently tall but not that wide. Western Forest Products has committed to not cut down any tree included on the BC Big Tree Registry, which is substantial—there are hundreds of big trees in the registry, and it's another reason to keep nominating trees. Of course, not all trees are of interest to a forestry company, but since they have the capacity to monitor vast land blocks with field surveys, drones, and lidar, their big-tree finds can be a welcome addition to the registry.

Whereas a laser (like the one I was using) is effective at measuring the heights of trees, lidar creates a "point cloud" through billions of laser pulses, more like radar. It can build a three-dimensional image of a tree—not just the height but the shape, the branches, and even the condition. Western Forest Products flies lidar across areas marked for reserve or for timber harvesting and then verifies any big trees through field assessments. Cedar can't be verified by lidar because it has multiple tops, so it has to be ground-verified. Lidar has other drawbacks: data points tend to miss a tree's leader (since it is so skinny) and tend to overestimate height if the tree is leaning, growing next to a canyon, on a cliff, uphill, et cetera.

After learning about the program in the boardroom for about an hour, we were all keen to get out into the field and see this big Doug-fir that WFP had located using lidar. I felt I was nodding and laughing at all the right places, pen scratching, finally feeling like a knowledgeable tree tracker who could hold my own in a room full of experts. As we headed out, I ran to the office washroom for another pit stop. Looking in the mirror, I realized that in the gas station washroom, I'd tucked my shirt into my sparkly rainbow underwear, which had been clearly visible above my pants all morning.

We piled in the trucks and drove to the same FSR near Sayward that I'd driven on a year earlier, but we turned left instead of right. Before the visit, the committee and I had chatted over email as to whether it would be possible to see the Champion yellow-cedar up by Sayward on the same outing. Bill confirmed that the tree was not in White River Provincial Park, where the gas station attendant in Sayward had pointed me, but that the park had some impressive Doug-firs. The film set for *The Scarlet Letter*, the 1995 film starring Demi Moore, is extant in the forest with wide boardwalks for phantom stagecoaches.

We pulled over, a line of white trucks on a stretch of FSR not too far from the village, and started talking safety procedures. The 94-meter Doug-fir was close to the road, growing in a ravine. When trees grow in a narrow valley or ravine, they compete for light, so they grow tall ("shoot up") and skinny. The Doug-fir was growing at an angle, next to the second-tallest Doug-fir they'd measured and a Sitka spruce with a dead top. The newly measured Doug-fir would likely now be the tallest Doug-fir in BC.

We put on safety vests and hard hats, and Jonathan from WFP said, "This is definitely a caulk boots scenario." I nodded, repeating *cork* under my breath. For liability reasons, we weren't able to get close to the tree, which was a crock. "If the tree is too dangerous, yes, it can be tackled another time, but [Western Forest Products] needs to understand this is what we do as big-tree hunters," Shaun wrote over email in advance of the field trip.

"We go into areas that are pretty crazy to find big trees since very few new Champions will be in easy flat locations." Even I was annoyed, as accessing the tree was as simple as fording a small ditch next to the gravel road we were standing on. But we carried on as respectful guests and admired the tree from afar.

The Douglas-fir is unique: not a true fir, it's defined as a member of the pine family despite its needles growing differently than typical pine clusters. As David Suzuki and Wayne Grady recount in their book *Tree*, "The Douglas-fir is not a fir or a spruce or a pine, as it has also been called. That is why Douglas-fir is hyphenated," to show it stands alone. The "mice" in the cones are actually bracts (they look like the rear legs and tail of a mouse sliding out between the scales of the cone) and are a primary way to identify this tree. The trunk generally grows straight but can sometimes have a slight bend or grow into gnarlier configurations; on the coast, its main boughs are near the top of the tree. Inland versions, which are less crowded by dense undergrowth, have boughs along the length of the trunk. Doug-firs are anchored to the ground with a deep taproot as well as side roots, giving them the ability to endure high winds. Doug-fir's brown-gray furrowed bark is exceptionally thick and corky, protecting the tree during wildfires; on older specimens, it's common to see burn marks from previous brush fires. Its wood is strong and valued as a building material and as firewood, and the tree is a popular Christmas tree variety.

This area, already designated as a reserve, seemed to be a good growing site, with cedars across the road that we estimated at over seventy meters high, really tall for a cedar. Since it was close to the road, it could make a good recreation site, like Avatar Grove in Port Renfrew. We talked about where stairs could be run up the hill, where to put a viewing platform, but I wondered how many trees would fall while that tourism infrastructure was being built. Sustainability is built over the long term, and any truly sustainable planning must engage with nature as existing within "deep time," a slower way of growing and changing over millennia and millions of years. Western Forest Products plans in 250-year cycles and is harvesting some second-growth forests now, but when planning for conservation, we need to think on a longer timescale: tree time, hundreds and thousands of years into the future, like the Indigenous worldview that considers the impacts on seven generations.

Consider that countries can form and dissolve before a tree achieves maturity. While we plan, we're actually counting down rather than building up reserves of time. As with a project, a weekend, a relationship—we have less time than we think. In *Four Thousand Weeks*, Oliver Burkeman notes that the average human life of eighty years amounts to an insultingly short time. He makes the case that in four thousand weeks, we can't accomplish everything on our to-do list, let alone our bucket list. I take some comfort, however morbid, in knowing that these Champion trees will likely outlive me, have already outlived me many times over. Scientists who study trees know that in many cases, their subjects will survive them; they're coming in for a small portion of the tree's life. "Even if a scientist dedicated her whole career to very old trees," writes Cara Giaimo, in an article on trees and immortality, "she would be able to follow her research subjects for only a small percentage of their lives. And a long enough multigenerational study might see its own methods go obsolete."

Trees are bastions of a longer perspective that sets its own pace. In *Orwell's Roses*, Rebecca Solnit considers the lasting effects of planting trees, flowers, and shrubs. When Solnit visits six eucalyptus trees in San Francisco, she reflects on the woman who planted them over a century earlier. "The trees made the past seem within reach," Solnit writes, "in a way nothing else could: here were living beings that had been planted and tended by a living being who was gone, but the trees that had been alive in her lifetime were in ours and might be after we were gone." It was a tree time trip-out if I ever read one. Solnit comprehends the apparent overlapping of time frames through the lens of saeculum, an Etruscan word "that describes the span of time lived by the oldest person present, sometimes calculated to be about a hundred years . . . Trees seemed to offer another kind of saeculum, a longer time scale and deeper continuity, giving shelter from our ephemerality the way that a tree might offer literal shelter under its boughs." Looking for the Champion trees felt like searching for an older world within this time, and they grounded me in their compression of scale. Big old trees allow us to confront the slow-slow-quick time of climate change, too: we are literally looking at rings of time, bound up in carbon, the destruction of which speeds up our own demise.

In *The Uninhabitable Earth*, a book on the climate crisis, David Wallace-Wells refers to the Aboriginal Australian concept of "'dreamtime,' or 'everywhen': the semi-mythical experience of encountering, in the present moment, an out-of-time past, when ancestors, heroes, and demigods crowded an epic stage. You can find it already by watching footage of an iceberg collapsing into the sea—a feeling of history happening all at once." That might be why we find big trees so calming—they confirm this deep time—and huge stumps, logs, and unfathomable climate change so upsetting—they upset our temporal scales.

Examine the rings of a tree and you'll see that not every year is one of immense growth. Tree rings can reveal what went into that year (for example, the nutrients from salmon guts that bears, eagles, and wolves leave in the forest, or that Coastal First Nations allow to return to the forest bottom, show up as

nitrogen in the rings) as well as what plagued the tree in a particular year (the soot from a forest fire). It's comforting to consider
our lives in the same way, with years of bounty and deprivation
equally valid additions. Having children, preserving crab apples,
planting cedars, investing in an RRSP, and betting on finding
these trees are all skewers in the side of death and environmental
catastrophe. Taking action on climate change doesn't necessarily shift the future as much as it improves the present, offering
us the chance to respond ethically to the greatest crisis we collectively face. Climate change and its effects are worsening,
biodiversity loss is increasing, old-growth forests are still being
cleared. The scale of the problem can be overwhelming. Perhaps
that's why when a large tree is cut down, we feel immeasur-
able grief, yet when we contemplate climate change, we feel
overwhelmed by the challenge of action and do nothing—
it's just too big. But as Robert Bringhurst and Jan Zwicky write
in *Learning to Die*, "To wallow in despair that the natural world
is dying is to fail to be aware that it is still, in many ways, very
much alive."

On the days when I'm feeling the strain of paying bills, keeping house, moving the muscles, and cranking out these words, I
imagine the stillness surrounding a moss-covered seven-hundred-
year-old western red-cedar and breathe a little easier. Staring
up at that 94-meter Doug-fir in Sayward, while the ecologists
and foresters milled about, I realized my life is a pleasingly small
element of the larger picture, and recognizing my insignificance
was my version of transcendence. It's good to feel small. "To
remember how little you matter, on a cosmic timescale," Burkeman writes, "can feel like putting down a heavy burden that
most of us didn't realize we were carrying in the first place." My
project was a Pop-Tart in the universal toaster.

I WAS FAMILIAR WITH coastal Doug-firs but not with the other version of them growing in the Interior called, you guessed it, interior Douglas-firs. Interior (or Rocky Mountain) Douglas-firs are a bit different from their coastal cousins: smaller, with upward-curving bracts in their cones (making them curly mouse feet), and blue-green needles. The registry accounts for these coastal and Interior varieties, and there can be separate Champion titles for varieties that grow in the Interior and on the coast, with the coastal cousins generally growing much bigger than the Interior.

A few years ago, my pal Cody moved out to Princeton to manage recreation programs for the small city in the foothills east of the Cascade Range. About three hours' drive from Vancouver, and at the intersection of the Tulameen and Similkameen Rivers, this region is semiarid and has more extreme temperatures than on the coast. Its grasslands and rocky hillsides make it an ideal location for ranching and, for my purposes, growing interior Doug-firs and ponderosa pines. The landscape changes dramatically as you move through the Fraser Valley and past Hope, into the Fraser Canyon and the mountains. The highway is dangerous to drive even in ideal conditions, with hairpin corners and a risk of landslides. In 1965, the Hope Slide, triggered by seismic activity, killed four people, and two bodies remain under the rubble. In November 2021, extreme flooding and rainfall in the Hope area triggered a mudslide that killed four people and stranded thousands.

I knew the Champion interior Doug-fir grew on a hillside just before Highway 3 entered Princeton. On a weekend visit to Cody, I saw a big fir growing above a ranch—it stood out among its fellow trees on the slope, but it didn't seem big *enough*. Once I was at home, I wrote to Shaun, who had seen the tree in 1995 and added it to the registry in the early 2000s. He confirmed it was the same tree: it looks small from the road and had been hit by lightning in the intervening years. When you're that big, you're a lightning rod. But he mentioned it's a beautiful tree and he'd love to know its condition and size, so a few weeks later, I returned.

Cody and I met by the tree, parking on opposite sides of the highway. He and I grew up on opposite sides of Royal Heights Park in Surrey and would often meet in the middle green or in the Fitness, so it was appropriate that we'd meet in the middle for this adventure. We held the barbed wire up for each other so we could step onto the ranch; unlike with the watershed, I was definitely okay with trespassing onto cattle country. The tree was growing at an angle on the sloping hillside of grass, loose rock, and dry soil, in the company of smaller Doug-firs and ponderosa pines. Hunks of charred wood the size of elephant trunks lay beside the giant, likely the top of this tree after it was struck. The whole tree was black from the lightning strike, though sap flow emerged atop the charred bole (trunk), and green needles grew. It was still alive. I sullied my d-tape with soot, and we took new measurements of the circumference at two different heights: at breast height (above a bulge in the trunk) and about a foot above the germination point, then I took the average of the two. This type of measurement is not easy on a slope, when at least one of the two people will be sliding and grasping for a hold. We made sure to measure on an angle with the tilt of the tree, rather than parallel to the ground, so we wouldn't distort our measurement.

As we were wrapping up our crown measurement, a rancher pulled up at the far end of the field, so we hightailed it back to Cody's vehicle rather than risk an altercation. We sat on the tailgate, pulling burrs from our socks and laces, and watching golden horses trotting in the rippling grass. He and I fell back into our old habits of bull-shitting each other and discussing the finer points of *Wayne's World*. Cody calls himself a big kid, always up for fun. His years of experience as a kayak guide on the west coast of Vancouver Island, plus his career in recreation and his outstanding cooking skills, make him an ideal travel companion. I handed Cody my plaid shirt and he removed the burrs while I took height measurements from the road, using the laser that UBC had loaned me, measuring the tree at 47 meters.

When I reported the measurements to the registry, Christine commended my measurement skills (score!) and told me the Doug-fir is no longer the Champion because it was reduced in size by the lightning strike. With several entries for most species in the registry, the trees are set up with an "heir and a spare" system, should the original Champion lose bulk or height, die, or be outpaced by another tree. The registry retains data on trees that have died or been burned, but it doesn't display that info online.

Shaun asked me to look for the runners-up, huge Doug-firs on Kane Valley Road that he'd seen in the '90s. So, a few weeks later, I drove back to Princeton. Before heading out, we stopped for air and filled the oil, Cody roaring when he realized that marmots had shit on his engine block. We filled up the six-CD changer (dope) and headed north toward Merritt. We figured we'd look for big ponderosa pines while we were at it, since the largest known pines grow in that region. We kept our pace leisurely, stopping at numerous big Doug-firs along the road outside Princeton, scrambling up and down steep slopes, measuring trees just for the hell of it.

Out near Lundbom Lake, we went looking for the Champion ponderosa pine, which Shaun had nominated in 2000, describing it as an "old gnarly giant with 3 massive limbs and a dead top." The area around Lundbom Lake is all golden grasses, creeks, and rolling hills. We stopped when we hit a logjam of cattle and when Cody's vehicle couldn't make it any farther on the rutted trail. We left a note on the car with our intention (safety always) and headed up and over a grassy hill, baked yellow in the sun, toward the Champion ponderosa, periodically facing off with cattle who refused to move off trail.

Ponderosa pines are magic. Their bark looks like the cracked top of a tray of brownies, sugary orange-brown lined with dark brown fissures. The bark separates into plates that resemble puzzle pieces or artist's palettes, falling to the ground amid their shed needle clusters and large seed cones. David George Haskell describes the odor of their bark in this way: "The golden sap between dark plates of ponderosa bark has the vigorous odor of rosin and turpentine: oily, acidic, and bright. But unlike the aggressive, spiky odor of other pines, ponderosa's aroma has smooth, sweet edges. A hint of vanilla or buttery sugar mingles in the resin." There is a reason for the aroma, Haskell tells us: "The scent is a deterrent against attacking insects. Sticky resin gums and traps woodboring insects, and resinous chemicals are poisonous in large doses." The name *ponderosa*—appointed by David Douglas—comes from *ponderous*, a reference to their large size. Ponderosa trunks are straight, their limbs slender and spindly, ending in sprays of bunched needles like fireworks against the sky, and draped pompoms when they fall. Indigenous Peoples have long used ponderosa pine for lumber, medicine, baskets, and canoes, and settlers later used the wood for railroad ties and buildings.

When I was with Ira at UBC, after we'd measured the Sitka alder, we'd wandered over to measure a ponderosa pine that was growing in the middle of the Ponderosa Commons student residence. The tree was saved when the building was constructed, but it looked a bit worse for wear when we saw it, brown needles indicating it wasn't getting enough water. Still, Ira surmised it was likely the largest ponderosa pine on the coast, growing out of its natural inland habitat, having been brought there for the original arboretum.

Using the GPS that UBC loaned me, Cody and I roamed all over the area but were unable to pinpoint the Champion. We didn't care, though: we were enjoying each other's company and the warmth of the day, rushing up to large trees regardless of whether they were pines or firs. We lost the light after about seven hours of searching and headed back to town for some comfort food, quoting *Pulp Fiction* at each other while we drove.

"Tell that bitch to be cool!"

"Be cool, Honey Bunny."

The next day, we took separate cars toward Kane Valley Road, where we hoped the runner-up Doug-firs still grew. We stopped where we could see tall firs jutting above the tree line. Big trees can sometimes be the flashing neon lights of the forest; towering above their neighbors, they don't stand a shot at hiding. Climbing over a low fence (we were again in private cattle country), we found ourselves in a grove of three huge firs—two standing and one that had fallen. The biggest of the two standing had a rich sap flow, and birds had pecked golf-ball-sized holes in its corky bark. This fir was more than 44 meters tall, with a 1.87-meter DBH and a 15.7-meter crown. I took a photo of the tree that had fallen down, just in case. When I later showed the photo to Shaun, he told me the fallen tree was likely the runner-up.

So, to recap: the tree on the hillside had been the Champion but was demoted after being damaged by lightning. The runner-up then became the Champ, until it fell down. So the third biggest moved into the Champion slot, until someone else measured a bigger one. Shaun later wrote to me, "You have to remember I measured these trees years ago. So much changes.

Cows rub up against the bark, lightning, etc." He told me to go find bigger firs "out around Logan Lake. Also you really need to get out to the Davis Lake area. Giant pines and firs. Maybe even a giant lodgepole pine. I can just feel it." Big-tree trackers are guided by their intuition, an uncanny sense combined with knowledge of ideal grow sites and use of Google Earth. But at this stage of learning to track trees, I still didn't have any tingling sense about where big trees would grow.

Cody was walking along the fallen tree and I was examining the sap flow of the standing tree when we heard a crashing in the bush and froze. My bear spray was at the ready as curious cattle whooped out of the shadows to watch us. A rainstorm had started while we were wrapping up our measurements, so we headed back to the cars and I drove to Vancouver.

Even though the lightning-hit tree was demoted, I still felt an affinity for it, having peered at it from the highway, sending its measurements, condition report, and coordinates to Christine. On future trips to visit Cody or travel farther inland, I would nod to it as I passed. I realized the former Champion had become a presence in my life, perhaps even a friend. It was my witness tree, like the ones that fire lookout folks have, that they keep track of as they return to their platform each year and that keep track of them. As author and lookout Trina Moyles told me, lookouts turn to witness trees for connection in an isolated landscape, and as a measure of time. "Lookouts often migrate back to the same towers, season after season," she wrote to me, "so we see those nuanced changes year to year in the boreal. Some lookouts witness the forest around them burn down, or be cut down, and regenerate. The impact of deforestation for agricultural expansion, logging, or oil and gas activity can be really psychologically tough on lookouts. Because we know how the forest serves as critical habitat for the wildlife we see and interact with." Indeed, the first fire lookout towers *were* trees—the tallest objects around. These lookout trees were common among the ponderosa pines of the Kaibab National Forest in Arizona, as well as in Washington and Australia. A ladder would be run up a tree, or rungs hammered into the trunk, and then watchers would sit in the tree and keep an eye open, or a platform might be created by cutting off the top of the tree and building a simple structure.

I realized that as my tree project continued, I was adding these witness trees, which I monitored in reality and through memory, to my mental landscape. I'd long used a remembered sit spot, a tongue of sandstone jutting into the bay on Hornby Island, as a mental reprieve. I'd spent countless hours on this rock during summer vacations as a teen, listening to the waves shape the rock as they have for millions of years. I return to the sandstone slip in memory whenever I need a moment of calm, or to assist relaxation in meditation or savasana. The western hemlock on Coliseum Mountain, the arbutus groves of Helliwell Provincial Park on Hornby Island, the former Champion interior Doug-fir beside Highway 3, even the patches of vine maples in Burnaby's Central Park all became timeless landscapes of my mind to which I could turn.

— 10 —

Slow and Low

GRAND FIR

"Don't get impatient. Even if things are so tangled up you
can't do anything, don't get desperate or blow a fuse and start
yanking on one particular thread before it's ready to come
undone. You have to realize it's going to be a long process
and that you'll work on things slowly, one at a time."
HARUKI MURAKAMI, *Norwegian Wood*

I SLOWED MY CAR AND STOPPED. A thick sheet of gray and
blue ice covered the access road curving out of sight. Kate and
I still had about seven miles to go before we hit the trailhead
that would bring us to a grove containing the largest grand fir in
BC, which officially made it the grandest. The Chilliwack Giant
was 74 meters high with a DBH of 2.16 meters and crown of
11 meters, which Randy Stoltmann had come across growing
along the Chilliwack River in the 1980s.

The sun was angling low over the hemlocks of the adjacent provincial park, and we'd eaten all the dill pickle chips.
We'd spent the morning at a gold-mining conference in downtown Vancouver. Kate had a press pass to attend, as she was
researching placer mining in northern BC. I was there for the
gold-panning demonstration and the freebies, loading up with
pens and an all-weather notebook. We'd worn matching green

plaid Patagonia shirts for the occasion, mine a gift from Kate, and were both feeling dressed up in our Patagucci.

"I'm not so sure Trouble can make it down here," I said to Kate, staring at the ice sheet, my left cheek ablaze with a rainbow I'd had painted on in the kids' zone at the conference.

"It will be fine, Sappy Pants," Kate said. "Just put on your chains." Kate, who biked the ice road to Tuktoyaktuk before they built an actual road, moved to Atlin after falling in love with the landscape at a glacier field school. She was used to wheels on ice. I'd earned the name Sappy Pants after sitting on a sap-covered bench while bike touring with Kate, forever marking my fleece camp pants.

I hadn't expected snow and ice in the Fraser Valley at this time of year—you know, January in Canada. I groaned. "I don't have chains." We'd driven almost three hours, screaming along with Beastie Boys most of the way, and I'd expected the search from here to be a cakewalk. We even had a map to the tree courtesy of Stoltmann's hiking guide.

I tried driving forward on the gently sloping hill and started sliding. "Nope," I said. "I'm not getting stuck down a remote road on a Sunday evening." I steered for the rough shoulder and reversed Trouble, letting out a heavy sigh.

"I would have done the same thing!" said Kate. I didn't believe her.

Giving up on the tree for that day, we parked next to the gates to the provincial park. Whiskey jacks hopped from branch to branch, hoping for handouts. I held on to Kate's arm for balance as she skate-stepped toward the lake, green and clear. We seated ourselves on driftwood cedars on the sandy shore and opted for a photo shoot on the way back to the car. In our green shirts, we blended into the forest, nouveau gothic.

"To find the tree, you must become the tree," Kate said.

To find the tree, you must become the tree

THERE'S A *GROUNDHOG DAY* QUALITY to tree tracking.

(car doors slam)

"Got the GPS?"

Yep.

"Got snacks? Bear spray?"

Double yep.

"Know where the tree is?"

Not a clue.

But each day you learn a little more, grow a bit, hopefully break the pattern. My friend Andre connected me with his long-time friend Dick, a retired vet who grew up in Chilliwack and knows its forests intimately. In September, I picked Dick up at his home overlooking the Chilliwack River. We fueled up with the burger family at A&w. I had a Beyond Meat veggie burger, which I nicknamed an Eccentric Aunt burger. It turns out I had the tendency to name everything. Before trying for the grand fir, we swung by his friends' place to measure a huge black elder-berry. As I shared some of my outings on social media, people began inviting me to come and measure trees in their yards.

They were starting to see me as some sort of tree expert, and they hoped they had a new Champion on their hands. While flattered, I didn't see myself that way and usually demurred, steering them toward an arborist or someone on the committee who could help. While Dick stepped through the brush to measure the trunk—"This is the biggest elderberry I've ever seen!" he called back—I hung back with the property owners, agreeing, "Yeeeep, that's plenty big all right."

We then drove to the Chilliwack River Ecological Reserve, about thirty-five miles southeast of downtown Chilliwack. We drove for half an hour on a paved road, past Chilliwack Lake Provincial Park where Kate and I had stopped, to an old FSR. On the other side of the rutted road, Chilliwack Lake glistened teal in the sun. This recreation site is popular due to the sandy lakeshore and the big trees in the reserve, which was set aside in 1980. The road to the trailhead was no joke and put Trouble to the test—lots of weaving around potholes and small boulders that had tumbled down. After fifty minutes of slow-going and bottoming-out, we came to a barricade. We walked about ten minutes along the road, past a regenerating cutblock. In the reserve, we were met by gigantic cedars, Douglas-firs, hemlocks, amabilis fir (Pacific silver fir), alder, grand fir, and a whole lot of devil's club. Devil's club is a slow-growing understory shrub with a long narrow stem, maple-like palmate leaves, and spikes growing on the stem and undersides of the leaves. It grows slowly but reaches to waist or chest level, and though it has numerous ceremonial and medicinal uses, it's a pain to walk through—the spines can pierce clothing and cause skin irritation.

When they're young, grand firs have reddish-brown bark that's fairly smooth apart from slight bumps; the bark thickens and grows rougher as the tree ages. From a distance, older grand fir can resemble Doug-fir, but grand fir branches often grow down the length of the trunk whereas coastal Doug-fir boughs only persist near the crown. Grand fir needles are dark green, shiny, and of uneven length, and their cones are large with smooth tightly packed scales and sit upright in the crown of the tree like matryoshka dolls; Doug-fir cones grow along the length of their branches and hang down. Grand fir pitch is used medicinally, its bark for canoes, and its boughs for mats and bedding. Its wood is useful for pulp, and the trunks offer homes for wildlife.

The Champion grand fir was supposed to be growing about twenty yards east of the riverside trail, near a sandbar. In addition to the map, we had coordinates and access notes. Following Dick's lead, I navigated the forest as a raccoon would, walking along fallen trees to avoid undergrowth and windthrow. "When a tree snaps in a windstorm," Nina Shoroplova writes, "it's called a *windsnap*. When a tree with shallow roots falls over, the roots tear out of the earth in a clump, bringing rocks and small plants with them; the tree is called a *windthrow* or *blowdown*, and its roots are called a *root wad*." Most of these walklogs were mossy but not slippery, as conditions had been fairly dry. The trail veered off, seemingly into the river, which we needed to traverse on logs. Dick scampered ahead, strong and capable. I felt less adept at log walking and my balance was thrown off by my pack. I stepped gingerly along a series of slick logs, a brown frog hopping ahead and keeping me company. When I was small, I'd scamper across logs in the ravine, but as an adult, I'd become nervous about using logs to cross water. Now, I went slow and low, fist pumping when I made it to the other side.

"Whether we find the tree or not, I've grown as a human by 23 percent today," I said to Dick. We kept on south (the tree was growing near the U.S. border) but eventually lost the trail and decided to turn back, try again when we had more light. We'd seen enough marvels—huge Doug-firs and cedars, and a western toad—to make the day a success. Returning to find the Champion would be a marvelous excuse to enter this ancient forest again, and with such an easy travel companion.

Later, as we traded photos of the day, Dick emailed, "I'm a little concerned with your 23 percent growth as a human, in one hike. At that rate, there is a serious concern that you might bubble over the top if you happened to do a long hike, or nimbly scampered along too many logs in a day." He attached a photo of a huge cascara he'd seen in Chilliwack. There are real big-tree trackers out there, doing it for the thrill of the hunt. I was enjoying myself more in the woods, and feeling proud of my skills, but I still didn't feel I belonged among their ranks.

MID-OCTOBER, I RETURNED TO the area with Dick and his son, Steve, who is a renowned local conservationist, as well as our mutual friend Andre. Andre picked me up at 6:30 AM in Vancouver, and we drove to meet Dick and Steve in a Tim Hortons parking lot.

Steve is built like his dad, not a spare bit of fat on him. A proud father of two girls, he is an experienced backwoods explorer and works in environmental services for the City of Chilliwack. Andre... well, Andre does everything. I know him because he was the manager of my friend's building, but he also works as a tutor and writer. He's tall and ropey, does the Grouse Grind (Nature's StairMaster, a gruesome hike on the North Shore) several times a week, and can outpace me any day.

The rains had arrived on the coast "like a wet rag on a salad," as Tom Robbins wrote in *Another Roadside Attraction*. "You picked a great day for a hike, Amanda!" said Andre. It had been raining all week, early onset Novembruary. We transferred to

Steve's suv for the journey to the trailhead. He took the entrance road at a fast clip, splashing through puddles.

"Dick's head is like a bobblehead!" said Andre next to me in the back seat, perhaps overlooking that his head was bouncing much the same.

"Anyone get car sick?" Steve asked.

I closed my eyes and willed myself to keep it down. The road that took me fifty minutes to drive in Trouble took Steve approximately ten minutes. We parked at the south end of Chilliwack Lake, began our own forms of preparation (me checking supplies, Dick gathering discarded beer cans), then walked to the trailhead.

Before heading for the grand fir, we went uphill away from the river to see the remnants of a silver mine from the early twentieth century. Steve and his friends found it after reading about it in an early settler's memoir of Chilliwack Lake. They scoured the hillside for two full days, looking for a scree slope where the mine was supposed to be located. Then, realizing that the landscape had changed since the time of writing, they accounted for the shift and found the mine, halfway up the slope. The area was grown over and mossy, with fairly young trees, and evidence of scree underneath the soil. We saw what looked like a corral for the mules that would have been brought up each day to carry down the silver ore.

The first part of the mine, with a wooden lintel across the entry, was a test site just five feet deep. The second was the actual mine. I walked through the narrow opening under a boulder, and stepped on planks on the left to stay above the water pooled at the entrance. Evidence of chiseling showed the rock was hand-hewn, and it went back about a hundred feet. How long had it taken to dig this far, how much energy, and for what payoff? We saw a vein of silver, which looked like a line of rust;

surprising, as I'd expected a line of glitter. We used our head-lamps in the pitch black, picking out lots of spiders and a few moths. Andre and Steve spoke about a fungus that grows in some of these mines and becomes a parasite in host bodies. I breathed as lightly as I could.

After descending from the mine, we moved from the inland trail to the river trail. "Go on a little bushwhacky," said Steve, plunging ahead into the thick devil's club. There was a lot of windthrow, including a root wad that was about twelve meters across and six meters high, actually a small copse that had blown over. "Vitally the human race is dying," D. H. Lawrence wrote in *Lady Chatterley's Lover.* "It is like a great uprooted tree, with its roots in the air. We must plant ourselves again in the universe." A treetop about five meters long had plummeted headfirst into the ground like a downed fighter jet, breaking off all its branches in the process. I knew the forest as a site of decay but not of so much destruction. The logs were slick, the moss a deep blan-ket dotted with almost translucent mushrooms, appearing like a dream forest in miniature. With the many varieties of fungi, it seemed an ideal spot for mushroom pickers. We bushwhacked through the marsh, me putting my log walking to the test. I was once again grateful to Jenny for suggesting the purchase of those gas-station gloves as I climbed over slick logs, grabbed hold of spiny devil's club, and swatted red osier out of my face.

We could still see salmon in the river this time of year. Steve explained that in August this river is filled with land-locked kokanee, the smaller version of the ocean-going sockeye. I noticed him pulling down tracking tape, orange and pink plas-tic tied to trees and branches by hikers and search-and-rescue crews. I could understand why he took down the flagging that identified the way to the mine, but what about on the existing trail? He said, "Oh, that's me and it's a bit controversial."

I said, "Controversy is fine," encouraging him to continue.

"I want people to earn these routes," he said, "to find deeper meaning that way, to work at it."

"Yeah," I said, "but what if someone doesn't want a deeper meaning? What if they just want to enjoy a day trip in a recreational area?"

"If someone can't tell the trail for themselves, with few markers," he said, "they shouldn't be in here."

While he was right in terms of backcountry safety, the overlap with big-tree tracking felt blatant. Where does that leave beginners who don't already possess advanced skills in log walking, bushwhacking, and map reading? Here we were with a map and coordinates, and we still couldn't find the tree, and now Steve was removing the trail markers. I felt slighted, as I probably couldn't find the trail without these markers, but I still deserved to be in here, enjoying the route and not earning it. Steve pointed out blazons, unobtrusive metal triangle- or diamond-shaped signs hammered into trees, as "good" flagging. "Those are set by people who know what they're doing, who set them at appropriate points where it's easy to get lost." He pulled down flagging that was set only a few feet apart, claiming that "it mars the landscape." He admitted he never removed natural markers, like cairns. Maybe it was less about earning the trail and more about reducing litter.

We hunted for hours, consulted the GPS, used Steve's tracking app, followed Stoltmann's map, and just looked up and through. The sandbar that had served as a landmark would likely have shifted over time and wasn't helpful to us now. I'd felt sure that with these experienced explorers, whom I'd privately nicknamed Trail Mix due to their assorted personalities, we'd find the tree. That confidence fell away as the day wore on. We saw huge cedars, which had been recorded in Stoltmann's book, but no massive grand fir. We walked on logs for a better viewpoint, me eagerly scrambling up onto the wide mossy mounds, and went off trail to look all over where the tree was supposed to be, periodically calling out to each other so we wouldn't get lost. We saw many skinny grand firs, likely sixty meters tall. Grand fir doesn't live that long (about 280 years max) but can grow to great heights in river valleys without crowding from hemlocks, the dominant tree in these forests.

After we'd been searching for several hours, Andre said, "I'm finally starting to understand that old saying: you can't see the tree for the forest." We did find one large grand fir, where the Champion was supposed to be, but it wasn't as big as our prey. When it was clear we wouldn't find the tree, Andre said, "It's frustrating!"

I said, "Welcome to my weekends. And usually I don't have this much to go on."

"With the amount of windthrow in there," Andre said, "it's entirely possible the tree blew down."

"But we would have seen it," Steve said.

"Not if it smashed and was covered in moss," I said, thinking of the other downed trees we'd seen. I had a sneaking suspicion that one of our walklogs was the grand fir that had fallen.

"What percentage are you now?" Dick asked, noting that I was cruising along logs without a care. I was so tired that my movements in the forest were automatic; I had no energy to waste on stressing about slipping.

"Fifty-six percent," I said, beaming even though I was dead to the world, privately counting down the hours until I could be home watching the BBC's *Victorian Farm*.

So, we went searching for the largest grand fir in BC and found instead:

- slug eggs laid in a wide circle on a log
- a silver mine

- bear puke (cream color, mostly liquid—Andre poked it with a stick)

- bear shit (black, greasy from salmon, not like berry-rich scat)

- partially eaten salmon (dark gray scales, heads, bones)

- an eagle's perching spot in a tree next to a deep fish pool in the river (more shit)

- windthrow and root wads

- tracks belonging to a big elk or a moose

- fungi and moss and ferns

- verrrry large cedars

- verrrry tall grand firs

Never a wasted trip, never wasted fertilizer.

"Amanda, you promised us rain!" said Dick as the skies opened up again. The rain bucketed down as Andre and I drove back on Highway 1, which resembled a silver river flowing below clouds. Later that evening, as I shook fir needles and black bark from my hair, an email landed from Andre.

Subject: Super day

A quick note of thanks for a super day. Hope the lack of a tree wasn't too much of a disappointment, but in my book the salmon carcasses, the slug slime, the windfalls, the moss, and the company made the day a rich and rewarding one.

This lovely note shifted my mood. Maybe it really was about the companions on the journey. In that way, I'd found what I was looking for without knowing I was seeking it.

THAT FALL, I WAS INVITED to join the BC Big Tree Committee AGM at the UBC Forestry building and present my findings to the group. We were assembled around a boardroom table: fabled big-tree trackers, ecologists, arborists, forest technicians—and me. Christine dimmed the lights, hit a button on her laptop, and my photo of the Scouler's willow flashed on the screen set up at the head of the table. I drew a breath, waiting for the "Nice job!" comments from the crew.

Matthew Beatty, arborist and canopy climber, immediately said, "That's not a Scouler's willow." I felt myself shrinking. I'd even gone back to the community center lawn the previous summer to grab coordinates and measurements for the registry. But as Suzuki Roshi said, "The essence of Zen is 'Not always so.'"

Christine buried her head in her hands. "I told you to ask Ralf to bring you there."

I said petulantly, "I haven't been able to get ahold of Ralf."

Ralf, sitting next to me, said, "We'll go."

IN LATE NOVEMBER 2020, Sean O'Rourke, an applied anthropologist and big-tree tracker in the Fraser Valley, was determined to put the Champion grand fir to bed. Following the map in Stoltmann's book, as well as additional resources online, he bushwhacked to find the original trail, now "in slightly rough shape and tricky to follow at times," he emailed me, Ira, and Shaun after his outing. He'd known we were interested in the status of the tree and had consulted with me for any tips in advance of his trip (me beaming at my computer, 100 percent growth).

Sean followed the coordinates to what was likely the remains of the tree. I thought for sure he had it. But he realized afterward that an approximately sixty-year-old hemlock growing out of the stump would mean this tree couldn't be the one

Stoltmann had located. In early December, he emailed, "I was pretty perplexed and believed the coordinates must be off, so I then attempted to use the directions described by Stoltmann . . . but could not definitively identify any landmarks. Anyways, not being able to find this tree is annoying the heck out of me. I am going to return a few more times." When I later asked Sean about what drives him to find big trees, he wrote, "I have an appreciation for novelty and uniqueness, and I like seeing beautiful things—big trees check all of those boxes. I am not really looking for the biggest tree though. I just enjoy getting outside, and intact ecosystems, where big trees are found, are some of the best places to visit."

And then in mid-December, Sean solved the mystery, finding the "remains" of a fallen grand fir with a "6.58m-ish circumference at breast height [2.09 m DBH] (and it was missing a chunk)." The new Champion was now officially the Totem Giant, the former runner-up that Ralf Kelman and Shaun Muc nominated and verified in 2006. It was last measured as 64.4 meters tall in 2020 and grows on the slope of Totem Park Ravine in Pacific Spirit Regional Park at UBC. The Totem Giant appears shorter than it is because its base is twenty meters below in the ravine.

I was disappointed with the news but relieved that I wasn't the only one concerned with the welfare of a tree. Like Sean with the grand fir, and Steve and his friends who'd spent days searching for a silver mine, I knew I'd gone the distance with this mission. Yes, it was still annoying to not find the tree standing, but how sweet it was to find that and more. I felt I was finally keeping up with these seasoned hikers and trackers, able to answer some of their questions about the tree and trail as we searched. And I was beginning to measure up to the expectations I'd set for myself as an adventurer in the woods.

— 11 —

Secular Pilgrimage

SUBALPINE LARCH, CHERRY, PLUM, BIGLEAF MAPLE, COASTAL DOUGLAS-FIR, ARBUTUS

"A drop of rain that lands on the leaf of a tree is not
the same as the drop that later falls down into the ground.
There's so much about it that we don't understand and
we don't have to understand it. It's not about understanding.
It's about our one life, our one and only life."

W. S. MERWIN

BY LOOKING FOR ONE TREE, I began to see the forest. As I stuck with it, each outing became less about conquering and more about appreciating, and in that way my journey felt like a secular pilgrimage. Wendell Berry explains that a secular pilgrimage "does not seek any institutional shrine or holy place; it is in search of the world." I didn't need to reach my original goal for spiritual reward, didn't need to "earn" these trees, didn't need to understand everything about the Champions in order to know them. To reinforce this stance, I sought out a common site of tree pilgrimage: Manning Park, when the larches turn gold. For a few weeks each autumn, this subalpine deciduous conifer's soft blue-green needles transform to gold tinsel. Then the needles drop and the trees appear diseased or dead until the spring, when the green reemerges.

On the Thanksgiving long weekend (October in Canada), I drove out to E. C. Manning Provincial Park, located in the Cascade Mountains on the way to Princeton, to meet with Cody for a hike up Frosty Mountain. The leaves were an overlay of red, green, and yellow on hillsides, beside creeks, and emerging from roadside ditches. The switchback trail up Frosty was coated with snow and ice, appropriate for the name but a few weeks early. We didn't have shoe grips or poles, so we slipped, slid, and held ourselves mostly rigid on the five miles up. On the drive, I'd stopped at Tim Hortons for a bagel and chili in my thermos, which was a brilliant companion at subzero temperatures in the backcountry hut. Whiskey jacks circled us as we ate chocolate-covered peanuts. A spruce grouse, unperturbed by our presence, calmly pecked away beside the path. We were off to a typical day of swearing, carousing, and *South Park* references.

"I'm not your buddy, guy."

"I'm not your guy, friend."

We met a few others on the trail, some there to hike the fourteen-mile roundtrip loop to the top of Mount Frosty, but most to see the larches. It's a tradition, as the larches tend to peak golden around Thanksgiving weekend. In the summer, this subalpine meadow is filled with a kaleidoscope of flowers, but now it shone, gold embroidery on white satin. Some of the larches were completely ablaze, some turning from green to gold, and some had already dropped their needles. Subalpine larches grow very slowly; a sign in the meadow told us that some of the skinny trees were up to two thousand years old. I soaked in the experience, not needing to know if they were the oldest or biggest in order to find communion. We took in the encircling jagged peaks dusted with snow, wandered in meandering circles with about twenty other larch pilgrims, everyone slowly turning in wonder.

We snapped goofy selfies in the frozen meadow, mementos of the day but also glorious shots that I planned to post later on social media, reinforcing our pilgrimage as a performative act. People hiking mountains and visiting pristine lakes for the likes can cause these sites to lose their luster. The outings become a mark of external validation rather than a path to internal reward. The rise of selfie culture has led to a rush on Instagrammable spots around the world—such as Joffre Lakes north of Vancouver, and Thailand's Maya Bay from the Leonardo DiCaprio movie *The Beach*—which has resulted in soiled sites, long lineups, brawls for parking spots, even accidents and deaths.

Lynn Canyon Park, near where Norvan's Castle grows on Coliseum Mountain, draws 500,000 visitors annually. Geotagging and hashtags, including Destination BC's own #ExploreBC, attract crowds to formerly obscure locations, so a site that used to be private or that was "earned" through an arduous hike becomes ruined and exposed. Trees may be sacred to an Indigenous group, and their locations concealed for spiritual or cultural reasons, so posting about their locations can be disrespectful. In a critique of social media's effect on the great outdoors, Joel Barde writes, "Exploring such places has traditionally been the reserve of a self-selected group of adventurers whose backcountry know-how and environmental ethic were forged in outdoor clubs or passed down through generations."

I found the same mindset in the big-tree tracking community, some of whom guard their knowledge of accessing the trees or feel the largest trees' locations should not be publicly available. For a long time, those who knew the site of Hyperion, a redwood in California that is taller than any other living tree (115.5 m), refused to disclose it for fear of visitors intention-ally or unintentionally damaging the tree. The risk was that too many visitors would trample the roots around the tree, damage the bark, create desire paths through the woods that upset the understory, or stress local search and rescue operations if they were injured or went missing. But, the Associated Press reports, "By 2010, visitors started trekking to see the tall, skinny red-wood after bloggers, travel writers, and others shared its exact location online." In August 2022, Redwood National Park closed access to the area due to damage and garbage (includ-ing human excrement), as officials had done with Maya Bay in Thailand for more than three years, citing extensive damage to the coral reef. Visitors who pushed on through to Hyperion would face up to six months' jail time and a $5,000 fine.

Barde notes that "geo-tagging certain areas or hikes online is now a serious faux pas in the outdoor community." Besides risk-ing the trees through overexposure, popularizing the location of large trees can also make them a target for timber poachers. As Lyndsie Bourgon covers in her book *Tree Thieves*, poachers can hack away parts of a tree, say its burl, or even take down the whole tree to sell on the black market. Poachers go after trees growing on both public and private lands, then sell this timber to mills or other outfits, concealing its provenance. Even that cord of wood you bought from a guy's truck beside the highway or on Craigslist might be suspect. The removal of these large trees not only destabilizes soils, reduces habitat, and contributes to climate change but also costs the economy millions. "In British Columbia," Bourgon writes, "experts put the cost of timber theft from publicly managed forests at $20 million a year."

In the case of the Golden Spruce, a culturally significant tree in Haida Gwaii, the tree's symbolism made it a target. This spruce's needles glowed golden as a result of a genetic mutation (chlorosis turned it yellow). The tree, called Kiidk'yaas was sacred to the Haida. It was also a valuable addition to local ecotourism in Port Clements. In an ill-advised protest in 1997, forest engineer Grant Hadwin cut the tree in such a way that it would fall in a high wind, and two days later it came crashing down. He regarded the focus on one tree as problematic: MacMillan Bloedel was using the retention of a notable tree to improve its public image. "We tend to focus on the individual trees like the Golden Spruce while the rest of the forests are being slaughtered," Hadwin was quoted in a newspaper shortly after confessing to the crime. He likened MacBlo's preservation of the Golden Spruce to Cathedral Grove on Vancouver Island, calling them both "freaks," but it was Hadwin who paid the cost. He was publicly lambasted and went missing during a winter kayak trip before his court date. In his masterful book *The Golden Spruce*, John Vaillant writes, "The collective reaction to the loss of the golden spruce ended up proving [Hadwin's] point: that people fail to see the forest for the tree."

Writer Robert Earle Howells calls social-media-driven runs to scenic spots "a growing brand of trophy hunting in nature." Howells, like Barde, outlines the numerous detrimental effects on established sites, like rivers or viewpoints. "But trees," Howells writes, "unlike swimming holes or scenic canyon ledges, are living things... It's worth wondering whether some of these one-of-a-kind trees should just be left alone. A first step toward discouraging trophy hunting might be to drop the practice of naming trees in the first place." Professor and redwood forest ecologist Stephen Sillett, who verified Hyperion's height and is famous for climbing into and studying the canopies of giant redwoods, agrees: "Publicizing names of champion trees is a mistake because it makes them targets of visitation." But the name itself is not the issue: it's what the naming represents. When a tree becomes a trophy, it is something to own or claim—a poster child for a logging company or a conservation group, a boon for tourism, a beacon for social media, or a Champion tree to collect on a spreadsheet. But in reality, it's a living being and exists in a delicate web.

At the beginning of my project, regardless of whether or not the tree had a name (not all do), I was out to claim them as trophies. As I went along, I gave up on the arrival fallacy, which writer Rainesford Stauffer defines as "the false illusion that once you attain a goal or reach a certain place, your happiness, your sense of stability, will be everlasting." The idea that I'd put such pressure on myself to find all the Champions now seemed laughable. Playwright Oscar Wilde wrote, "The secret of life is to appreciate the pleasure of being terribly, terribly deceived." But really, the secret is to manage your expectations. Early on, I'd realized that my Champions project would take longer than a year, and that what I'd learned about trees had set me up for a lifetime of observing them—their size, their individual characteristics, their larger context. Now I no longer felt compelled to seek out the Champions and decided to wrap my project well short of my initial goal. I'd saved the biggest trees for last, and these would be for pure appreciation: the Doug-firs, Sitka spruce, and western red-cedars on southwestern Vancouver Island. I planned to visit that grand bastion of solitude, Big Lonely Doug near Port Renfrew, and come full circle at the Randy Stoltmann Commemorative Grove in Carmanah Walbran Provincial Park.

But before that, in December 2019, I set out for a nine-day solo hike along the Kumano Kodo in the Kii Mountains of Japan. This traditional pilgrimage route is a UNESCO World Heritage Site and one leg of Japan's intricate pilgrimage network. I wasn't roughing it on that trip—I was soaking in a hot bath and sleeping in ryokan (family-run inns) each night—but the confidence I'd gained on the trails around BC gave me the final push to achieve this lifelong dream, my red backpack and hiking boots accompanying me across the Pacific. Once home, I began plotting my trip to see the biggest trees in the spring. I emailed my dad and invited him to come with me on a father-daughter tree-tracking trip. He wrote back, "Enthusiastic YES!!!!!" If Jenny could wangle time away from the kids, she'd come too. Ken Wu, executive director of the Endangered Ecosystems Alliance, offered to guide us to some old-growth groves when he visited from Montreal. I also planned to join a group climb into the local forest canopy, witnessing these trees from a new perspective. It had taken me over a year to realize that with others I could go farther, longer, higher—and the trips were better as a result.

THE FIRST DAY OF 2020, Jason and I biked to VanDusen Botanical Garden. Fresh flowers are one of Jason's essential joys, so we tried to go about once a month, to monitor the changing flower conditions and learn more about the trees in the arboretum. In winter, we studied their bark and the shape of their branches, which could facilitate easier identification in the field during other seasons. Jason didn't often come with me on tree-tracking trips, but he was a huge supporter of my project. Flowers made from upcycled plastic water bottles adorned white fairy lights lining paths for that evening's Festival of Lights. Around the witch hazel and ferns we smelled a mix of jasmine and lilac. Early rhododendron and magnolia buds risked a late frost, but this smell pointed to something sweeter. Wandering around the paths, a few steps forward, back a few, we finally found it: a low shrub with small star-shaped white flowers and glossy purplish-black berries. Sweet box, a shrub from China.

"You found it!" Jason said.

"We found it," I corrected. "Though I'm pretty good at finding plants of note."

"Yes, you've had a lot of experience in recent months," he said. "Do you think it's the biggest? Will you start a registry?"

"Noooo, Jason, I won't. Because people will ask, 'How big is the biggest sweet box?' And I'll say, 'Not too big, about this big, bigger than that one.'"

We walked on, saw an even bigger sweet box spreading alongside the path, and inhaled deeply.

AT THE END OF FEBRUARY 2020, I started making near-daily pilgrimages to monitor the development of the cherry and plum blossoms on Trinity Street, near my apartment in East Van. The annual hanami—the act of viewing cherry (sakura) or plum (ume) blossoms—is for me what writer and professor Robert Macfarlane calls an "anchor-point," a feature of the natural world that is mentally grounding. In a few weeks, the street would be lined with photographers and their tripods, parents and their newborns, grads in their dresses and tuxes, posing under the pink tufts. I preferred the streets before they were overrun, the blossoms when they were starting to bud, small spots of pink on dark reddish-brown twigs.

But as the cherry and plum trees began cresting, another wave swept the city. We started hearing murmurs of a new potentially fatal coronavirus that was spreading quickly. The World Health Organization declared a pandemic, and we were suddenly all jellyfish at low tide. We didn't know if we could touch delivered packages, share elevators, breathe the air after a stranger had passed us on the street. On March 12, when the "Is this really happening? Yes, it is" conversations were taking place in hospitals, schools, and offices, I popped into my local drugstore to stock up on supplies. I was sweating and had a headache from the worry that I was already sick; as Gary Shteyngart wrote in *The New Yorker* a few weeks later, "I don't have the virus. I have the fear."

While pondering the purchase of a spearmint and euca- lyptus "stress-reducing" candle (reader, I bought it), I ran into my friend Jens Wieting. Jens is the senior forest and climate campaigner with the Sierra Club BC, the local branch of the international conservation group, and we'd met years before in a social change training program at a retreat center on Cortes Island. "I've been meaning to interview you about deforesta- tion," I said, at that moment not wanting to in the slightest, as I couldn't stomach more devastation. A woman with frantic eyes passed us with a cartload of cleaning supplies.

A few days later, looking over scraps of paper on my dining table, I realized I'd written at the top of my March 12 to-do list "reassess everything." Our office shut down that weekend, and I was lucky that I could move my work home. We were liv- ing bigness on the scale of the pandemic as we made our lives smaller, balancing safety with apprehension and—for those lucky enough to still be pulling a check, not working on the front lines, not homeschooling kids—a creeping sense of boredom.

I was reluctant to hike on the nearby trails—they were steadily becoming overrun, as they offered a safer form of rec- reation. I happily settled for the circuitous life of walks to local trees of all sizes, native and imported. The two dogwoods in front of our building started to leaf and bud, their leaves curling to the gray skies. I looked forward to them filling out, small cups made of bracts, gently containing a cluster of spaghetti ends. Green and red leaves studded fractals like the bleeding bots and ghostly animals of musician John Lurie's watercolors. Within a week, the moss thickened on the two silver maples outside my apartment, and the canopy bushed out. There were glints of green everywhere, emerald globules, perfectly round emoji trees. New growth shot straight up to the sky, and mugo pines flipped us all off. Painted rocks appeared around the neighborhood, lining sidewalks and atop posts: Minions, M&M's, faces, or inspirational quotes. *You're doing great. We'll get through this. It's a beautiful day.* Where had all these optimists come from? Didn't they know we were in a pandemic?

We were more linked and fractured than ever, tossed around by our mortality and fear. We became isolated, antisocial organisms who threatened as much as relied on each other. I learned about the Pando Grove, which seemed a reasonable symbol of our interconnection. A stand of quaking aspen, known collectively as the Trembling Giant and covering 108 acres in Utah, its root system is thousands of years old, and the trees reproduce through cloning. When a stem or trunk dies, another takes its place. There are currently more than forty thousand stems in Pando, and the whole organism weighs almost six thousand metric tons. Pando looks like separate trees, but it's all the outgrowth of one organism—just as we're all one global family that depends on each other for survival and community.

Horse chestnuts began to bud, their flowers on tiered stem clusters reaching to the sky like candlesticks. I stopped in my tracks in the smelly alley behind my apartment when I came face to bud and noticed the intricate beauty of their white petals with blushes of pink and yellow, bearing so much resemblance to catalpa flowers. Magnolias opened in large pink blossoms or explosions of smaller white flowers. The blossoms unfurled in staggered waves across the city, and we gushed over first, second, third waves of pink. I saw honeybees alighting on cherry and plum, learned to tell which tree species were which by the bark, leaves, and blossoms. The winds and birds gifted me small conifers in herb planters on my balcony. A skunk roamed along a hedge while I ogled a laburnum near my building. I watched wasps fly into my window pane, perhaps looking for an entry point. A couple summers earlier, a hornet had flown through the crack in my sliding door and diligently built a small hive deep in my closet, adhered to the honeycomb-like knit of an Aran sweater. I found the quarter-sized hive after the hornet had laid eggs.

"Were there always northern flickers here?" Jason asked, about the medium-sized brown and white birds that often peck for insects where the lawn meets the sidewalk.

"Yes," I said. "In pairs." I was used to their chatter.

"Are you sure? A guy told me they all moved in recently."

"They've always been here. People just haven't noticed them."

I began to watch Silver with increasing intensity, the crows mobbing a red-tailed hawk in its branches, a family of raccoons sleeping atop the main trunk before it divided. I looked past Silver and Silas to spot other varieties of maples: sugar maple, red maple. A bigleaf maple a block from our building dropped a limb, and a circle of neighbors formed to bear witness, standing six feet apart. California lilacs bushed out on their stems, producing mounds of intoxicating flowers, and apple blossoms unfolded in a gentle blush. Dove trees, with their handkerchief-like bracts, bloomed throughout East Vancouver, and mountain ash bore white ball flowers.

In mid-March, Ken let me know we'd need to postpone our trip because daycares in Montreal would be closed until May 1 at the earliest. Provincial Health Officer Dr. Bonnie Henry encouraged us not to visit small communities on the islands and Sunshine Coast, so we wouldn't overwhelm the small hospital systems. BC Ferries, citing an 80 percent drop in ridership, reduced their sailings, so I was essentially grounded in the Lower Mainland. The canopy tours, a group activity, were canceled, and the Capilano Suspension Bridge Park was temporarily closed. I now had a grander mission than searching for big trees: navigating and surviving a pandemic.

I played with scale in my goal, shifting to the local again, as I had when the registry was unreliable and I was getting my feet wet as a big-tree tracker. Since I couldn't get to Vancouver Island, I looked for smaller versions of the Champions in the parks and streets around my house. The western red-cedar next to my balcony, which laid the escape route for the gray squirrel chased by crows, became a stand-in for the six-meter-wide Cheewhat Giant, the largest tree in Canada and (it goes without saying) the Champion western red-cedar in BC. Instead of going to Port Renfrew to see Big Lonely Doug, I walked around Pacific Spirit Regional Park with Jason, appreciating the Douglas-firs of all sizes growing near the beaches of Vancouver. We studied how young trees "ate" the nurse stumps that gave them nutrients, and how the new tree, with the nurse stump gone, appeared to stand on spindly legs. Without looking solely for bigness, we could take in smaller details, use them to ask more intricate questions. Forest ecologist Suzanne Simard tells us, "We think that most important clues are large, but the world loves to remind us that they can be beautifully small."

The trees I was supposed to visit had always been trees of the mind, in that I had to imagine them before I found them, or picture them in absentia. From a meditation perspective, if you're always mindful—of every breath, word, interaction, movement—then your whole life becomes your practice, not just when sitting in formal meditation. I was no longer going out of my way to find wonder; I realized it was all around me. Sally Mann, a photographer from the American South, said, "It's always been my philosophy to try to make art out of the everyday and ordinary… it never occurred to me to leave home to make art." The longer I stayed in one place and focused on my tree project as art, the more I felt I was coming home to myself.

I explained to my sister how the project was shifting. "I started big, and now I'm ending small."

"I don't know," Jenny said. "COVID is pretty big."

AROUND THE CORNER FROM our building, I found Doug-fir cobbles covered in creosote, revealing themselves through a gash in the concrete. These wooden squares began to peer out where the road cracked, once walked upon by horses, a palimpsest of petals atop ancient tree rings. A carpet of pale pink blossoms formed a Rorschach test on the sidewalks, gathered on the windshields of parked cars, fluttered around us as we walked in bonded pairs. The city's cherry blossom festival was canceled, and in its place an online festival bloomed, a rough simulacrum. The organizers encouraged us to follow the city's bloom on a website, across neighborhoods, through maps, a photo contest, a haiku invitational.

Like millions of others during the pandemic, I tuned in to Tree.fm to listen to recordings from forests around the world. As I write this, I am listening to a forest vibrating with insects in Kamienna Góra, Poland, a town of just over nineteen thousand people. When I click "next forest," I am transported to a forest in Nelson Lakes National Park, New Zealand, where I can hear what sounds like a bird calling. The soundscapes were crowd-sourced, and I can search by locations on the map, if I want to zero in on a landscape I'd like to visit or a place I've been.

I listened to the sounds of crashing waves reverberating through a Sitka spruce (a popular wood for musical instrument soundboards) that had hollowed out and lay on the shore. Sound tracker Gordon Hempton recorded the sound, calling it "The Ocean Is a Drum." He is on a mission to preserve spaces free from noise pollution and record natural soundscapes before they are drowned out by human-made sounds: airplanes, traffic, industry. As Hempton says, "Silence is not the absence of something but the presence of everything." I'd planned to visit the Hoh Rainforest in Olympic National Park in Washington State, a UNESCO site and sound preserve that is an inspiration to Hempton. This park used to be logged but was protected in 1938. Then the border closed, so this recording and others from the Olympic National Park served as an acoustic stand-in.

Another stand-in for a true forest experience was possible through AR and VR. As part of the *Anthropocene* exhibit at the Art Gallery of Ontario in 2018, there was an augmented reality (AR) representation of Big Lonely Doug, a miniaturized version of which you could project into your hand. Augmented reality uses a process similar to lidar—whereas lidar uses laser points, AR uses thousands of photos from every angle. This exhibit also allowed visitors to experience in 3D the last male northern white rhino before he died in 2018. Do we have a responsibility to capture these images, a duty to look at these big trees and rhinos, which we bear responsibility for destroying? And how much can we expect a big tree to hold for us—our hopes, our guilt? Almost eight hundred kilograms of carbon dioxide were created just from my return flight to hike the Kumano Kodo. Virtual visitations make it possible to experience the world without burning carbon to get there, but what do we miss by not visiting the forests along the west coast of Vancouver Island, by not standing in a cathedral along the Camino de Santiago while dawn light streams through stained glass?

You can't beat the healing effects of an actual forest walk, with its aerosols, breezes, and dance of light, but you can try.

In a 2010 study from the University of Waterloo, researchers demonstrated that playing an RPG, *The Elder Scrolls IV: Oblivion*, which involves images of nature including forests, resulted in benefits similar to viewing nature through a hospital window, an oft-cited study of the role of nature in healing. In response to playing the game, Lewis Gordon writes in the *Washington Post*, "Positive emotions rose while telltale signs of anxiety—heart rate and skin conductivity—decreased." Studies in Taiwan and Switzerland using VR nature also recorded healing effects. Exposure to virtual nature might be as simple as listening to the sound of a forest or watching a video recording of a forest walk. But an advantage of video games and VR is they can go big. "Development studios have created near-photorealistic recreations of nature," Gordon writes, "simulating not just its minutiae but larger phenomena such as towering redwoods, rolling valleys, and vast, star-filled skies. Crucially, such environments often instill the same sense of wonder we feel outside." And there's some benefit to feeling miniaturized in relation to that vastness. Alice Chirico, a postdoctoral researcher in psychology at Catholic University of the Sacred Heart of Milan, says, "This diminishment of the self isn't just a way to feel annihilated, it's a way to find your place in the universe. By doing that, you feel more connected."

OPPORTUNITY STRUCK AND MY ART PROJECT responded to the times, scales shifting again like a slowly turning kaleidoscope. The ferry was set to resume regular service in early June, so my sister and I planned to go to the Champions on Vancouver Island before the likely second wave in the fall. Ken was flying out to bring Endangered Ecosystems Alliance supporters to a few key groves, and he offered to personally guide us to some of the most spectacular forests around Port Renfrew. Jenny and I loaded up her green camper van, Lichen, and slowly made our way from Bowser to an RV park in Port Renfrew, two hours southwest of Victoria. Missy Elliott or The Band blaring, me handling snacks, we were right back in high school, only Jasper's baby booties hung from the rearview, and we'd traded in our former duds for outdoor gear. Back then, Jenny would be decked out in knee-high oxblood boots, a Danzig patch on her army surplus jacket. I favored bell bottoms, Chuck Taylor high-tops, a tie-dyed shirt, and an army surplus bag with a patch of Shaggy from *Scooby-Doo*, the strap of which I'd lengthened with fake fur.

Now calling itself the Tall Tree Capital of Canada, Port Renfrew is in the process of transforming itself from a primarily logging-based economy to one that runs on ecotourism, namely big trees and sport fishing. The line that the trees are "worth more standing" is not just a catchy slogan but has been borne out in an economic valuation of old-growth, with a focus on Port Renfrew. In the late 1990s and early 2000s, mills began closing throughout BC for several reasons, including the end of appurtenance (a rule that trees had to be processed in the communities where they were cut, supporting local economies) and an increase in raw-log exports after mills failed to adequately retool equipment to handle smaller logs and create value-added products. Many of the towns that had prospered in the heyday of forestry in the second half of the twentieth century, like Port Alberni and Youbou, took a hit economically. The government is still pulling in high revenues through stumpage fees (the price companies pay to harvest timber on Crown land) for old-growth. And we are running out of prime trees to harvest. As Ben Parfitt writes in *The Tyee*, "In 15 years, logging rates have fallen 25 per cent. In three more years [2025], they will be barely half of what they were in 2007... We have stripped our forests of much of their green gold."

Port Renfrew has large trees just outside town, rather than down a teeth-chattering FSR, and is not yet overrun by tourists, the way Lynn Canyon now is. Many visit Port Renfrew to see the easily accessible Avatar Grove and "Canada's Gnarliest Tree," a burly cedar, with *gnarl factor* referring to "an arbitrary scale used to compare the gnarliness of trees," Robert Van Pelt tells us in his glossary. Some tourists venture farther along the FSR, past Avatar Grove, to visit Big Lonely Doug.

Jenny and I slept in and then shoved food down our gullets as we drove to meet Ken. We were so intent on getting to our destination that we didn't recall it was my birthday until halfway to a certain-numbered telephone pole on the highway. While we waited, Jenny braided her thick chestnut hair and sorted through her supplies, her routine honed from years in the bush. Ken showed up in his rental car with Celina Starnes, the operations and outreach director for Endangered Ecosystems Alliance. Their enthusiasm for trees and creatures was infectious. Ken is jovial and super knowledgeable about these forests and the threats they face, and he works regularly with government and First Nations to lay out conservation plans. Like other big-tree enthusiasts, Ken has a tendency to speak in superlatives and rankings—"this is the third-biggest cedar in BC" or "I need to bring my number two biggest supporter on a forest walk tomorrow."

We started by visiting Jurassic Grove off Highway 14, which the Ancient Forest Alliance named in 2018, next to the Juan de Fuca Marine Trail. This 130-hectare (320-acre) stretch of forest follows the convention of naming after blockbuster Hollywood films, but it does feel primordial with its mix of colossal cedar, Sitka spruce, and Douglas-fir. Both Jurassic Grove and Eden Grove, near Big Lonely Doug outside Port Renfrew, are leased to timber companies under tree farm licences. Each TFL has a thirty-year term so, generally speaking, timber companies have no long-term investment in managing the land sustainably. (Some companies, like Western Forest Products, are building their own long-term sustainability plans.) That's where conservation groups like the Ancient Forest Alliance and Endangered Ecosystems Alliance come in, working with First Nations to manage the land in a more sustainable way with a longer view.

While Ken and Celina turned over logs looking for salamanders, Jenny and I wandered slack-jawed, gazing up at the trees and stepping inside hollow cedars.

"Look," Ken said, "there's a vagina tree!"

"Step inside for a photo," Jenny said to me, "right under the man in the canoe."

Born again in a vagina tree on my happy birthday

"Is that what it's called?" Ken said.

"Take it from us," I said, reaching upward as I was born again.

What I like most about this project is that it makes me feel like a kid again. Not just on a scale level—being surrounded by huge old-growth Doug-firs, western red-cedars, and Sitka spruce would make anyone feel small—but the experience of playing for hours in the woods. Years later, I'm doing the same thing, but I've turned the dial to eleven.

We then drove to Mossome Grove, a now-rare old-growth forest of bigleaf maples and Sitka spruce. Big spruce were extensively logged along the north and south coast in the early twentieth century and then in the valleys—their light strong wood ideal for airplanes in the two World Wars. The name *Mossome* is a combination of *mossy* and *awesome*, and the grove's bigleaf maples are draped in long moss and licorice ferns. It was glorious to wander in that glowing green. The grove is home to bears, wolves, Roosevelt elk, and copious mosquitoes, which created a ring of bites around Jenny's ankle where her socks didn't reach her leggings. This grove is less than an hour's drive from Port Renfrew on Crown land, and the Pacheedaht First Nation have logging interests in the area.

First Nations increasingly have more leverage in how forestry is run in this province, from controlling woodlots to partnering with forestry companies. In 2022, for example, the Huu-ay-aht First Nations in partnership with Western Forest Products announced that they will retain big trees in Tree Farm Licence 44 (Alberni Valley), based on DBH and/or a significant height: 70 meters. In a woodlot managed by First Nations, the Nation can contract out any work in the forest, but they can't lease the land to anyone else; to compare, Crown land can be leased to a forestry company under a tree farm licence.

Then Jenny and I left Ken and Celina and headed to Avatar Grove. Boardwalks and railings ringed the trees, reminding me of Cathedral Grove and preventing close access. I felt less like a tree tracker and more like a tourist as I grumpily posed in front of the Gnarliest Tree, a large cedar with a ten-foot-diameter burl on its lower trunk, and then I yelled at a man to stop throwing rocks at a wasp nest.

We headed back to the RV park to plan our final full day on the road. I wanted to see the Red Creek Fir (74 m tall, 4.2 m DBH), the biggest known Douglas-fir in the province and situated in an Old-Growth Management Area. A logging-road survey crew came across the tree in 1976. According to a story told in Stoltmann's posthumous hiking guide, the crew stopped for lunch at what they thought was a cliff face covered in moss; turns out they were leaning against the huge tree. But Ken had told us that the Red Creek Fir access road wasn't in great shape, and the tree was almost dead, just a sprig of live growth like an asparagus stalk at the top. I was determined to visit the Randy Stoltmann Commemorative Grove in Carmanah Walbran Provincial Park, but upon reviewing access notes from Ken and checking the map, Jenny and I knew we would need to add an extra few nights or a week to fully appreciate the park. Now that I'd given up on the deadline for my project, I looked forward to returning another time to see these trees for what they were, rather than for their Champion status. We'd been zipping from grove to grove, but such fast travel didn't feel appropriate, especially in a pandemic when time no longer made sense.

Our campsite backed onto a ravine in the center of the RV park, a dark crater of dampness. We smoked a joint and cooked s'mores over the campfire for my birthday.

"This is my number one best s'more," I said, liquid marshmallow threatening to fall on my lap.

"Number two biggest s'more fo sho," Jenny said, preparing another mound of graham crackers and chocolate.

The next morning, Jenny and I drove past Avatar Grove and parked Lichen at the top of a hill, before a sideless bridge spanning the Gordon River. Jenny was scared of walking on the bridge, even in the middle, in case she fell off—"I know! It's irrational!"—so we linked arms. Jenny also fears she'll pull off her shoes and throw them overboard on the ferry, but she hasn't done it yet.

"What would you do if a man emerged from the bush on a quiet road like this?" I asked as we walked on the gravel FSR after the bridge.

"Use my pepper spray," she said immediately. "Or run. A guy wandering up to me on a road like this can only mean trouble."

"You ever poop when you're scared?"

"Nope."

"Me either. I was just asking."

When we reached the clear-cut, there was no mistaking the tree. Harley Rustad's description is apt: "In the middle of the clear-cut, the giant fir stood like an obelisk in a desert." Big Lonely Doug is the second-largest Doug-fir in Canada, at 66 meters tall with a 3.79-meter DBH, and it's estimated to be around one thousand years old. Its straight trunk and broad crown of dark green boughs make it the Platonic ideal of a Doug-fir. Ken Wu told me that he'd long used names for trees as a way to grab media attention, beginning with his time in the Western Canada Wilderness Committee in the '90s. In 1999, he saw a huge Douglas-fir in the Walbran Valley. This fir was all by itself among western red-cedars, so he named it Big Lonely Doug. People had forgotten about the name by 2014, when TJ found this solo tree near Port Renfrew, so when they sent the press release a few weeks later, the AFA reused the name for this sentinel.

We posed for photos on the road above the cutblock, holding Big Lonely Doug in our palms the way you might the Eiffel Tower (or the VR image), then walked down into the cutblock, stepping around cedar stumps, easily maneuvering along walklogs, seeing the green slowly returning: salmonberry, huckleberry, and saplings growing back amidst the slash. We stood on a hemlock stump cut at Big Lonely Doug's roots, rested our hands against the tree's wide base, peered into its crown, ran our fingers along the scar in its bark where the loggers turned the tree into a spar for hauling out other trees. We could dedicate our full concentration to it as One Big Tree, but that is not how to appreciate a tree.

Trees are all things to all people, and Big Lonely Doug's symbolism for the environmental movement was launched when TJ Watt stumbled on the tree in cutblock 7190 while out looking for large old-growth near Edinburgh Mountain, outside Port Renfrew. The tree, growing at the foot of the mountain, had been spared in 2011 when Dennis Cronin, a forest engineer, tied a green ribbon around its circumference. The ribbon bore the words *LEAVE TREE*. Usually this ribbon is used for trees that aren't worth removing, low in timber value due to rot or a twist in their trunk. But this tree was a perfect specimen, and Cronin estimated its value at about $50,000. The lumber in this cutblock under TFL 46, leased by Teal-Jones, was worth about $1 million at that time. There are numerous reasons why foresters might leave big old trees standing: to serve as seed trees to help repopulate the cutblock; because they were growing twisted or had a low fork, which would be dangerous to cut; or because they were growing in a hard-to-access area, like a steep canyon or a boulder-strewn slope. In fact, there are several trees like Big Lonely Doug standing in nearby cutblocks, serving as seed trees. But standing there and gazing up, it was undeniable: there is something special about Big Lonely Doug. According to a quote in Rustad's *Big Lonely Doug*, Cronin saved the tree for another reason than seeding the lot: "Because I liked it."

The irony is that a lot of big trees were found by foresters, those looking for ideal specimens to cut—and in some cases, save. When I started my project, I learned that the common name for those who look for big trees is *big-tree hunter*. I clearly wasn't out to kill the tree, but I still used hunting terminology: *bag, quarry*. In her early twenties, Suzanne Simard, working for a forestry company, was sent to scout a site for clear-cutting near Lillooet in the Interior of BC. Finding big Doug-firs on the edge of the designated patch, she asked her cruiser companion if they could leave them. "Not only were big elder trees an important seed source for the open ground," she writes in *Finding the Mother Tree*, "they were favorite perches for birds, and I'd seen bear dens under the necks of the roots." But her partner, Ray, understood the value of such stately trees for the logging company and the mill. In a way, Simard, who came from a family of loggers—though they logged by hand, selectively— got it. "I understood the pride of claiming what was grandest, the temptation—green-gold fever. The handsomest trees captured top prices. They meant jobs for the locals, mills staying open. I checked out this one's immense bole, seeing the cut through Ray's eyes. Once you start hunting, it's easy to get addicted. Like always wanting to snag the tallest peaks. After a while, your appetite can never be sated."

Without a buffer of other trees, Big Lonely Doug is more susceptible to windstorms, though there is evidence the tree has survived at least one colossal storm over a century ago. Big Lonely Doug also lacks a community of trees with which to trade nutrients and life-saving signals—that's one reason for its loneliness, and staring at it, growing alone, I could empathize even without anthropomorphizing it.

The cutblock where Big Lonely Doug stands is currently a recreational reserve, but Rustad argues in favor of it being made a provincially protected recreation site—a park that would receive promotion and marketing by the provincial government, no different from Cathedral Grove. "Parks are lovely to hike through and camp in, but, apart from the odd educational placard, they are rarely provocative and challenging in their own right," Rustad wrote in an op-ed in the *Globe and Mail*. Big Lonely Doug was already protected in the reserve but received additional protection when, in July 2019, the New Democratic Party provincial government protected fifty-four "notable" trees in the province, as well as a one-hectare (2.5-acre) buffer around each tree. These big trees were growing on Crown land and already listed in the BC Big Tree Registry—at the time, accounting for around one in six of the 347 trees in the registry. Longtime BC big-tree tracker Mick Bailey spelled it out on his blog: "Most of those trees were already unofficially protected, but that status had simply not been formalized yet. Designating them was basically a token gesture, meant to appease the many people vehemently protesting old-growth logging."

Then, in September 2020, the BC NDP brought in its Special Tree Protection Regulation policy, which automatically protects fourteen species once they reach a certain DBH, with a mandatory one-hectare circular buffer around every tree. This legislation aims to conserve about 1,500 big trees in the province, though only about two hundred are at the moment protected (including the fifty-four marked in 2019). What's important about this preservation legislation is that it's based on the size of the tree: the bigger the tree, particularly in diameter rather than height, the more likely it will be protected. Western Forest Products' big-tree policy thresholds for conservation, like BCTS's Coastal Legacy Tree Program, are better (i.e., lower) than the provincial thresholds, which have a significantly higher minimum DBH for each species. That results in very few trees being protected under this regulation. What this means, by an example Greg Herringer of BCTS shared with me, is that WFP's and BCTS's programs protected close to eight hundred trees in one geographical area, whereas the government's regulation in the same area protected only 154 trees.

But only assigning trees significance based on their size misses the mark when considering their role in the ecosystem. Do we want a province of "special trees" standing alone like Big Lonely Doug (the charismatic megaflora of the forest) or an interconnected ecosystem? Sally Aitken made precisely this point back in WFP's boardroom, the day we visited the 94-meter-tall coastal Doug-fir: when we rush to protect the largest trees, we miss protecting the smaller elements, including the not-quite-big-enough-to-retain trees.

Trees show us what we value when we plant them, when we protect them, and when we cut them down; in doing so, they're a reflection of our desires and our worldviews. A large cedar that Indigenous Peoples have respected as a Grandfather or Grandmother Tree for centuries could be valued by foresters as a source of timber and economic security; by scientists, as a source for clones of superior trees; by conservationists, as a marker of what could be again; by tree trackers, as an objective or the makings of an adventure. As eco-philosopher Timothy Morton argues, "Use value isn't 'what things really are for,' but 'what things are for humans.'" And the founder of the BC Big Tree Registry, Randy Stoltmann, reminded us back in 1987 that true conservation must account for the things that can't be measured, a multitude of values including wildlife habitat and beauty. Saving trees based on their size quantifies the trees rather than considers their roles in carbon capture, air filtration and cooling, oxygen creation, soil stability, biodiversity, propagation and reseeding, tourism, and cultural use.

The glaring problem is that we might cut down future Champions while we're working on legislation. To base the conservation of a tree solely on its size, and only one element of its size at that (DBH), misses the whole point. *Pace* Odell, it is a tree without context. The size requirements don't take into account how the light falls on dried moss or the elegant drape of a bough. We know that many of the biggest trees have already been cut down, with only stumps, oral histories, and sometimes photographic evidence indicating they had existed.

Big-tree tracker Robert Van Pelt notes that when Darius Kinsey took a photo of a western red-cedar at the turn of the twentieth century, the tree had a 6.7-meter DBH, and Van Pelt describes it as "the largest known recorded western red-cedar." Kinsey often took photos of logging operations, and this photo shows three loggers cutting down the tree, one standing to each side of the cedar with the third lying on his stomach in the cut, his saw hanging down past a ring of springboard plank cut marks and an axe lodged in the trunk. Big trees are still out there, ready to be measured and ideally conserved. In 2001, when Van Pelt published his influential book on giant trees of the Pacific Northwest, he wrote that "Vancouver Island and the upper British Columbia mainland... have vast (albeit dwindling) unexplored areas of cedar forest, such as Clayoquot Sound and neighboring areas." When I'd started nosing around Lynn Valley in North Vancouver for trees at the beginning of my project, I'd often hear that the area hadn't been completely searched and that there might be huge cedars that had up to now gone undetected. And then in June 2022, local tree trackers Colin Spratt and Ian Thomas, both in their twenties, came across a two-thousand-year-old western red-cedar in Lynn Valley, west of Lynn Creek, which I'd hiked along to find Norvan's Castle. The tree is growing in the unceded territories of the Tsleil-Waututh and Squamish Nations. They named the tree the North Shore Giant, and early estimates gave its DBH as 5.8 meters. The diameter of cedars is notoriously hard to calculate, due to burls and base flare, but members of the BC Big Tree Committee went out for another measurement and assessment. The committee determined the DBH is closer to 3.75 meters, a discrepancy mostly based on the position of the tape. But it really doesn't matter to Spratt, who has been trolling Vancouver's parks and forests (including all of Stanley Park during the pandemic) looking for the biggest trees in the Lower Mainland, sometimes hidden and sometimes in plain sight. "My goal has been to show people that in Vancouver it's still possible to find Canada's largest trees still alive and growing," he said. "I'm glad to keep the dream very much alive that much bigger trees still hiding out there [are waiting] to be found." This tree, growing in a park, is protected.

The shared goal of big-tree registries is education and conservation. Registries are a useful way to compare vegetation and landscapes too. At a glance, you can see which trees grow best in which area. That's especially useful in BC, with its fourteen distinct biogeoclimatic zones giving rise to a range of flora and fauna. The more trees that are recorded, the more people will hopefully get to see them, either in person or through media.

In his wonderful book *The Once and Future World*, J. B. MacKinnon points out that we're living in a 10 percent world. This figure comes from numerous studies about "what's left" in the natural world compared to when plants and animals were at their most populous. "In the oceans," MacKinnon writes, "the world's biggest fish, from tuna to cod to swordfish to sharks, have been reduced to an estimated 10 percent of their past abundance." The same is true of whales and to a greater or lesser extent of land-dwelling mammals. This loss of population points to our temporal presence within the sixth extinction and to large-scale extirpation (when species relocate from an area, so they appear extinct where they once dwelled). MacKinnon goes on: "Twenty percent of the earth is still covered with ancient forests, but more than 50 percent of nations no longer have any old-growth forests at all, and fully half of the forest cover that has vanished in the last ten thousand years worldwide has been lost in just the past century."

We become used to the forests we have, thinking they're representative of what was always there. The remaining species are much smaller, with the largest being hunted or fished out of existence, thus further shifting our baseline of what bigness means within a particular species. To illustrate, MacKinnon references a study by Loren McClenachan, a marine biologist and professor, that uses archival "big-game fishermen's photos" to demonstrate that fish caught in the Florida Keys were remarkably larger in the 1950s than in the early 2000s. "In the old black-and-whites," MacKinnon writes, "the biggest fish, strung up on the dock, are as tall and wide as the fishermen themselves... By 2007, the catch is dominated by snappers that measure just a little longer than a grade-school ruler." And in both sets of photos, the fishermen look like the cat who caught the canary: "the same wide smiles, the same backslapping-with-Hemingway pride." We've adapted to a smaller world, reduced our understanding of big by removing examples of bigness. It stands to reason that even the biggest trees that remain, while not white rhinos, are likely smaller exemplars than what came before and were cleared. By gazing upon what remains, we consider what was and might be again, the "once and future world" of MacKinnon's title.

The way I see it, the greater purpose of a registry is to make itself obsolete. If we stopped cutting down big trees, we wouldn't need to record them—they would be a staple in our forests. In that way, registries are a symptom of the Anthropocene, and big trees—whether left standing or cut for timber—are symbolic. I know how important symbols can be for conservation— Big Lonely Doug, the turtle with a plastic straw up its nose, a polar bear on a dwindling ice floe, or a duck covered in oil. But it feels unfair to these quietly flourishing trees that we see them as symbolic or pit them against each other in the registry to claim a position. Couldn't they simply exist? Singular big trees become a stand-in for ancient forests, when in reality they point to what sustains them: the surrounding forest. Perspective is key when looking at these trees: depending on the beholder, a big tree can be a portal to transcendence, a canoe in the making, jobs for mill workers, community wealth and self-reliance, habitat, a wayfinding beacon. A single tree reduced to a stump is also a marker—of greed, capitalism, and shortsightedness.

ON MAY 10, 2017, Yoko Ono tweeted about her *Ceiling Painting* (1966), sometimes called her ladder piece or *Yes Painting*. "I was depressed at the time," she reflected. "So I wanted to give some positivity to my life." For this installation, she'd printed YES in small sans serif capital letters on a framed piece of paper and hung it on the ceiling of London's Indica Gallery. Visitors would climb a ladder and use a magnifying glass to read the word. It was at that show, or more accurately the day before the show opened, that John Lennon met Ono in 1966. As Louis Menand recounts in an overview of the influence of Ono's famous husband on the art world's perception of her output, Lennon climbed the ladder and later said, "It's a great relief when you get up the ladder and you look through the spyglass and it doesn't say 'No' or 'Fuck you.'"

Arbutus trees fill me with that feeling of YES when I spot them bending gracefully in coastal forests. And I'm not alone. When

I started my tree-tracking project, the most commonly asked question was "Where is the biggest arbutus?" This sinewy red-skinned tree (also called madrone in the U.S., and sometimes called a refrigerator tree due to the coolness of its trunk) has been my favorite since I was a teen, wandering arbutus groves on Hornby Island. It's a thin-skinned deciduous tree with waxy green leaves, peeling bark, red berries, and curving branches. It grows in drier coastal rainforests, like the east coast of Vancouver Island, the Sunshine Coast, and the Gulf Islands, alongside Douglas-fir and Garry oaks. The berries are edible but not commonly eaten, and the wood is valued as firewood. Arbutus is experiencing a range of threats, from fire suppression (fire is how the arbutus regenerates) to drought and fungus.

A year earlier, Jason and I had gone looking for the Champion, which grows in Nanoose Bay, near Parksville on Vancouver Island. This area has numerous large arbutuses growing along the highway. We parked on the shoulder and walked back to the access road to a woodlot. Each end of the woodlot was blocked with a locked gate, one end marked "forestry access" and the other marked "no trespassing, you consent to being searched, DND." After a quick search online, I thought the area was an aviation field for drones and private aircraft. When I returned home, I emailed PDQ Flyers, an amateur flying club, and the VP agreed to bring me there the next time I was in the area—but yes, it was Department of National Defence land.

Before Jenny and I left on our Port Renfrew trip, I learned that the tree grows just *outside* the DND fence, and we could access it unescorted and without having to sign the DND guestbook. The morning after our Big Lonely Doug visit, Jenny and I parked off the highway and walked up an FSR. Douglas-fir seed trees growing in the cutblock were paintbrushes against the blue sky. The road turned into a dirt path in the forest, obviously a popular walking and biking path. We kept our eyes peeled as we walked deeper into the forest, near the Five Amigos trail, expecting to hit the DND fence.

"There's a big tree," I said, peering through some underbrush at what, in the dappled sunlight, I thought was a wide Doug-fir.

"That's a *huge* arbutus," Jenny said.

YES.

This Champion arbutus has a 2.26-meter DBH and is 27 meters tall, with a crown of 25.6 meters. It's a total beauty, with scaly thick bark at its base rather than the thinner skin higher up on the tree; the thicker bark is an indicator of age. I knew from previous repeat attempts to see other trees— Norvan's Castle, the Chilliwack Giant—that searching for the tree again caused it to loom even larger in my imagination, and hopefully in reality. As a species I had long revered and one that populated my mental landscape, this Champion grew in my estimation—a positive sign as if magnified through a glass.

In her classic book *The Living Mountain*, Nan Shepherd writes of her experience of slowly coming to know the Cairngorm Mountains over decades: "I began to discover the mountain in itself. Everything became good to me, its contours, its colours, its waters and rock, flowers and birds. This process has taken many years, and is not yet complete. Knowing another is endless... The thing to be known grows with the knowing." With this arbutus so close to the highway, I could easily return to take in more of its details whenever I was in the area, experiencing the joy of knowing it more each time.

— 12 —

The
Pointed Forest

SITKA SPRUCE, LOG HOUSE,
WESTERN HEMLOCK GROVE

"Once there were brook trout in the streams in
the mountains... They smelled of moss in your hand.
Polished and muscular and torsional."
CORMAC MCCARTHY, *The Road*

IN 1970, SINGER-SONGWRITER HARRY NILSSON released the
concept album *The Point!* This joyful collection of narration and
songs teaches us to embrace diversity, work through problems,
and look at the world from a new perspective—for these reasons,
and because its main character is a boy named Oblio, it has
the feeling of a kids' musical. Oblio is born without a point on
his head in a world where everyone has a point. Because of his
round head, Oblio and his dog, Arrow (who has a point), are
banished from the Land of Point to the Pointless Forest. There
Oblio discovers that the trees, and the branches on the trees, and
the leaves on the branches have points. The forest isn't pointless at all. Nilsson's inspiration for the album came from a little

chemical support. "I was on acid and I looked at the trees and I realized that they all came to points, and the little branches came to points, and the houses came to [a] point. I thought, 'Oh! Everything has a point, and if it doesn't, then there's no point to it.'"

I'd realized that rushing past trees on my way to bigness missed the point: the forest as a whole sustains bigness, and we have the ability to support or destroy that forest. Since we love to assign numbers to trees—their ranking in the registry, their value as timber—let's quantify it. British Columbia has 11.1 million hectares (27.4 million acres) of old-growth, but not all of that is made up of the large coastal trees that have such ecological and cultural values. Only about 400,000 hectares (1 million acres) of BC's old-growth forests are considered "high-productivity"—sites where most of the forest giants grow. Of the forests that the BC government defines as old-growth, 68.5 percent are unprotected; within that amount, 23 percent are recommended for immediate deferral, of which 22 percent falls under the purview of BC Timber Sales. Understanding where potential cutblocks lie, amid buffer zones and parks, is a challenge. So when Ken Wu asked me to join a Labor Day weekend outing to an ancient Sitka spruce and bigleaf maple forest whose future was undetermined, I said yes immediately.

This forest grows west of Lake Cowichan in the unceded territory of the Ditidaht First Nation on southern Vancouver Island. The Endangered Ecosystems Alliance is planning to work with local First Nations to see what conservation measures can be enacted here. One way to preserve this old-growth forest would be through a Ditidaht-managed Indigenous Protected and Conserved Area, run on Indigenous principles of stewardship. As Ken explained to me, an IPCA is not a legal designation, but its tenets can be achieved through provincial conservancy legislation or a federal National Park Reserve designation, which means that lands are reserved for specific practices, such as hunting, gathering, and cultural cutting of big cedars for long houses and canoes. In an IPCA, the Nation would manage or comanage the land and protect it from industrial extraction. Ken told me that we need a combination of legally protected areas and regulatory protections (like an Old-Growth Management Area) and First Nations decision-making authority at every level as well as compensation for logging on their lands.

Jason and I drove to Lake Cowichan to meet with Ken and Celina, as well as members of the BC Big Tree Committee, and Ian Thomas, a six-foot-four graduate student in biology and research and engagement officer with the Ancient Forest Alliance. (He and Colin Spratt registered the big cedar mentioned in the previous chapter.) Ian had located this patch of old-growth Sitka spruce and bigleaf maple using first Google Earth and then ground-truthing. Jason had come with me as moral support, as I felt shy of being in the company of all these tree trackers, and he and I nibbled on cheesy buns while Ken outlined the plan to the group assembled in the parking lot of the grocery store. Traveling as a convoy, we drove about forty minutes out of town, through Youbou and down a dusty FSR. Eventually the recreational vehicles sharing the road thinned out, and it was just us. We parked to the side of the FSR, and I could clearly see the complex old-growth on one side of the road, with its rich understory and light filtering through the canopy, and the monoculture second-growth on the opposite side, shaded and lacking vibrancy. We descended a steep hillside, using Doug-fir roots to support us on the slope, until we came to a level area rich in undergrowth. Salmonberry, stink currant, sedge, rush, and foam flower grew with abandon. Christine, the registrar, gushed over the delicate maidenhair fern. "My favorite!"

Sword ferns released their spores into the humid air as we walked, and dust from the undergrowth hung in the rays that cut through the canopy. Albert Camus said, "Autumn is a second spring when every leaf is a flower," and this forest of bigleaf maples was in full bloom, transitioning toward winter. We walked under curtains of moss and falling leaves as we sort of followed elk trails throughout the flat site—"sort of" because elk don't cut strong trails, so we were bushwhacking through prickly stands of salmonberry, the leaves of which obscured depressions. Where possible, we moved along the mostly dry streambed rather than through the undergrowth. We peered at tiny Pacific chorus frogs and larger red-legged frogs hiding in leaf litter.

We saw a couple of western red-cedars and Doug-firs, but the forest at this level, below the road, was mostly Sitka spruce and bigleaf maple. Andy MacKinnon, a member of the committee and our resident forest ecologist with a specialty in fungi, told us that spruce and maple grow better than cedars and Doug-fir in a low floodplain like this one; these conifers have a hard time establishing themselves in flowing water. Andy used to work with BC Forest Services and then moved into teaching and serving in municipal government. I'd been carrying my all-weather notebook and pencil to make ready notes, and now I hooked the spiral notebook over my backpack's chest strap and wove the pencil into my braid. I kept up with the group, angling over low branches and walking along dry but mossy logs. Jason was a good sport, but big trees aren't really his thing, and he hates mosquitoes, of which there were plenty in the shadows. In a stand of trees, I spotted a wildlife tree, filled with holes made by a pileated woodpecker. I pointed it out, and Jason beamed— Woody is his favorite bird.

We kept stopping to ask Andy identification questions.

"What's this, Andy?" I said, pulling back some leaves, thinking what looked like red balls might be insect eggs. Its closest approximation to my sushi-eating, coast-dwelling eyes was fish roe.

"That's pink coral fungus," he said excitedly.

"Is it rare?" asked Christine.

"A little rare," he said.

Ken got us back on track: we were here to see big trees, not tiny fungi. "Is this the most direct route?" Ken asked Ian, forging on up ahead. Ian was trying to recall where he'd seen the large spruce on his last expedition.

"Don't follow me!" Ian said, laughing and legging along in gum boots. "There's no direct route."

We gathered at the first big spruce and started measuring. Ira wandered away a distance to take a laser measure while his girlfriend, Sharlene, held a reflective vest up the tree to catch the beam. Christine called out requests to take photos, datum, GPS, elevation, and crown spread. The Endangered Ecosystems Alliance and the committee could use this data when speaking with governments about protecting the area. This site, if preserved, could become the next Avatar Grove for the conservation movement. But for the area to be conserved, the province would need to compensate the Ditidaht for the income they would have generated from logging old-growth.

"Look at this monster!" said Shaun, referring to the spruce with a three-meter diameter.

"That's not as interesting as lichens," Andy said.

"Let's get a photo of all the big-tree people up there!" Ken said, pointing to the base of the second big spruce. Ira, Christine, Shaun, and Andy moved toward the tree.

"Come on, Amanda!" Shaun called. I hesitated a moment and then climbed up for the photo. Shaun had been telling me to join the committee for basically my whole time looking for big trees, and I'd demurred.

"Why wouldn't you join?" Jason had asked a few months earlier.

"I can't ruin my journalistic integrity," I said, shocked.

"You're not a journalist!" Jason said.

Now, in this grove, Andy asked, "Why aren't you on the committee?" I stumbled for a response and he cut across with "Shaun, don't you think she should be on the committee?"

"Yes, indeed I do, Andy," Shaun said as we found our footing around the tree, "so long as Ira agrees."

I winked at Jason, standing off to the side. While we hammed it up for the lens, Andy and Shaun talked about the early big-tree committees, not just in BC but in Washington State, Oregon, and elsewhere. Shaun joked that the early registry committees were mostly made up of guys competing with each other through the size of the trees they located, a friendly international competition between U.S. and Canadian registries that amounted to "Mine is bigger than yours."

We climbed back up the slope, and Jason and I shoved our backpacks in Trouble's trunk, where the road dust had permeated. Then we headed to Nanaimo, where we'd catch the ferry to Gabriola and spend the night with my parents. I kept trying to get the "Brooklyn of Nanaimo" to catch on as a nickname for the small island, but so far no takers. Over dinner, we filled my parents in on the outing.

"Those guys were really into measuring," Jason said. At one point, I'd pulled out my trusty d-tape to contribute to the Sitka measuring, and Shaun said, "No need." He pulled out the biggest tape I'd seen, the reel as large as a dinner plate. "They seemed really concerned with how big trees are," he continued. "I don't see the point."

Jason couldn't see the point of big trees at all. Jason is a quantitative assessor—data is his thing, capital-t Truth his guiding light—but I had to agree with him here. I didn't share in the other big-tree trackers' passion for data, but how could Jason stand in front of a huge Sitka spruce or bigleaf maple and feel nothing?

IN NOVEMBER 2020, photographer and AFA campaigner TJ Watt posted before and after photos of old-growth cedars cut down in the Caycuse watershed near Lake Cowichan. On the left, a majestic tree in a flourishing ecosystem; on the right, the same tree reduced to a stump backed by clearing. He'd last been to the area earlier that year, in April. Teal-Jones had logged these old-growth cedars in the meantime and had a government-granted license to do so. The photos went viral internationally, even appearing in *The Guardian*. I realized the photos bore a sorry resemblance to the before-and-after diptychs of the Kiyu Creek forest in the Nimpkish Valley in 1981 and 1985, which Stoltmann included in the introduction to his 1987 guide. The times, they were not a changin'.

When I was a kid, our TV was always tuned to the news at dinner, and that's where I learned about the Clayoquot protests in 1993, when I was ten. The first so-called War in the Woods was a series of protests against clear-cutting old-growth rainforest in Clayoquot Sound on western Vancouver Island. I wanted to be part of the action, especially when I saw other kids taking part (and later being arrested), but there was no way my parents could bring us over there with their work commitments, and we didn't know any other families taking part. Besides, Vancouver Island might as well have been a world away. The protests involved a series of blockades between 1984 and 1994, with a significant standoff in Carmanah in 1988 and a huge turnout of protestors at Clayoquot Sound in 1993. The campaign in Carmanah, in which Stoltmann and the WCWC participated, eventually led to the conservation of the area as Carmanah Walbran Provincial Park. Of the approximately 12,000 people who showed up to the Friends of Clayoquot Sound (FOCS) Peace Camp in the summer of 1993, 856 people were arrested.

The protests began in 1984 when members of the Nuu-chah-nulth and FOCS, objecting to MacBlo logging Meares Island off Tofino, blockaded logging roads. They were opposed to industrial logging in the area, which wouldn't benefit the local First Nation and would jeopardize their drinking water. That year, the Tla-o-qui-aht announced that Meares Island would be protected as the first Tribal Park, run under a Tla-o-qui-aht model of stewardship. Blockades and arrests in the late '80s and early '90s set the stage for the 1993 blockades. This summer of demonstrations included supporters from all walks of life, elders and children, activists from Greenpeace and FOCS, and First Nations. In 2000, part of Clayoquot received a UNESCO biosphere reserve designation, which is important recognition but confers no legal protection. The Nuu-chah-nulth bought the TFL for half of the logging rights to the area, forming Iisaak Forest Resources Ltd., and MacBlo pulled out of the area as the protests and ongoing boycotts of its products were damaging its reputation. First Nations, with federal and private conservation funding, have now designated the vast majority of old-growth forest in Clayoquot Sound off-limits to commercial logging and are waiting on provincial alignment and recognition. Clayoquot set the stage for the Great Bear Rainforest Agreement in 2006, which concerned a 6.4-million-hectare area (15.8 million acres; the size of Ireland) on the central and northern coast of BC. Of that region, about 38 percent is protected, and about 85 percent of the forests are off-limits to logging.

But logging old-growth on Vancouver Island didn't stop in the intervening years. In 2018, the Sierra Club BC noted, "On average, nearly 9,000 hectares of old-growth were logged annually from 2011 to 2015... In 2016, that annual amount jumped to nearly 11,000 hectares, the equivalent of 26 Stanley Parks." Which brings us to Fairy Creek in 2021.

This watershed in southwestern Vancouver Island is on the unceded territory of the Pacheedaht First Nation, abutting the territory of the Ditidaht and Huu-ay-aht First Nations. Teal-Jones has harvest rights to roughly half of the watershed, and the remaining amount is reserved under an OGMA. The government can remove portions of the OGMA but it's difficult to do so; it happens more often in the Interior than on the coast. The area licensed to Teal-Jones was of interest to the protesters, in particular old-growth yellow-cedars at higher elevation. After Teal-Jones built a road up the ridge, the Rainforest Flying Squad moved into the area in August 2020. Their goal was to protect a thirty-two-acre stand of old-growth, approved to be harvested by Teal-Jones. But the Pacheedaht were divided on the issue and the presence of the grassroots activists. Pacheedaht Elder Bill Jones supported the protest, calling the land defenders "allies" in the quest to stop old-growth logging. But the elected leadership and Nation-recognized Hereditary Chief of the Pacheedaht, Frank Queesto Jones, as well as the leadership of the Ditidaht and Huu-ay-aht, were opposed to the protestors' presence. They see the protestors' criticism of the First Nations for allowing old-growth to be cleared as a mark of ongoing colonialism. Over the past decade-plus, the Pacheedaht have taken back their logging rights, harvesting the land themselves or selling the rights to timber companies including Teal-Jones. As Chief Jones told Sarah Cox reporting in *The Narwhal*, "Why are the logging trucks going by our community and not stopping?

Why aren't we benefiting from the resources that go out of our territory? For the last decade or so we've been slowly turning it around."

In April 2021, Teal-Jones was granted a court injunction against the blockades, so they could continue clearing their approved cutblock under TFL 46 (the same TFL in which Big Lonely Doug and Avatar Grove are situated). The RCMP moved in to remove protestors, eventually arresting over 1,100 protestors in both the Fairy Creek and Caycuse watersheds throughout the summer, the arrest numbers making it the largest act of civil disobedience in Canada's history. In June, the Pacheedaht, Ditidaht, and Huu-ay-aht First Nations made the Hišuk ma c̓awak Declaration; Hišuk ma c̓awak means "everything is connected," and the document declared "our responsibility to decide what is best for our lands." In response to a request from the Nations, the BC NDP government granted a two-year deferral of logging in 2,000 acres of the Fairy Creek watershed, plus an area of Central Walbran, while the Nations determined their plan for the area. Deferrals aren't permanent protections, merely actions that can be deployed quickly.

Old-growth trees are immense carbon stores—once we log these trees, we cannot recover this carbon. But old-growth logging can currently be the best economic alternative for some rural First Nations. The government has a responsibility to make other alternatives—like logging second-growth forests, high-value wood processing, and milling—as economically appealing, while encouraging a broader economy that includes tourism and clean energy.

The Fairy Creek protests followed the release of a strategic review on the status of old-growth in BC ordered by the provincial government. In this review, registered professional foresters Garry Merkel and Al Gorley call for a "paradigm shift" in how we regard and manage forests and ecosystems, namely that forestry plans need to involve Indigenous decision-makers and communities; that not all old forests are renewable; and that forests are for the benefit of all beings, not just humans. The review calls on the BC government to implement fourteen recommendations for ensuring the health and biodiversity of all forests within the province. But at the time of writing, the three-year framework that Merkel and Gorley laid out in 2020 has not been implemented, despite the majority of British Columbians (85 percent, according to a survey) wanting to stop all logging of old-growth forests.

I BECAME INVOLVED IN TREE TRACKING at a prime moment in BC's big-trees story. The limited extent of old-growth forests in the province was becoming evident through the 2020 strategic review, and the Fairy Creek protests in the summer of 2021. Even amateur dendrophiles and newbie climate change believers were making the connection between deforestation, intensifying climate disasters, and flooding. It was obvious when the sky was orange, and in each compounding weather cycle, we learned the terrifying language of *heat dome, atmospheric river, bomb cyclone.*

Thanks to the popularity of Big Lonely Doug on social media, and the pandemic restrictions that meant more people were exploring forests closer to home, word got out about the BC Big Tree Registry and nominations began pouring in. In December 2020, eighty-five trees were added to the registry, and in December 2021, hundreds of trees, the most ever. Among the new nominations:

- the tallest ponderosa pine on record, at 58.7 meters, growing in Castlegar, nominated by a BC Timber Sales employee, and called Lieutenant Dan, the nickname for Dan Upward, who first noticed the tree and told the measurer about it

- a new western red-cedar on the coast called the Duncan Mother

- a new interior western red-cedar Champion, the Big Tree, growing in Ancient Forest Provincial Park

- a new Champion western white pine (56 m tall) named Target because of a blue circle spray-painted on it

- and a huge new Champion subalpine larch nicknamed Grand Daddy Subby (my personal favorite name)

Though I had already realized I could never complete this project, it was now decided for me, like being laid off when you have resolved to quit. That my completionist goal was foiled by a new crop of big-tree hunters in BC, tracking the giants that haven't yet been measured, added a nice touch of irony to a project that originally had me competing with myself. Sebene Selassie explains in *You Belong* that it's a developmental trait for children to measure—we compare and rank while we learn to tell objects apart and describe them—but this tendency to compare ourselves to others, or even to earlier or imagined versions of ourselves, follows us through life and inhibits our capacity for connection. "When comparison is rooted in separation," Selassie writes, "it becomes competitive."

The fact that so many new nominations continue to come in means there really could be bigger Champions out there, something the committee believes wholeheartedly. As Andy said, "I'm absolutely convinced that the biggest trees in the province aren't on the registry yet, and it's just a matter of finding them." Consider that Hyperion, the tallest tree in the world, wasn't measured until 2006 in Northern California; the tallest tree in the Amazon, a *Dinizia excelsa* (or angelim vermelho), wasn't verified until 2019.

Scientific research is slowly catching up to Indigenous wisdom about forest stewardship, like the importance of periodic burns to prevent wildfire in drier ecosystems, or the role of big trees—some of them Mother Trees—in supporting the larger forest. Suzanne Simard, the researcher credited with the idea of the Mother Tree—a hub tree in a forest that supports other trees by sharing nutrients and communicating along mycorrhizal (fungal) networks—notes that Indigenous populations already had this information. As she said in an interview, "If you go back to and listen to some of the early teachings of the Coast Salish and the Indigenous people along the western coast of North America, they knew that already. It's in the writings and in the oral history. The idea of the Mother Tree has long been there. The fungal networks, the below-ground networks that keep the whole forest healthy and alive, that's also there. That these plants interact and communicate with each other, that's all there."

That we would cut these trees down before understanding them burns the library, sullies our home.

BETWEEN CHRISTMAS AND NEW YEAR'S EVE 2020, Jason and I called it quits, like so many other couples during the pandemic. A few months after that, I bought a log house on Gabriola Island, in Snuneymuxw territory. My home is most likely made of second-growth Douglas-fir. Downy woodpeckers and insects peck and gnaw into the logs, and who can blame them? Log houses take an extra level of care when it comes to pest control and wood preservation, but as Kurt Vonnegut wrote in *Hocus Pocus*, "Another flaw in the human character is that everybody wants to build and nobody wants to do maintenance."

Gabriola has its own big-tree registry, a regional collection distinct from the BC Big Tree Registry. Located within the coastal Douglas-fir zone, the island's cedars, grand firs, and Doug-firs are smaller than those in the cooler and wetter areas on Vancouver Island and the mainland; none appear on the main BC Big Tree Registry. But Garry oak and arbutus, which appreciate drier climates, grow especially large here, and I often wander their groves of scraggy gray and peeling red corkscrew trunks in Drumbeg Provincial Park, an intertidal ecosystem.

Native trees fill a corner of my front yard: western red-cedar, Pacific willow, Doug-fir, red alder, and arbutus. A large Doug-fir with a pleasing bend to its trunk stands guard over the smaller trees I plant in my backyard: hazelnut, apple, plum, Saskatoon berry, and the yellow-cedar that I raised from a seedling on my balcony in East Vancouver. I welcome those who build nests of needles under the beams of my house, and I hang syrup feeders for the hummingbirds who create round nests of spiderwebs and moss in the surrounding cedars. A large cedar near my house is peppered with holes made by a red-breasted sapsucker, appearing like an upright cribbage board. I now say trees' names with confidence, cataloging their presence. When I gently correct my new friend Moe's tree identification on a walk together, she comments that I know a lot about trees, and I agree with her.

Over the first summer, I stacked cords of firewood for my woodstove. When I said to my architect friend Em that it felt wrong to be burning the same material as my walls, she said, "Yeah, it's like feeding eggs to a chicken." That first summer, the Fairy Creek summer, I became more watchful than participatory. Oliver Burkeman writes in favor of using your strengths to respond to global crises, and I had previously combined my interest in books and activism to build a niche as an editor of books about the environment and social change. Now, I combined my strengths as an observer of big trees and ecosystems, with my wariness of overloading myself, my discomfort at protests, and my continuing fear of the coronavirus pandemic. I couldn't tend to my small patch of trees, watering them against the dryness of the summer, and be at Fairy Creek. I didn't need to see the big trees to know they were there and worth saving.

As winter set in, I developed a new connection to trees through firewood, and how carrying my heat source into the house brings so much outdoors in: wasps, spiders, gray moths, lichen, moss, splinters. In winter, I try to spot the wasps, hibernating with their jaws holding tight to the wood, but they are wily and hide because they are fucking wasps. They wake up in the warmth of the house and fly around, drawn to the low lights of evening. Sometimes I catch them in a mason jar and release them back into the cold world; otherwise, I later find them lying legs up.

Islanders stop their cars to ask you, on a walk, if you want a ride up the hill. My neighbor met me at the community mailboxes and asked if I'm dating yet. I reminded her I just got here. "Well," she said, "the thing about Gabriola is the odds are good, but the goods are odd." Ravens use the sky paths above the road instead of maneuvering through the dense forest, and the deep swoosh of their wings cuts through the silence of the day. Turkeys, less a wild variety and more escaped domestics gone feral, live here in packs. Cars yield to the birds. Why did the bachelor turkey cross the road? To live in my backyard for a week, eat all my green strawberries, shit everywhere, and make friends with my cat.

Walter Murch said, "I've found that your chances for happiness are increased if you wind up doing something that is a reflection of what you loved most when you were somewhere between nine and eleven years old." I drop into a steady rhythm that is less a new ritual born of the pandemic and more how I spent my youth: wandering in the woods, beachcombing, making art. I had qualms about moving to an island where my parents live, but Simard tells us, "Roots didn't thrive when they grew alone. The trees needed one another." Besides, my dad makes excellent eclairs. My parents school me on organic gardening, help me establish veggie beds and a compost, hang a clothesline, and install cisterns to catch rainwater.

I'd hoped my big-tree project would make me tougher and help me live up to my exceedingly high expectations for myself, which demanded I not only get it right but quickly and on my own. That's how capitalism operates, not the forest. Capitalism thrives on competition by making us feel we are individuals; the forest models collaboration and evolution. As Richard Powers said in an interview with the *Los Angeles Review of Books*, "We have all completely habituated to the first tenet of commodity-individualism: meaning is entirely something we make for ourselves ... But there is, of course, a meaning of and for trees, a meaning to the hugely interconnected living world that cares very little for human meaning."

A few years spent peering closely at the forest is not a lot of time to learn about trees, or to transform yourself. But being in the presence of these giants did change me—not through achieving transcendence, but through reveling in insignificance and the community I found along the way. Constantly failing to find the Biggest Things in the Forest allowed me to lighten up on myself, trust myself enough to let others in. I moved to a practice rather than a goal. Now when my friend Greg texts me "You up for a tree outing on Friday?" I don't even check the map. Big-tree trackers have a well-honed instinct that helps them find good grow sites, but I'm riding on my own intuition that lets me grow into my potential by easing up. I had originally confused commitment with achievement, not taking the project seriously by refusing to plan, research, or ask for help. When I relaxed the outcome and went searching for all the runners-up (i.e., the forest), I gained more skills and tree knowledge.

By looking for a Champion, nominated, verified, and even named, I was following a path set by others, certainly not by the tree. Rather than crossing off trees in a spreadsheet or building my brand or social capital, I am more interested in seeing where smaller dreams take me. Besides, capitalism weakens in the face of antiproductive goals like big-tree tracking for the hell of it— in other words, acts that are creative. On his podcast *Object of Sound*, the poet and culture critic Hanif Abdurraqib asks the multi-instrumentalist Taja Cheek (L'Rain), "It is one thing to talk about collaboration with others, but I'm also really curious about collaboration with the self... How do you not just chase after everything that your abilities tell you that you can do?" I started out with forty-three options and a bottomless well of self-pressure, the choice to pursue this tree and not that one, or to close on a tree before looking for another one. I realized in hindsight that my bouncing from tree to tree, which in the moment felt like fear and perhaps looked to others like vacillating, was self-kindness.

By paying attention to nature, loving being in my body, looking for trees of all sizes, I reclaimed my time and my life. Jenny Odell might call this "doing nothing," as a way of rejecting the algorithm that skews toward extremes including bigness. "To capitalist logic," Odell writes in *How to Do Nothing*, "which thrives on myopia and dissatisfaction, there may indeed be something dangerous about something as pedestrian as doing nothing: escaping laterally toward each other, we might just find that everything we wanted is already here."

IN LATE WINTER, I headed out to see not one tree but a whole grove of monumental western hemlocks just above sea level, in the surf town of Ucluelet on the west coast of Vancouver Island.

I took the crack o' dawn ferry from Gabriola to Vancouver Island and drove to northern Nanaimo to hop into Mick Bailey's car. Mick is a retired landscaper and has been tracking trees since the 1980s, many around where he used to live in Lynn Valley. We drove to meet Greg Herringer and Sean O'Rourke in Port Alberni. Greg had cleared our visit in advance, receiving permission from the Ucluelet First Nation for us to be tree tracking. Greg is a forest technologist with BCTS and lives in Port Alberni. He adopted the BCTS Coastal Legacy Tree Program and took over administration of it on the south island. He is also a certified horticulturist, and before he joined BCTS, he worked for ten years as a tree planter in these forests. Sean, based in Hope, is the applied anthropologist who came across the remnants of the grand fir in the Chilliwack River Ecological Reserve. He works for the Kanaka Bar Band, a Nlaka'pamux community in the Fraser Canyon.

Greg and I had been keeping up a steady conversation on Instagram, where all tree trackers go to emote. "Oh, I see we got the Stanfield's memo!" I said to Greg as we met each other for the first time. He and I were dressed in the unofficial uniform of Canadian foresters: a thick gray Henley sweater, though I had festooned mine with orange needle felting in the copious moth holes. While we waited for Sean to emerge from Greg's house, we loaded up Greg's dogs, a German shepherd named Ben and an English springer spaniel named Angus. Ben reared up on Greg's white truck tailgate, and Angus shyly moved in for a head scratch. "Oh, Angus, we have the same energy," I whispered, shying from Ben's exuberance.

After a quick caffeine fuel-up, we drove out to Florencia Bay in Ucluelet and began donning our rain gear in the fine drizzle.

The three men geared up with waterproof bib overalls, and I admired their foresight to bring truck clothes and bush clothes; I'd be wearing my wet clothes and muddy boots home.

"I didn't bring any bear spray or GPS, as I figured you guys would have it," I said.

Mick, grinning, motioned to the dogs. "We won't need bear spray with them," he said. A GPS hung from his backpack strap.

While we laced up our hiking boots and caulks, Mick ribbed another tree tracker who wasn't forthcoming with details on their visits and wouldn't answer email. We talked about how helpful others' knowledge is on these tree-tracking journeys, and how one bit of info from someone who's been there can lead to new discoveries for someone else. "We're supposed to help each other. It's a brotherhood!" Mick said.

"Personhood," I said.

"Whatever," Mick said.

I joked that I wanted to call this book *I Heard It From a Guy.* They snickered, and I exhaled... The day was going to go just fine. I was struck that all those "failures" I'd not posted about in my early days as a tree tracker could have been put to use, helping other trackers. In not sharing, I'd been contributing to the old-school idea that you need to "earn" your tree by solving riddles, like a real SOB tree tracker.

We hit the boardwalk for a spell, then veered off into the woods, Greg leading the way. He'd been to the area a few weeks earlier with his wife, Janet, and mapped out the location of three huge western hemlocks on his water-protected tablet. These trees wouldn't be cut down, growing as they were in a sliver of protected Treaty Settlement Land—culturally significant to the Ucluelet First Nation—between cutblocks. None of the hemlocks was the Champion—that title still belonged to Norvan's Castle—but these trees were especially large for hemlocks so close to sea level; they usually grow to these sizes only in the mountains.

With Greg and Mick leading the way, hiking poles akimbo, we thrashed through salmonberry stems and thick salal for a couple hours, the salal stalks sometimes as thick as rebar and twelve feet high. We were walking parallel to the shore; when we paused, we could hear the crashing of waves. I saw a small white and gray bird fly into a nest in a tree and wondered if it was a marbled murrelet, the seabird that nests in canopies and was a key species in the fight to save Clayoquot. Deer fern grew everywhere, including on the soil "wall" of a twelve-foot-high root wad. Small hemlock and light brown Sitka spruce cones littered the forest floor, evergreen huckleberry leaves glistened in the undergrowth, and moss lay in thick pillows on the upper branches. Stepping around salal and salmonberry required fancier footwork than my Thursday night tap class. There were a few walklogs, and logs we had to scurry under or climb over. At one point, I attempted to hold on to a small log while dropping from a larger log on to the forest floor, only to pull the smaller log down with me. Mick and Greg began calling me Bushwhacker Lewis.

Greg forged on ahead, sometimes calling to the dogs to come back in from their solo adventures. His trademark waxed-cotton packer hat was covered with debris from our trek. My wool tuque was sopping and anointed with bark, moss, and cedar bits.

"Ever heard of gorp core?" Sean asked as we walked.

Mick chimed in. "It's for people in Vancouver who wear expensive outdoor clothing but never go outside." They all laughed, and I felt suddenly proud of my sap-covered fleece pants, gray sweater with orange tufts of needle felting, and home-patched Mountain Equipment Co-op jacket circa 1995 that Mom had found for me at a yard sale.

We came to the runner-up hemlock, which was entered in the registry in 1998. We were there to calculate new measurements and assess its height.

"What a beauty!" Sean exclaimed.

"It's bigger than I thought," said Mick.

Its DBH measured 2.56 meters, but the hemlock had lost its top in the coast's high winds, and it lay shattered next to the tree. Once our official measuring business was done, we reveled in being in the forest together, joking and swapping tales, and measuring the other large western hemlocks in the grove. Some were in the top five in the registry, but my favorite wasn't big enough to nominate—a hemlock with one candelabra leader covered in ferns, and the other twisted to resemble a mudra, a meditative hand position.

"I've never seen such gnarly hemlocks," I said to Mick. "I usually think of them as a bit boring, growing straight."

"Hemlocks don't get any respect," said Mick.

The Nation had requested photos and info on any big cedars, and I helped Greg measure the DBH and crown of two cedar sisters. "Amanda, your hand is going to be famous," he said as he took a photo of the tape wrapping around the cedars, me holding the tape in place to provide a clear record. Occasionally I'd hear him call "I need those Vanna White hands!" and I'd rush over to carry the tape around a tree, stepping over roots and slipping around the tree's base.

We found a clearing and stopped for lunch. Angus had better luck begging sandwich bites from the guys; I told the crew I'd be in charge of the small army of kittens we were bound to find in the woods. I had stuck a box of old-fashioned glazed doughnuts in my grocery cart the day before, and it was just the thing to warm these tree trackers' hearts.

"Hey, did you ever see that Champion shore pine in Esquimalt?" Sean asked as we passed around the doughnuts.

"Yeah!" I said. "An easy get." I'd headed to this older residential area early on an overcast Sunday morning, shortly after resuming my original pace once the registry was up and running. I eased my car into the parking lot behind a low-rise with pale yellow vinyl siding. The registry indicated that the Champion shore pine, in Esquimalt near downtown Victoria on Vancouver Island, was on private land, but I felt that my trespassing wouldn't be noticed. The shore pine before me (18 m high, 1.03 m DBH, and 15 m crown) was straight with stout branches and a burst of needled arms projecting over the street.

"What an underwhelming tree!" Sean said. He looked dejected. So it seemed that even seasoned big-tree trackers could be unimpressed.

The last of the hemlocks in the grove measured, we turned back, taking a new route. That's when we saw a huge hemlock previously unknown to Greg and not listed on the registry. The tree had been through the wars, its thick bark partially covering exposed cambium, so that I initially couldn't tell if I was looking at a cedar, fir, or hemlock. Stoltmann noted in 1987, "Often record trees are not the perfectly formed specimens sought out by the foresters, but rather the gnarled, scarred survivors of centuries." This tree had endured many windstorms, refused to die, and lost its top but sent up four vigorous leaders. We guessed the tree was about 80 percent dead but also, crucially, 20 percent alive.

We fell hard and fast and measured its DBH at 2.48 meters. Mick said admiringly, "Look at this freak show!" Sean and I said that was a bit mean to the tree. We tossed around naming suggestions: Old-Fashioned Glazed, the Four Tops, eventually settling on PT Barnum. I hoped we could later reassess that name in consultation with the Ucluelet First Nation, if they wanted to name the tree.

"Is this your first nomination, Amanda?" Greg asked.

"Yes, I guess it will be," I said, tickled. A name does emphasize the individual over the collective, the tree over the forest. But a conomination recognizes community, and I was delighted to have recognized this tree in such fine company. Solo tree tracking, like writing and editing, can be lonely, self-questioning work. As an editor, I work in service of the writer and the reader, and that dynamic flows between having more of a hand in developing the idea and fine-tuning every word and sitting back and asking the occasional question. Over time, I have come to favor editing as cocreation, an exchange of ideas with an eventual cap: a word limit, a production schedule, the author's and editor's energy.

Close to PT Barnum was a keyhole walk down to the long beach, a welcome reprieve from bushwhacking. Under an overcast sky, we wandered the sands back to the parking lot, Ben getting out his zoomies, Greg finding an abalone shell for Janet. Sean and I noticed a dead crab on its back, seeming to ooze an orange fungus from its lower body. I poked it gently with a stick, and we both jumped as it waved its arms, prompting us to flip it right side up. "You are having a terrible day, my friend," I said to the crab. I found a couple log rounds for my newest pastime, making heavy-duty doorstoppers, and carried one while Sean and Greg carried the other for me, looped in Ben's leash.

"Well, you guys got to see what a big nerd I am," I said as we packed up the truck.

"We had an inkling," said Mick.

"My kids call me a big nerd," said Greg.

"My daughter asks, 'Does this story have to do with trees?' and then tunes me out," said Mick.

"People who like big trees are nerds through and through," said Sean.

On our way back to Port Alberni, we pulled into Canoe Creek next to the Kennedy River to measure a giant western red-cedar at Shaun Muc's suggestion. The tree is well known, a short walk down a level path strewn with toilet paper from highway pit stops, but it's not in the registry. That's often the case with big trees in popular tourist areas: they're so "everyday" that we assume they have been measured. Greg and I took diameter and crown measurements while Sean measured the height with his laser.

Mick walked around the cedar to check out its root health. "You can really see the effects of the pandemic on this tree," he said. "With more people coming out here, all the vegetation and soil have been cleared away. There's much less since the last time I visited." Later, in an interview about BCTS and the Coastal Legacy Tree Project, Greg told me he has mixed feelings about big trees like Big Lonely Doug being made into spectacles. "People are killing it with kindness," he said, as they walk on its roots and erode the soil. "But we need to have these sacrificial trees that people experience at this size because that's what saves the trees." He reminded me that tree lovers don't want to stay away, behind fences, looking at the trees—they want to touch them.

The three men stood on the bank and looked across the creek to a hillside covered in trees.

"There have got to be bigger ones over there," Mick said.

"Like that huge cedar growing right there, in the middle," Sean said, pointing. Another trip was in the works, once the creek dried up a bit to cross.

"There's something special about this place," Mick said. "Even though it has been devastated by logging, all the way down to the creek, you can feel its vibe. You can see what a special place it once was."

And I could see it too. Like spotting springboard cuts in trees as a kid and old skid roads as a hiker, I saw the forest anew. I widened my lens past the huge cedar, moved back in time to settlers cutting the timber all the way to the creek, with little regard for the health of the waterway, and before that, the forest under Indigenous stewardship. I regrew the cedar stumps and added more bigleaf maples. The sunlight broke through the canopy and lit the moss so it glowed a brilliant green, catching the eyes of a Douglas squirrel as it dislodged a seed cone. The tributary creek, dried up now, flowed inland over boulders. The salmon returned, and ravens called. A thick layer of duff spotted occasionally with Roosevelt elk droppings and the odd bone covered the forest floor, and conks leaned out from ribbed bark. A buttressed opening in a cedar trunk was lined with dried sword ferns a black bear had pulled in for its summer den. I could see how all parts of the forest supported each other. I imagined the mycorrhizal networks underground, and the pheromones floating tree to tree. I saw nurse logs ushering in younger trees, hemlock atop cedar, rows of leggy trees that had outgrown their perch. There was evidence of a fire in the charred corky bark of a wide Doug-fir, but the forest had bounced back. Salmonberry, thimbleberry, salal, and wood sorrel grew thickly in the understory. I saw the Mother Tree at the center of it all, perhaps even the large cedar we'd measured. A showstopper or a sapling, each tree played its part.

I took a deep breath as I moved from focusing on One Big Tree to a Pointed Forest. If I could reclaim this forest in a matter of seconds, surely we could preserve these forests where they stood, if we worked together. My spreadsheet, and then the structure of this book, suggested a democratic forest, but one based on individual bigness and striving: Champions side by side in data cells, competing for the title. But here was a true forest, integrated and whole. I realized late in the process that I was following the same trajectory of Stoltmann, in whose footsteps I'd been walking. In his posthumous guide, Stoltmann writes, "My initial interest [as a big-tree tracker] must have grown out of a child-like fascination with bigness—to find new records—but as I ventured beyond the local parks into wilder forests, I gradually became aware of something far more complex of which these great trees were a part."

We drove back to Greg's house for a debrief. The dogs tucked into their dinner while we picked out beers from Greg and Janet's basement fridge. Speaking in the superlatives common to big-tree trackers, Mick said it was the most joyful day in the woods ever and the biggest hemlocks at sea level ever. I jotted some notes so I wouldn't forget the day.

"What are you writing down, Amanda?" Greg asked. "Are you recording our conversation?"

"That's right," I said, pretending to scrawl in my all-weather notebook. "*Greg can't get any respect, no respect at all.*" We all laughed. Angus sighed from his bed in the corner of the kitchen.

As I drove up island that night to stay at my sister's for the weekend, I was proud of myself for holding my own. Bushwhacker Lewis indeed. Sure, I still confused hemlocks and Sitka spruce before carefully considering their cones and bark. (Pro tip: Sitka spruce bark looks like potato chips.) But who cared? There's a Zen teaching: "When you start on a long journey, trees are trees, water is water, and mountains are mountains. After you have gone some distance, trees are no longer trees, water no longer water, mountains no longer mountains. But after you have travelled a great distance, trees are once again trees, water is once again water, mountains are once again mountains."

So how do you know when you've completed a goal, and when it's yet unfolding? You lose ten pounds, and then try to maintain that weight. You pay off your debt, and then track your spending. You achieve a promotion, and then look for your next opportunity. In his essay "Structure," John McPhee writes, "People often ask how I know when I'm done—not just when I've come to the end, but in all the drafts and revisions and substitutions of one word for another how do I know there is no more to do? When am I done? I just know. I'm lucky that way. What I know is that I can't do any better; someone else might do better, but that's all I can do; so I call it done."

I set out to see all the Champion trees, and in some ways I didn't succeed. But I didn't need to be the best tree tracker, best editor, best writer. I could respect the land and the people who host me, and look after my small patch of it. I'd need to reach these Champions in the company of friends, over and over, and happily so. I'd learn along the way, calling on the help of experts.

Besides, who wants to be outstanding in their own field? That's a good way to get hit by lightning.

Acknowledgments

A BOOK IS NEVER *REALLY* DONE, until it is—for better, for worse, for distribution deadlines. I have a number of folks to thank for helping me build the folly or, in my wildest dreams, the ha-ha. These people supported me as I lived through the arc of this narrative, during the hellscape of 2019 to 2022, with the climate crisis playing out to spectacular effect in the Pacific Northwest (and apologies to everyone I've forgotten to mention here).

Above all, thank you to my beloved family, without whom none of this is possible. To my parents, Seán and Angie Lewis, for their love, sacrifices, and eclairs. To Jenny, Tony, Jasper, and Eddie Botica, for living adventure. To Christina, Alvin, Áine, Kieran, Maeve, and Clare Caleb, for enthusiastic support.

Thank you to the BC Big Tree Committee for welcoming this novice tree tracker with open arms. The entire committee as well as individual trackers, especially Sally Aitken, Mick Bailey, Christine Chourmouzis, Greg Herringer, Ralf Kelman, Andy MacKinnon, Shaun Muc, Sean O'Rourke, and Ira Sutherland, were enormously helpful to me from the start, patient with my questions and errors, and encouraging.

The irony of writing a book praising shallow experience is it involves a lot of research, and I have learned more about trees in the process. Thanks to those tree experts who took the time to vet these words; all remaining errors are my own. Special thanks to John Deal at Western Forest Products for talking to me about their big-tree program, and to Sally Aitken, Mick Bailey, Bill Beese, Christine Chourmouzis, Greg Herringer, Jens Wieting, and Ken Wu for reading in whole or in part, and answering my many questions. Thanks to Lyndsie Bourgon, Jake Tobin Garrett, Bernadette Macdonald, Trina Moyles, Steve O'Shea, and Mick Short at the Riverview Horticultural Centre Society for updates and verifications.

Thank you to my dear friends for being the forest that sustains me, many of whom generously gave of their time and brain power to talk through these ideas with me: Karen Benedikt, Sarah Carr-Locke, Paul Fowler, Kathy Friedman, Rony Ganon, Hiromi Goto, Arno Kopecky, Jennifer Lum, Joanna Reid, Carol Shaben, Annemarie Tempelman-Kluit, Lisa Thomas-Tench, Susan Traxel, and Kendra Ward.

Special thanks to my sister Jenny for being my companion on the road and for answering so many of my book-related questions; Sabrina Bowman for deep friendship (marry me); Fiona Jones for being a mountain-dwelling queen; Diandra Ships for supporting me on every level; Kate Harris for suggesting the Champion trees idea, for vetting questions as my Ideal Reader, and for enriching my life with poetry and goofiness in equal doses; and Diana Beresford-Kroeger for being a valued mentor and this book's fairy godmother.

Thanks to these friends for being the community I needed in the woods: Andre, Celina, Christine, Cody, Colin, Dick, Fiona, Greg, Hiromi, Ira, Janet, Jason, Jenny, Jon, Ken, Laura, Mick, Sean, Shaun, Stephen, Steve, Terry.

I worked on the final chapters of this book under the ponderosa pines at Yasodhara, an ashram on Kootenay Bay in eastern BC.

Thanks to Dr. Luschiim Arvid Charlie and Dr. Nancy J. Turner for permission to draw on *Luschiim's Plants*.

Thank you to the Canada Council for the Arts. The grant I received was a life-changer, allowing me to take time away from my day job to dig deeper than ever and finish this book.

Thanks for inspiration: Beastie Boys, Bill Callahan, Tony Hoagland, J Dilla's *Donuts*, Kirsten Johnson's *Cameraperson*, Kyo Maclear's *Birds Art Life*, Harry Nilsson's *The Point!*, Jenny Odell's *How to Do Nothing*, Michael Ondaatje's *The Conversations*, Seth Rogen's *Yearbook*, and Alec Soth's photobooks and videos.

Thanks to my publisher, Greystone Books, for believing in this project despite an ambitious proposal and many missed deadlines. Thanks to Jennifer Croll, Jen Gauthier, and Rob Sanders for steering this book through publication. Special thanks to my editor, Paula Ayer, for being a clear-eyed companion while I was thrashing through metaphorical salal. Paula, you were a valued cocreator in this process—I could not be more grateful for your mind, heart, and sharp edits. Thanks also to Crissy Calhoun and Alison Strobel for your excellent editing. Thanks to the marketing team, especially Megan Jones and Makenzie Pratt, for getting the word out, and to Belle Wuthrich for a terrific cover and interior design.

From the start, Stephanie Sinclair understood this project and, crucially, believed in my ability to finish it. Thank you.

To the memory of Randy Stoltmann. Stoltmann knew the power of trees to transport us in our daily lives, that trips into the forest were worth the effort, and that it was important to preserve what was left. Thanks for laying tracks.

And finally, thank you, dear reader. Books are tricky things, and I'm grateful you stuck it out and even read the acknowledgments, which editors always read, but we love a bit of flattery.

Notes

Author's Note:
In Which I Get Away With It

like squeezing Jell-O: I first heard this expression in reference to protesting pipelines, in that a new project seems to start just as an existing one is canceled. I can't recall which activist said it, but I am indebted.

1: Norvan's Castle

Lynn Headwaters Regional Park: Randy Stoltmann, *Hiking Guide to the Big Trees of Southwestern British Columbia* (Vancouver: Western Canada Wilderness Committee, 1987), 73; correspondence with Mick Bailey, April 2022. The Lynn Valley area used to be a watershed and closed to the public until a 1981 storm damaged the water intakes. The park was created in 1985, preserving all the trees within it.

Lower Lynn Valley: There are still big trees out in Lower Lynn Valley, as Colin Spratt and Ian Thomas demonstrated when they registered a huge western red-cedar in June 2022. See chapter 11 for more.

the Lynn Valley Tree: Robert Van Pelt, *Forest Giants of the Pacific Coast* (Vancouver: Global Forest Society, in association with Seattle: University of Washington Press, 2001), 128.

the logging had stopped here: Stephen F. Arno and Ramona P. Hammerly, *Northwest Trees: Identifying and Understanding the Region's Native Trees* (Seattle: Mountaineers Books, 2017), 83. The loggers in Lynn Valley would have hauled out anything that had value. Possibly the logging occurred before forestry companies realized the value of western hemlocks as a timber tree; before around 1920, they thought that eastern hemlock had more value.

"You can't catch fish": Norman Maclean, *A River Runs Through It* (Chicago: University of Chicago Press, 1989), 42.

This western hemlock is the fourth biggest: Big-tree tracker Mick Bailey writes on his blog, "Norvan's Castle is, by volume, the fourth largest western hemlock on the planet. Its nine foot diameter at breast height also makes it the widest one on record! The three trees that are of larger volume are all south of the border on Washington State's Olympic Peninsula." Mick Bailey, "Finding Norvan's Castle," BC *Tree Hunter* (blog), December 20, 2019, bctreehunter.wordpress .com/2019/12/20/finding-norvans-castle/#more-5932.

BC Big Tree Registry: The BC Big Tree Registry includes trees that have been planted, so long as they're native species.

the mountains remain largely intact: Mountains do grow over time, but they also erode. What changes more quickly is our ability to take precise measurements, as was done of Mount Everest in December 2020. Ankit Adhikari and Joanna Slater, "It's Official: Mount Everest Just Got a Little Bit Higher," *The Washington Post*, December 8, 2020, washingtonpost.com/world/asia_pacific/ mount-everest-height-nepal-china/2020/12/08/a7b3ad1e-389a-11eb-aad9- 8959227280c4_story.html.

The term bending the map*:* I'm grateful to Wade Ellett for his explanation of the term: "Stop Bending the Map: Rule #81," *Intrepid Daily*, June 10, 2019, intrepiddaily.com/stop-bending-the-map/.

this Champion was likely more than three hundred years old: Arno and Hammerly, *Northwest Trees*, 81–82.

"multiple tops": Van Pelt, *Forest Giants*, 128.

"Amateurs know that contributing": Austin Kleon, *Show Your Work! 10 Ways to Share Your Creativity and Get Discovered* (New York: Workman Publishing, 2014), 16.

2: The Seed

his name is appropriately repeated: Shaun Muc, another tracker, who fell in love with big trees in the 1990s when visiting Meares Island off Tofino, never met Randy Stoltmann, but he named his oldest son after him (middle name). Correspondence with Shaun Muc, April 2022.

he launched the registry in 1986: Harley Rustad, *Big Lonely Doug: The Story of One of Canada's Last Great Trees* (Toronto: House of Anansi, 2018), 194. The BC Forestry Association later became Forest Education BC and then FORED BC Society. BC Big Tree Website, "About," The University of British Columbia, Faculty of Forestry, bigtrees.forestry.ubc.ca/about/.

Lyell Island (Haida Gwaii) protests: Thanks to Greg Herringer for pointing out the significance of Lyell Island (Haida Gwaii) in the history of logging protests in BC.

support the understory: If left alone, replanted forest eventually ages into old-growth forest, the designation clear through age as well as the complexity of the ecosystem. Foresters can speed up this process by removing the tops of trees and thinning them out to allow more light to reach the forest floor. I learned about this shift from second-growth to old-growth forests in this video: *Bringing Back the Light: Restoring the Life to Canada's Temperate Rainforests* (Wyatt Visuals, 2015), vimeo.com/131506757.

the Interior Wet Belt: Herringer review.

Tragically, Stoltmann died: Useful for my research on Stoltmann was this brief bio: "Randy Stoltmann, #269," Bivouac.com, bivouac.com/UsrPg .asp?UsrId=269.

A grove in the newly formed Carmanah Walbran Provincial Park: Heaven Grove was renamed the Randy Stoltmann Commemorative Grove in 2015 ("Randy Stoltmann, #269," Bivouac.com). Mick Bailey shared with me that the Randy Stoltmann Wilderness Area, which covers the upper Elaho to Meager Creek, is also named after him. Manuscript review by Mick Bailey, August 2022.

protecting land as a provincial park: Mick Bailey, "Protecting Ancient Trees in British Columbia," BC *Tree Hunter* (blog), August 29, 2021, bctreehunter .wordpress.com/2021/08/29/protecting-ancient-trees-in-british-columbia/.

After his death, the physical records: Rustad, *Big Lonely Doug*, 195; BC Big Tree Website, "About."

The committee now maintains the registry: Thanks to Sally Aitken for her help with this section. Big-tree registries are maintained by a range of groups from universities and governments to nonprofits and registered charities. Canada doesn't have a national registry, only local registries. American Forests holds the National Register of Champion Trees across the U.S., and there are additional state-specific registries. The Tree Register of the British Isles has a database of over 200,000 notable trees, with more than 69,000 Champions across Britain and Ireland. The Archangel Ancient Tree Archive, cofounded by David Milarch, also gathers Champion trees but in a more literal sense than a digital registry: the team collects cuttings from the largest and oldest trees and stumps, clones them, and replants them to create a living library around the world. Their aim is to reproduce the strongest, longest-living trees and reforest groves to help reverse the effects of climate change.

Fred Besley: Jim Robbins, *The Man Who Planted Trees: A Story of Lost Groves, the Science of Trees, and a Plan to Save the Planet* (New York: Spiegel & Grau, 2012), 17–18. The term *Champion* is well used among other big-tree registries. Fred Besley came up with the formula for determining the tree score, and in 1925 he compiled the first list of Champion trees (Rustad, *Big Lonely Doug*, 196; BC Big Tree Website). Besley was inspired to create the Champions list in response to logging out old-growth, specifically big trees, in the state of Maryland. Francis Zumbrun, "Fred W. Besley," Maryland's Conservation History, dnr.maryland.gov/centennial/Pages/Centennial-Notes/MFA_ Event_Zumbrun2.aspx.

Champions are assessed using a score: Tree score is formally referred to as the U.S. Champion Tree Score. American Forests refers to the tree score as AF or AFA points. The tree score is distinct from the tree volume, which refers to the amount of wood and is measured in cubic feet. Diameter at breast height assumes a height of 1.37 meters above level ground or the germination point of the tree, above the natural flare of many trees; it is to be measured on the higher side of the tree if growing on a slope. There are other considerations to take into account when the tree is growing at an angle (leaning), has burls (large bulges at root level), or is multistemmed.

"There's no reason why": *Giant Tree Hunters*, written, directed, and produced by Sean Horlor and Steve Adams (Telus/Storyhive, 2017), youtube.com/ watch?v=TmIo6pF-R90.

"Life shrinks or expands": Anaïs Nin, *The Diary of Anaïs Nin, 1939–1944* (San Diego: Harvest/HBJ, 1969), 125.

3: Hit It and Quit It

The Sweetness of a Simple Life: Diana Beresford-Kroeger, *The Sweetness of a Simple Life: Tips for Healthier, Happier and Kinder Living From a Visionary Natural Scientist* (Toronto: Vintage Canada, 2015). For more on Diana, I highly recommend her memoir, *To Speak for the Trees*, and her classic *The Global Forest*.

Tudor-style building: The community center site includes Aberthau Mansion, a Tudor-style home that's now a popular wedding venue; its name is often used interchangeably for the location.

I was looking for a Scouler's willow: Mary Jewell nominated the Champion Scouler's willow. She is an artist and a good friend of big-tree tracker Ralf Kelman. Mick Bailey, "The Grove That Time Forgot," *BC Tree Hunter* (blog), February 22, 2019, bctreehunter.wordpress.com/2019/02/22/ the-grove-that-time-forgot/#more-4162.

Scouler's leaves are "velvety" and "oblong": Arno and Hammerly, *Northwest Trees*, 153. David Tracey, *Vancouver Tree Book: A Living City Field Guide* (Vancouver: Pure Wave Media, 2016), 180.

beginner's mind, or shoshin: Shunryu Suzuki, *Zen Mind, Beginner's Mind* (Boulder, CO: Shambhala Publications, 2006), 1.

"the mind that is innocent": Zenkei Blanche Hartman, "The Zen of Not Knowing," *Tricycle*, January 6, 2022, tricycle.org/trikedaily/zen-not-knowing/.

"We are not practicing to become good meditators": Sebene Selassie, *You Belong: A Call for Connection* (New York: HarperOne, 2020), chap. 3, Overdrive/Kobo.

"Summit moments are private affairs": Bernadette McDonald, *Winter 8000: Climbing the World's Highest Mountains in the Coldest Season* (Sheffield: Vertebrate Publishing, 2020), 117.

Shaun Muc: Shaun and Ralf often tracked trees together, beginning in the '90s.

This Champion towered above: Bitter cherry and chokecherry are related, but chokecherry and bitter cherry count as separate native species in the registry. This bitter cherry was likely a variety called *P. emarginata* var. *mollis.* Arno and Hammerly, *Northwest Trees,* 193.

bitter cherry bark is traditionally used: Dr. Luschiim Arvid Charlie and Nancy J. Turner, *Luschiim's Plants: Traditional Indigenous Foods, Materials and Medicines* (Madeira Park, BC: Harbour Publishing, 2021), 110. The thirst-quencher fact also comes from this book.

there's a good chance its days are numbered: I learned from Ralf Kelman in April 2022 that the lot was cleared when they redeveloped the Phibbs Exchange. In August 2022, I verified that the tree is gone.

There are no automatic protections for Champion trees: Bailey, "Protecting Ancient Trees."

"The first step to conserving": Forest ecologist Andy MacKinnon, a member of the committee, notes in *Giant Tree Hunters,* "People have taken the list [of trees] and used it in campaigns to try and save some of these trees, some of these groves of trees, and sometimes valleys."

"Trees grow, die": Gerald B. Straley, *Trees of Vancouver: A Guide to the Common and Unusual Trees of the City* (Vancouver: UBC Press, 1992), xiii.

"Humans are a species adapted": David George Haskell, *The Songs of Trees: Stories From Nature's Great Connectors* (New York: Viking, 2017), 64.

"trees are not only embodied recorders": Dalia Nassar and Margaret M. Barbour, "Rooted," *Aeon,* October 16, 2019, aeon.co/essays/what-can-an-embodied-history-of-trees-teach-us-about-life.

"If I go out to record a door-slam": Michael Ondaatje, *The Conversations: Walter Murch and the Art of Editing Film* (Toronto: Vintage Canada, 2002), 234.

CW&T, a design duo in Brooklyn: CW&T, "Personal Body Unit Index," Kickstarter campaign, November 19, 2016, kickstarter.com/projects/cwandt/personal-body-unit-index.

Champions usually aren't identified: The Red Creek Fir does have a sign indicating it's the Champion Douglas-fir in Canada.

Stuart Roosa: NASA estimates two thousand seeds or more were brought on the 1971 lunar launch, but other accounts say several hundred or five hundred.

Moon trees, living and dead: The Wikipedia article is excellent on the topic of Moon trees: en.wikipedia.org/wiki/Moon_tree. Also helpful: Jessica Leigh Hester, "Whatever Happened to All the Moon Trees?" *Atlas Obsura*, February 1, 2019, atlasobscura.com/articles/what-happened-to-moon-trees; Marina Koren, "We Almost Forgot About the Moon Trees," *The Atlantic*, January 31, 2022, theatlantic.com/science/archive/2022/01/nasa-moon-trees-apollo/621395/; Dr. David A. Williams, "The 'Moon Trees,'" NASA, last updated August 12, 2022, nssdc.gsfc.nasa.gov/planetary/lunar/moon_tree.html.

"I always feel such curiosity": Jori Lewis, "The Eternal Tree," *Emergence Magazine*, March 17, 2022, emergencemagazine.org/essay/the-eternal-tree/.

4: Like Shooting Fish in a Barrel

its slogan was City of Parks: Surrey's official slogan is now *Progressio per diversitatem*, though its former slogan, The Future Lives Here, is still more often on signage.

Nina Shoroplova: Nina Shoroplova, *Legacy of Trees: Purposeful Wandering in Vancouver's Stanley Park* (Victoria: Heritage House, 2020), front flap.

Stanley Park was officially named: Shoroplova, *Legacy of Trees*, 13–15.

The tallest known tree in Vancouver: Ira Sutherland named Second Chance Grove. With Flora Hugon, he measured this tallest known tree in Vancouver using lidar and ground-truthing (verifying measurements with "boots on the ground" inspection). Ira Sutherland, "The Stanley Park Forest," *Vancouver Big Tree Hiking Guide*, vancouversbigtrees.com/stanley-park/.

Despite the fires: Correspondence with Ira Sutherland, June 2022.

some of the largest bigleaf maples: Sutherland, "The Stanley Park Forest."

Bigleaf maples can generate: To learn more about how old the "mats" of bigleaf maples can be, check out Karen Price, Erica B. Lilles, and Allen Banner, "Long-Term Recovery of Epiphytic Communities in the Great Bear Rainforest of Coastal British Columbia," *Forest Ecology and Management* 391 (May 1, 2017), 296–308, doi.org/10.1016/j.foreco.2017.02.023. Licorice fern also grows on alder and rocks, and the roots can be used to make tea (Charlie and Turner, *Luschiim's Plants*, 36–37). The Hul'q'umi'num' name for licorice fern growing on bigleaf maple is tl'usiip-s tu ts'alhulhp.

fifteen-meter-high western red-cedar stump: The Hollow Tree is burned out and "has the greatest diameter of any tree—living or dead—in Stanley Park, nearly 18 feet, 5.5 metres." Stoltmann, *Hiking Guide*, 43. Ira Sutherland agreed that it's likely the widest tree in the park, but there is a close contender. Correspondence with Ira Sutherland, June 2022.

the Hollow Tree, into which you can easily walk: For the history of the Hollow Tree and efforts to save it, see Harold Kalman and Lorne Whitehead, "Conservation of the Hollow Tree in Vancouver's Stanley Park," *Apt Bulletin* 42, no. 4 (2011), apti.org/assets/docs/Kalman-42-4.pdf. Kalman and Whitehead put the tree's age at one thousand years; another report says eight hundred. Chad Pawson, "Douglas Coupland's Golden Tree Unveiled in Vancouver," CBC News, August 7, 2016, cbc.ca/amp/1.3710622.

the Chandelier Tree: "Chandelier Tree," Wikipedia, en.wikipedia.org/wiki/Chandelier_Tree; "Shrine," Famous Redwoods, famousredwoods.com/shrine/.

The Hollow Tree became a popular spot: The Hollow Tree died in about 1875. Kalman and Whitehead, "Conservation of the Hollow Tree."

Historical photos: Kalman and Whitehead, "Conservation of the Hollow Tree"; *The Hollow Tree* (Ramshackle Pictures), vimeo.com/62641764. Meg Stanley mentions the bar at 7:11 in the video.

"when we were first born": Charlie and Turner, *Luschiim's Plants*, 73–74.

Stripped-bark trees: It's sometimes difficult to tell the difference between a cedar that grew with the inner bark exposed in a strip and a CMT. If there are branches growing on the strip, it's likely not a CMT. A cedar can be considered a CMT if it's altered in one or more of these ways: with a strip or plank removed, or with a small piece of bark removed to examine the health and strength of the wood.

BC's Heritage Conservation Act: This government publication is a terrific resource on CMTs: BC Ministry of Small Business, Tourism and Culture, *Culturally Modified Trees of British Columbia* (Resources Inventory Committee, 2001), for.gov.bc.ca/hfd/pubs/docs/mr/mr091/cmthandbook.pdf.

Typhoon Freda: The Hollow Tree (Ramshackle Pictures); Maryse Zeidler, "Typhoon Freda Slams BC Coast in 1962," CBC News, October 15, 2016, cbc.ca/news/canada/british-columbia/archives-typhoon-freda-1962-1.3806345. Typhoon Freda was downgraded to a tropical storm by the time it reached BC. Storms that knock down big trees open spaces in the canopy for light to stream through, allowing smaller trees the opportunity to grow.

Vancouver Park Board and arborists: The Hollow Tree (Ramshackle Pictures), 7:55.

In early 2008: Footage from Global News in *The Hollow Tree* (Ramshackle Pictures).

received permission from the Park Board: The Hollow Tree (Ramshackle Pictures), 8:55.

Called the Golden Tree: Douglas Coupland, "Golden Tree," coupland.com/
golden-tree/.

stump-inspired art within Vancouver: Thanks to Ira Sutherland's *Vancouver
Big Tree Hiking Guide* for highlighting *Trans Am Totem* by Marcus Bowcott and
Your Kingdom to Command by Marina Roy.

The artwork pays homage: "Trans Am Totem," Vancouver Biennale,
vancouverbiennale.com/artworks/trans-am-totem/.

She found the nurse stump: In an artist's talk, Roy notes that the 1886 fire that
leveled Vancouver traveled as far as Maple Ridge, and she reckons that some of
the huge stumps she played in as a kid in Coquitlam were the result of that fire.
I suspect that a lot of them were left over from logging the area. "Artist's Talk:
Marina Roy," Vancouver Art Gallery, June 7, 2016, vimeo.com/179779281.

In her artist's statement: Marina Roy, "Your Kingdom to Command,"
marinaroy.ca/art/your-kingdom-to-command/.

two hundred to three hundred years old: Arno and Hammerly, *Northwest Trees*, 206.

the "helmet" was not as intact: Stoltmann notes that the trunk is hollow.
Stoltmann, *Hiking Guide*, 43.

Alder typically blends in: "This multiple trunked tree likely began its life as a
cluster of saplings which over the years grew together at the base." Stoltmann,
Hiking Guide, 41.

Male catkins are brownish: Arno and Hammerly aptly describe the male catkins
as "tassels." *Northwest Trees*, 166.

The male catkins are edible: Arno and Hammerly, *Northwest Trees*, 166.

likely forty to sixty years old: "Red alders attain their maximum height of 100 to
110 feet (30 to 33 m) in about sixty years and then lose vigor as heart rot sets
in. On good sites, red alders can reach 70 to 80 feet (21 to 24 m) in height by
age twenty, outgrowing all other trees except black cottonwood." Arno and
Hammerly, *Northwest Trees*, 166–167.

5: Here Comes Trouble!

MacMillan Provincial Park: In 1944, H. R. MacMillan donated 336 acres
to the province to become a provincial park. This land had been stewarded
by the K'ómoks, Snaw-naw-as, and Te'mexw since time immemorial.
"Cathedral Grove, MacMillan Provincial Park," Parksville Qualicum Beach,
visitparksvillequalicumbeach.com/things-to-do/parks-nature/cathedral-grove/.

Stoltmann noted in 1987: Stoltmann, *Hiking Guide*, 120.

Mountain Equipment Co-op: RIP Mountain Equipment Co-op, which has since
been sold and rebranded as Mountain Equipment Company.

Cascaras aren't valuable as timber: Arno and Hammerly, *Northwest Trees*, 213–215. Dr. Luschiim Arvid Charlie writes about gathering and selling bark as medicine. Charlie and Turner, *Luschiim's Plants*, 101.

the cascara Champion in the registry: Shirley Ward nominated the tree in 2003, and its Champion status was verified the same year.

the province sold a parcel of the forest: Andrew Findlay, "$73 Million Crown Land Sell-Off Revs Up," *The Tyee*, March 26, 2004, thetyee.ca/ News/2004/03/26/%2473_Million_Crown_Land_Sell-off_Revs_Up/.

cleared part of the forest in 2010: Char Olson, "Lannan Forest destruction" comment, Animal Advocates Watchdog, February 15, 2010, animaladvocates.com/ watchdog.pl?md=read;id=13262.

Residents have resisted the sale: George Le Masurier, "Brooklyn Creek: It's Surviving but Faces Old and New Threats From Upstream Development," *Decaf Nation*, December 10, 2018, decafnation.net/2018/12/10/brooklyn-creek-its-surviving-but-faces-old-and-new-threats-from-upstream-development. The Brooklyn Creek Watershed Society is active in restoring this area (brooklyncreek.ca).

Sir Daniel Samson: Wayne Nikolaisen and Tyson Knowles nominated Sir Daniel Samson in 2005 and named it after Nikolaisen's cousin. Correspondence with Christine Chourmouzis and Bill Beese, August 2022.

largest known yellow-cedar in the world: "World's Largest Yellow Cedars Are on Vancouver Island," *Vancouver Island Big Trees* (blog), May 3, 2015, vancouverislandbigtrees.blogspot.com/2013/05/worlds-largest-yellow-cedars.html.

"an interesting incentive for people": Giant Tree Hunters.

"Thousands around [Canada] mailed": Rustad, *Big Lonely Doug*, 101.

"For some reason, it's difficult": Jordan Kisner, "A Theory of Immortality," *Thin Places: Essays From In Between* (New York: Farrar, Straus and Giroux, 2020), Kobo.

often given military names: Other significant trees are named after the presidents in office when the tree was measured, like Lincoln (a sequoia, the fourth largest tree in the world), or are assigned names retroactively. A tree named in the 1990s is the Franklin Tree after Benjamin Franklin "as it fits in with the Founding Fathers theme already present in this section of the forest, as well as with the obvious physical similarities"—"stout, balding, and aged." Van Pelt, *Forest Giants*, 13.

"Giant sequoias were discovered": There have been challenges to this naming practice, as Van Pelt points out regarding General Sherman, the largest known living single-stem tree in the world: "The fact that the world's largest tree is

named after a brutally savage yet brilliant general does not sit well with many people." General Sherman was, for a time, named after Karl Marx. Van Pelt, *Forest Giants*, 4.

General Grant: "General Grant (tree)," Wikipedia, en.wikipedia.org/wiki/ General_Grant_(tree).

General Sherman: "General Sherman (tree)," Wikipedia, en.wikipedia.org/ wiki/General_Sherman_(tree).

Admiral Broeren: The runners-up for biggest yellow-cedar are in the Sayward Valley. Local foresters named them Admiral Broeren (second biggest) after Menzies Bay forester Martin Broeren, an avid boater, and General Buxton (fifth biggest) after Ken Buxton, the general foreman of the area. Van Pelt, *Forest Giants*, 88.

General Buxton: Van Pelt, *Forest Giants*, 92.

Sergeant RandAlly: "The 'sergeant' in the name comes from their desire to call it after the highest enlisted rank, as they were engineers and not management" (Van Pelt, *Forest Giants*, 89). Beese recommended a buffer around Sergeant RandAlly to protect it (Van Pelt, *Forest Giants*, 89). Sergeant RandAlly fell naturally due to windthrow or ice and snow over the winter of 2003–2004. "World's Largest Yellow Cedars," *Vancouver Island Big Trees*.

Castle Fire of 2020: Alex Fox, "Fire Destroyed 10 Percent of World's Giant Sequoias Last Year—Can They Survive Climate Change?" *Smithsonian Magazine*, June 11, 2021, smithsonianmag.com/smart-news/ fire-destroyed-10-percent-worlds-giant-sequoias-last-year-180977947.

Treebeard, a cedar: "Ancient Forest/Chun T'oh Whudujut Provincial Park," BC Parks, bcparks.ca/explore/parkpgs/ancient-forest.

"We don't have the luxury": Justine Hunter, "For Vancouver Island's Old-Growth Explorers, Naming Trees Is a Delight but Saving Them Is a Challenge," *The Globe and Mail*, January 7, 2020, theglobeandmail.com/canada/ article-for-vancouver-islands-old-growth-explorers-naming-trees-is-a-delight.

He's one of the minds: Andrew Findlay, "A Closer Look at B.C. Forestry and Tall Tree Tourism," *Douglas*, October 3, 2019, douglasmagazine .com/a-closer-look-at-b-c-forestry-and-tall-tree-tourism.

The Pacheedaht First Nation's name: Barb Sligl, "In B.C., the Biggest Sights Include Massive Ancient Trees. Here's How Tourism Can Prove They're 'Worth More Standing,'" *Toronto Star*, August 14, 2021, thestar.com/life/ travel/2021/08/14/in-bc-the-biggest-sights-include-massive-ancient-trees- heres-how-tourism-can-prove-theyre-worth-more-standing.html.

"wide bluff overlooking the river": Lisa C., "The Sanctity of Avatar Grove," *Victoria Guest Services Network* (blog), April 28, 2020, vgsn.ca/post/the-sanctity-of-avatar-grove.

It was their fishing camp: Rustad, *Big Lonely Doug*, 131.

That's the problem with OGMAs: "Some OGMAs are intact groves untouched by commercial logging, while others are younger second-growth stands that are off limits to logging and maintained to achieve old-growth characteristics." Rustad, *Big Lonely Doug*, 139–140. Thanks to Ken Wu for reviewing this section in August 2022.

Avatar Grove was declared a recreation site: Rustad, *Big Lonely Doug*, 139–143.

"I used to name them": Correspondence with Sean O'Rourke, April 2022.

Finding and naming the tree: "Activist organizations often defend the language by saying that their 'discovery' is not to say they were the first to ever see the tree or walk the grove, but that they are the first to recognize the tourism or recreation potential and significance of the trees." Rustad, *Big Lonely Doug*, 131.

it might be regarded as sacred: I have heard of these large trees referred to as Grandfather or Grandmother Trees in different Indigenous traditions.

"Things are what you call them": Ahmir "Questlove" Thompson and Ben Greenman, *Mo' Meta Blues* (New York: Grand Central Publishing, 2013), chap. 17, Overdrive/Kobo. He was referring to his own self-appointed hip-hop name but also the name of his band, The Roots, which evolved over time, and their album titles.

old-school method of tree tracking: For an account of using clues to find Hyperion, the tallest tree in the world, see Mario D. Vaden, "Hyperion Coast Redwood," *Coast Redwood Adventures* (blog), mdvaden.com/redwood_hyperion.shtml. In BC, big-tree trackers have been trying to piece together the location of a huge cedar measured by Maywell Wickheim, who did not divulge its location before his death.

yellow-cedar's foliage: Arno and Hammerly, *Northwest Trees*, 125–129. "Yellow-cedar's foliage is dark bluish green and hangs limp, giving the tree a weeping appearance." Arno and Hammerly, *Northwest Trees*, 125.

The thin metal tape: Generally, it's helpful to take a photo of the d-tape in situ, making the measurement of the tree visible as further proof of its girth.

The Indian Act: Bob Joseph, *21 Things You May Not Know About the Indian Act: Helping Canadians Make Reconciliation With Indigenous Peoples a Reality* (Vancouver: Page Two Books), 2018.

The treaty recognizes: "Understanding the Treaty," Nisga'a Lisims Government, nisgaanation.ca/understanding-treaty; "Nisga'a Nation," British Columbia, www2.gov.bc.ca/gov/content/environment/natural-resource-stewardship/consulting-with-first-nations/first-nations-negotiations/first-nations-a-z-listing/nisga-a-lisims-government.

crush invaders: Metal as fuck. "Gitwangak (Kitwanga)," Simon Fraser University, sfu.ca/brc/virtual_village/gitxsan/gitwangak.html.

dozens of big cottonwoods: Along with colleagues from the BC Big Tree Committee, and building on fieldwork done by Ralf Kelman, Will Koop, Shaun Muc, and Randy Stoltmann in the 1980s and '90s on Skumalasph Island in the Stó:lō Nation, applied anthropologist Sean O'Rourke located a larger single-stem cottonwood. O'Rourke, interim report, April 2022.

Cottonwood is often used: Dr. Luschiim Arvid Charlie writes about its uses as a face cream, salve, and shampoo. Charlie and Turner, *Luschiim's Plants*, 106.

"Only those that start life": Haskell, *The Songs of Trees*, 165–166.

it must be the Champion: Mike Plunkard, an arborist in Terrace, BC, nominated the tree in 2014 and verified it in 2015.

"the ordinary furniture of daily life": Sean Sheehan, "Selections From William Eggleston's Masterwork, *The Democratic Forest*," *LensCulture*, lensculture.com/articles/william-eggleston-selections-from-william-eggleston-s-masterwork-the-democratic-forest.

"democratic" nature of Eggleston's project: For more on Eggleston's process, Holborn's role as editor, and the differences between the single-edition photobook and the ten-volume edition, see Alec Soth, "Rambling Through Eggleston's Democratic Forest," YouTube video, February 5, 2021, youtube.com/watch?v=Kj6efh1msH4&t=3s.

Douglas maples: Arno and Hammerly, *Northwest Trees*, 208.

Indigenous Peoples of the islands: Charlie and Turner, *Luschiim's Plants*, 86, 88.

Trees are protected if they grow: Bailey, "Protecting Ancient Trees."

Coastal Legacy Tree Program: BC Timber Sales has twelve operating regions, and Greg Herringer and others at BCTS are pushing to expand the Coastal Legacy Tree Program province-wide.

BCTS voluntarily retains the tree: Among the four species in the Coastal Legacy Tree Program, if the tree is larger than that species' tenth largest in the Big Tree Registry, BCTS will nominate the tree for the registry, which isn't necessarily a good thing. Being included on the registry doesn't automatically save the tree, and a larger DBH pushes the threshold higher. In recent years, BCTS has come under fire for auctioning some old-growth timber for harvest, such as huge trees that were cleared in the Nahmint Valley in Hupacasath territory and Tseshaht territory. Judith Lavoie, "The Government Agency at the Centre of B.C.'s Old-Growth Logging Showdown," *The Narwhal*, July 15, 2019, thenarwhal.ca/the-government-agency-at-the-centre-of-b-c-s-old-growth-logging-showdown; Chad Pawson, "Logging Watchdog Probes Government Agency Over Felled B.C. Old-Growth Trees," CBC News, December 23, 2018, cbc.ca/news/canada/british-columbia/british-columbia-forest-practises-board-nahmint-valley-logging-1.4957637.

The tree was nominated: Brandin Schultz nominated and verified the maple in 2001.

"My regular routine here": Barry Lopez, *Horizon* (New York: Knopf, 2019), 220–221.

"You are not breathing pollution": Naomi Klein, "In a Summer of Wildfires and Hurricanes, My Son Asks 'Why Is Everything Going Wrong?'" *The Intercept*, September 9, 2017, theintercept.com/2017/09/09/in-a-summer-of-wildfires-and-hurricanes-my-son-asks-why-is-everything-going-wrong.

6: Attention Grows

"I think about trees all the time": Giant Tree Hunters.

"I have a bit of a GPS": Giant Tree Hunters.

"I must admit that not all blues thrill me": Maggie Nelson, *Bluets* (Seattle: Wave Books, 2009), 14.

Oliver Burkeman: Oliver Burkeman, *Four Thousand Weeks: Time Management for Mortals* (Toronto: Allen Lane, 2021), 143.

Aldous Huxley: Aldous Huxley, *Island* (London: Vintage, 2005), chap. 14, Overdrive/Kobo.

Gina Rae La Cerva: Gina Rae La Cerva, *Feasting Wild: In Search of the Last Untamed Food* (Vancouver: Greystone, 2020), 23–24.

In How to Do Nothing*:* Jenny Odell, *How to Do Nothing: Resisting the Attention Economy* (Brooklyn: Melville House, 2019), 81.

"After birds, there were trees": Odell, *How to Do Nothing*, 122.

"We might seek to incorporate": Burkeman, *Four Thousand Weeks*, 158.

Katie Arnold: Katie Arnold, "An Elite Athlete's Real-Life Training Plan," *The New York Times*, July 9, 2019, nytimes.com/2019/07/09/well/move/leadville-katie-arnold-ultramarathon-training-parenthood.html.

Dr. Kaeli Swift: @corvidresearch, Instagram post caption, May 17, 2020, instagram.com/p/CATMHtyAXQ_/.

an arborist on Instagram: Thanks, Matthew Beatty!

"Attention is the beginning": Mary Oliver, *Upstream: Selected Essays* (New York: Penguin, 2016), chap. "Upstream," ebook.

"Attention . . . just is life": Burkeman, *Four Thousand Weeks*, 91.

Walter Murch: Ondaatje, *The Conversations*, 10.

Kirsten Johnson: The Criterion Channel, "Masterclass: Kirsten Johnson," filmed at Traverse City Film Festival, 2016, criterionchannel.com/masterclass-kirsten-johnson.

three significant botanical gardens: The botanical gardens that include arboreta are VanDusen Botanical Garden and Queen Elizabeth Park, which both border Shaughnessy, and the UBC Botanical Garden.

Todd considered hundreds of tree species: Alwyn Rutherford, "The Shaughnessy Heights Landscape: Symbolizing the Power of the CPR Company in Vancouver, 1887–1914," British Columbia Society of Landscape Architects, 2021, bcsla.org/sites/default/files/Tattersfield-A-Rutherford%5B1%5D.pdf; Vancouver Heritage Foundation, "Places That Matter: The Crescent," placesthatmatter.ca/location/the-crescent/; City of Vancouver, "Shaughnessy (History and Heritage)," vancouver.ca/news-calendar/shaughnessy.aspx.

arboreta used to be grown: Michael Hickman and James H. Soper, "Arboretum," *The Canadian Encyclopedia*, last edited March 4, 2015, thecanadianencyclopedia.ca/en/article/arboretum.

Arboreta date back: "Arboretum," Wikipedia, en.wikipedia.org/wiki/Arboretum.

"'peopling' of the forest": Kyo Maclear, "A Small Walk," *Brick* 102, November 27, 2018, brickmag.com/a-small-walk.

Braiding Sweetgrass: Robin Wall Kimmerer, *Braiding Sweetgrass: Indigenous Wisdom, Scientific Knowledge, and the Teachings of Plants* (Minneapolis: Milkweed Editions, 2013), 54.

If a maple is an it: Kimmerer, *Braiding Sweetgrass*, 57.

"Can we unlearn the language": Robin Wall Kimmerer, "Speaking of Nature," *Orion*, June 12, 2017, orionmagazine.org/article/speaking-of-nature.

her students in field school: Kimmerer, *Braiding Sweetgrass*, 224.

UBC's Point Grey campus: For more on the history of UBC's construction, see "A Brief History of UBC," The University of British Columbia, last updated May 27, 2022, archives.library.ubc.ca/general-history/a-brief-history-of-ubc/.

Kwikwetlem First Nation's name for the area: "The Place of the Great Blue Heron" has replaced "Riverview" in Google Maps and is now the dominant name, also used by BC Housing (sumiqwuelu.com). Learn more about the role of the Kwikwetlem First Nation in determining the future of the site: "səmiq̓ʷəʔelə—Place of the Great Blue Heron," Kwikwetlem First Nation, March 10, 2021, kwikwetlem.com/blog/Place-of-the-Great-Blue-Heron.htm. "Apart from their stunning beauty, the trees are also a valuable gene pool. A recent assessment put the trees' individual worth at over $50 million, but as a collection the arboretum is worth far more than that." Crawford Kilian, "Riverview Hospital's Secrets," *The Tyee*, August 1, 2007, thetyee.ca/ Views/2007/08/01/Riverview/. See also "Riverview Hospital (Coquitlam)," Wikipedia, en.wikipedia.org/wiki/Riverview_Hospital_(Coquitlam).

After World War II: Straley, *Trees of Vancouver*, xv.

the Old Arboretum a bit forgotten: Correspondence with Ira Sutherland, June 2022.

crossed into the arboretum zone: Straley, *Trees of Vancouver*, xv. UBC has come under fire for clearing trees, some of them large and old. Ira Sutherland wrote an obituary for UBC's tallest tree, the Wesbrook Sentinel, a 60.5-meter Douglas-fir cut down to build condos: "Letter: An Obituary for UBC's Tallest Tree," British Columbia Community Forest Association, March 6, 2020, bccfa.ca/an-obituary-for-ubcs-tallest-tree.

Straley noted of the Sitka alder: Straley, *Trees of Vancouver*, 77.

Sitka alder commonly grows: Suzanne Simard, *Finding the Mother Tree: Discovering the Wisdom of the Forest* (Toronto: Allen Lane, 2021), 122–123. "Only occasionally, where this species descends to lower elevations in canyons west of the Cascades, does it become a small tree, up to 30 feet (9 m) tall." Arno and Hammerly, *Northwest Trees*, 167.

Jessica Francis Kane's narrator: Jessica Francis Kane, *Rules for Visiting: A Novel* (New York: Penguin, 2019), 182–183.

"A tree is not always a definite entity": Straley, *Trees of Vancouver*, xiii.

7: Three the Hard Way

an episode of his marketing and culture podcast: Seth Godin, "Ignore Sunk Costs," *Akimbo* (podcast), August 29, 2018, play.acast.com/s/akimbo/ignoresunkcosts.

the reserve of the Royal Navy: Matt Humphrey, "Tourist in Your Town: Burnaby, B.C.'s Central Park," CBC News, July 13, 2017, cbc.ca/news/canada/ british-columbia/burnaby-central-park-1.4204093; "Central Park (Burnaby)," Wikipedia, en.wikipedia.org/wiki/Central_Park_(Burnaby).

the National Audubon field guide: "The scientific name [*Acer circinatum*], meaning 'rounded' or 'circular,' refers to the leaf shape." National Audubon Society, *Field Guide to Trees: Western Region* (New York: Knopf, 1998), 530.

Marni Jackson: Marni Jackson, "What I Learned From a Summer of Not Catching a Single Fish," *The Walrus*, June 24, 2019, thewalrus.ca/ what-i-learned-from-a-summer-of-not-catching-a-single-fish/.

John Zada: John Zada, *In the Valleys of the Noble Beyond: In Search of the Sasquatch* (New York: Grove Press/Atlantic Monthly Press, 2019), 107.

In The Snow Leopard*:* Peter Matthiessen, *The Snow Leopard* (New York: Penguin Classics, 2008), 88.

"That the snow leopard is": Matthiessen, *The Snow Leopard*, 238.

the black hawthorn in the same area: Mary Jewell nominated the black hawthorn, as well as the Scouler's willow.

The wood is hard and useful: Roberta Parish and Sandra Thomson, *Tree Book: Learning to Recognize Trees of British Columbia* (Victoria: Ministry of Forests, n.d.), 126, for.gov.bc.ca/hfd/library/documents/treebook/treebook.pdf. For the face paint reference, see Charlie and Turner, *Luschiim's Plants*, 131.

Its Latin name, Crataegus douglasii*:* Arno and Hammerly, *Northwest Trees*, 198.

He built trails in the '90s: "Artist Searches for Giant Trees," *Wilderness Committee Educational Report* 16, no. 6 (Summer/Fall 2017), wildernesscommittee.org/sites/ all/files/publications/1997%2010%200ur%20choice.pdf.

8: Yew Complete Me

Tree *by Matthew Battles:* Battles tells us that "Today, we mostly do the yew as a woody shrub and an edge planting; but yews in the West have a long history of entanglement with humans: their springy wood was traditionally used in archer's bows, and long-lived individual trees are often found in the yards of medieval churches." Matthew Battles, *Tree* (New York: Bloomsbury, 2017), 59.

The vascular cambium and bark: "It takes 2000 Pacific yew trees to produce 0.5 kg (1 lb) of taxol." Randy Stoltmann, *Hiking the Ancient Forests of British Columbia and Washington* (Vancouver, BC: Lone Pine, 1996), 82.

"When the anticancer qualities of the yew": Simard, *Finding the Mother Tree*, 276.

"Churches and monasteries throughout Ireland": Robbins, *The Man Who Planted Trees*, 150.

planting a toxic yew: Found throughout Western Europe, churchyard yews are among the oldest living things in the world, some of them surely dating to pre-Christian times. This may speak to lost sacral meanings of the yew, as early European churches often were built at sites holy to Celtic and Germanic tribes... [I]t may [also] reflect the yew's useful toxicity, with trees cultivated to dissuade herdsmen from pasturing sheep and cattle in church burial grounds." Battles, *Tree*, 59–60. Also thanks to Seán and Angie Lewis (yes, my parents) for sharing this idea about toxic yews as a helpful "fence."

The area was logged extensively: Stoltmann, *Hiking Guide*, 49.

"I saw wilderness staring back at me": Kate Harris, *Lands of Lost Borders: Out of Bounds on the Silk Road* (Toronto: Knopf Canada, 2018), 116–117.

"I was completely swallowed up": The Rachel Carson Center, "Q&A with Jessica J. Lee," *Seeing the Woods* (blog), March 5, 2018, seeingthewoods.org/2018/03/05/qa-with-jessica-j-lee.

"It forced me not to be in my head": Shelagh Rogers, "Jessica J. Lee on 'Turning: A Year in the Water,'" *The Next Chapter*, CBC Radio, 2017, cbc.ca/news/jessica-j-lee-on-turning-a-year-in-the-water-1.4289355.

the forty-four wards: The ward system has since been revised and there are now twenty-five wards in Toronto.

"I think, as humans": Correspondence with Jake Tobin Garrett, January 2020 and August 2022.

"That was an enjoyable waste of time": Davis Vilums, "Cycling Through All the Streets in Central London," davis.vilums.me/all-the-streets.

Arlin ffrench: Tamara Baluja, "Vancouver Man Says He Cycled Every City Street Over 3 Years—Then Had His Bike Stolen," CBC News, November 17, 2019, cbc.ca/news/canada/british-columbia/biking-every-street-vancouver-1.5362107.

Jason Polan: Gideon Jacobs, "Artist Jason Polan Is Trying/Failing to Draw Every Person in NY," *Vice*, September 5, 2014, vice.com/amp/en_ca/article/qbexjm/jason-polan-405.

cautionary tale of Dr. Steve O'Shea: Grann, "The Squid Hunter."

"It's a fucking catastrophe": As Dr. Steve O'Shea told me over email in July 2022, in response to my request for an update on his quest to find a giant squid paralarva, "Yes, we were successful in capturing them, but not in ongrowing them."

9: Heir and a Spare

While WFP wasn't pressured: Special thanks to John Deal of Western Forest Products for reviewing this section and helping me understand the nuances of the standard.

VP of fiber supply: Titles are current at the time of writing and don't necessarily reflect their titles then.

not all trees are of interest: John Deal told me in August 2022, "Our standard includes a total of 11 tree species."

The film set for The Scarlet Letter*:* "White River Provincial Park," BC Parks, bcparks.ca/explore/parkpgs/wht_river.

newly measured Doug-fir: Here's an aside about another tree and another forestry company: the Carmanah Giant, a 96-meter Sitka spruce on western Vancouver Island that was measured in 1988, was the poster child for environmentalists working to protect the area from MacBlo's logging in the 1990s. Ironically, MacBlo had measured and named the tree. Rustad, *Big Lonely Doug*, 93–96.

The Douglas-fir is unique: The Douglas-fir bears the name of David Douglas, a botanist. The first half of its Latin name, *Pseudotsuga menziesii*, appointed in 1950, means "false hemlock," and the second half is after Archibald Menzies, botanist on the HMS *Discovery*, Captain George Vancouver's ship. "Menzies had been the first European botanist to document the tree when he encountered it on Vancouver Island." Rustad, *Big Lonely Doug*, 43. See also Rustad, *Big Lonely Doug*, chap. 3, and David Suzuki and Wayne Grady, *Tree: A Life Story,* rev. ed. (Vancouver: Greystone Books, 2018).

As David Suzuki and Wayne Grady recount: Suzuki and Grady, *Tree*, 30.

Doug-firs are anchored: Unlike Douglas-firs, redwoods have a mat-like web of shallow roots that interweave with their neighbors' roots, ensuring sturdiness through community.

Sustainability is built over the long term: Cf. David Wallace-Wells, *The Uninhabitable Earth: Life After Warming* (New York: Tim Duggan Books/ Crown, 2019), 78.

"Even if a scientist dedicated her whole career": Cara Giaimo, "Can Trees Live Forever? New Kindling for an Immortal Debate," *The New York Times,* July 27, 2020, nytimes.com/2020/07/27/science/trees-immortality.html.

"The trees made the past": Rebecca Solnit, *Orwell's Roses* (New York: Viking, 2021), chap. "Day of the Dead," Overdrive/Kobo.

"that describes the span of time": Solnit, *Orwell's Roses*, chap. "Day of the Dead," Overdrive/Kobo.

a book on the climate crisis: Wallace-Wells, *The Uninhabitable Earth*, 79.

the nutrients from salmon guts: Simard, *Finding the Mother Tree*, 289–292.

"To wallow in despair": Robert Bringhurst and Jan Zwicky, *Learning to Die: Wisdom in the Age of Climate Crisis* (Regina: University of Regina Press, 2018), 51.

"To remember how little you matter": Burkeman, *Four Thousand Weeks*, 210.

The registry accounts for these coastal and Interior varieties: There are currently forty-three species in the registry and fifty-five Champions, but more Champions will be added when Interior trees are nominated.

a reason for the aroma: Haskell, *The Songs of Trees*, 125.

The name ponderosa: Arno and Hammerly, *Northwest Trees*, 27.

Indigenous Peoples have long used ponderosa pine: Arno and Hammerly, *Northwest Trees*, 30, 32.

someone else measured a bigger one: In 2020, Terry Nelson nominated a bigger one, now the Champion.

Trina Moyles: I am grateful to author and lookout Trina Moyles for telling me about witness trees. Correspondence with Trina Moyles, February and July 2022.

A ladder would be run up a tree: Watchers lived in accommodation at the base of the lookout tree. "Lookout Tree," Wikipedia, en.wikipedia.org/wiki/Lookout_ tree. The Kaibab lookout trees were initially a budget-friendly measure, with platforms perched atop ponderosa pines; these were replaced with human-made structures in the 1930s. WhiskeyBristles, "Kaibab Lookout Trees," *Atlas Obscura*, December 12, 2018, atlasobscura.com/places/kaibab-lookout-trees.

10: Slow and Low

a huge black elderberry: I later confirmed with Christine Chourmouzis that elderberries are not included on the registry because they're considered a shrub.

This recreation site is popular: Stoltmann, *Hiking Guide*, 75.

"When a tree snaps in a windstorm": Shoroplova, *Legacy of Trees*, 63.

"like a wet rag on a salad": Tom Robbins, *Another Roadside Attraction* (New York: Bantam, 2003), 247.

"It is like a great uprooted tree": D. H. Lawrence, *Lady Chatterley's Lover* (London: Vintage, 2011), 24.

Grand fir doesn't live that long: Arno and Hammerly, *Northwest Trees*, 98.

Suzuki Roshi: Hartman, "The Zen of Not Knowing."

"I have an appreciation for novelty and uniqueness": Correspondence with Sean O'Rourke, April 2022.

It was last measured as 64.4 meters tall: Correspondence with Sean O'Rourke, November and December 2020.

The Totem Giant appears shorter: Ira Sutherland, "UBC's Forests and Big Trees," *Vancouver Big Tree Hiking Guide*, vancouversbigtrees.com/ ubcs-forests-and-big-trees/.

11: Secular Pilgrimage

Wendell Berry: Wendell Berry writes, "But it is a pilgrimage nevertheless because it is a religious quest." By *religious*, he doesn't mean within the confines of a religion: "[a] better term than religious might be worshipful, in the sense of *valuing* what one does not entirely understand, or aspiring beyond what may be known." Wendell Berry, "A Secular Pilgrimage," *The Hudson Review* 23, no. 3 (Autumn 1970), 401–424, sites.evergreen.edu/ politicalshakespeares/wp-content/uploads/sites/321/2015/09/Berry-Secular-Pilgrimage.pdf.

500,000 visitors annually: Joel Barde, "How Selfie Culture Ruins the Great Outdoors for Everyone Else," *The Walrus*, May 16, 2019, thewalrus.ca/ how-selfie-culture-ruins-the-great-outdoors-for-everyone-else.

Trees may be sacred: When CBC News covered the "discovery" of a large cedar in North Vancouver (see later in chapter 11), Squamish Nation Hereditary Chief találsamkin siyám (Bill Williams) spoke with journalist David P. Ball and pointed out that the Nation already knew about the tree (which grows on the unceded territory of both the Squamish and Tsleil-Waututh Nations).

In a critique of social media's effect: Barde, "How Selfie Culture."

By 2010, visitors started trekking: Associated Press, "California: Visitors to World's Tallest Tree Face $5,000 Fine and Possible Jail Time," *The Guardian*, August 2, 2022, theguardian.com/us-news/2022/aug/02/ california-redwood-hyperion-worlds-tallest-tree.

officials had done with Maya Bay: Barde, "How Selfie Culture"; Apinya Wipatayotin, "Maya Bay to Close Again for 2 Months," *Bangkok Post*, May 7, 2022, bangkokpost.com/thailand/general/2306110/maya-bay-to-close-again-for-2-months.

six months' jail time and a $5,000 fine: Associated Press, "California."

"experts put the cost of timber theft": Lyndsie Bourgon, *Tree Thieves: Crime and Survival in North America's Woods* (Vancouver: Greystone Books, 2022), 6–7.

He likened MacBlo's preservation: John Vaillant, *The Golden Spruce: A True Story of Myth, Madness and Greed* (Toronto: Vintage Canada, 2006), 138.

"The collective reaction to the loss of the golden spruce": Vaillant, *The Golden Spruce*, 139.

Robert Earle Howells: Robert Earle Howells, "Should We Hide the Locations of Earth's Greatest Trees?" *San Francisco Chronicle*, July 3, 2018, sfchronicle .com/travel/article/Should-we-hide-the-locations-of-Earth-s-13046894.php.

Stephen Sillett: Stephen Sillett is a focus of Richard Preston's wonderful book *The Wild Trees: A Story of Passion and Daring* (New York: Random House, 2007).

Chris Atkins and Michael Taylor nominated Hyperion in 2006, and Sillett climbed it to measure it.

the arrival fallacy: Rainesford Stauffer, "The Obsession With 'Getting Ahead' in Your Twenties Is Failing Young People," *Catapult*, May 27, 2021, catapult.co/stories/the-obsession-with-getting-ahead-in-your-twenties-is-failing-young-people-rainesford-stauffer.

the Randy Stoltmann Commemorative Grove: A separate tree is named after Stoltmann: the Stoltmann Cedar at Kennedy Lake near Tofino. Robert Van Pelt named this tree. Van Pelt, *Forest Giants*, 39.

"I don't have the virus": Gary Shteyngart, "Adjusting to the Prophylactic Life, Under Coronavirus Quarantine," *The New Yorker*, April 6, 2020, newyorker.com/magazine/2020/04/13/the-prophylactic-life.

more than forty thousand stems in Pando: "Pando (tree)," Wikipedia, en.wikipedia.org/wiki/Pando_(tree).

"We think that most important clues are large": Simard, *Finding the Mother Tree*, 15.

Sally Mann: Malcolm Daniel, "Southern Exposures: The Photography of Sally Mann," The Museum of Fine Arts, Houston, February 14, 2019, mfah.org/blogs/inside-mfah/southern-exposures-the-photography-of-sally-mann.

Like millions of others: "Travelers Turn to Tree.fm to Experience the Forest During the Pandemic," *Here & Now*, NPR, March 3, 2021, wbur.org/hereandnow/2021/03/03/tree-fm-forest-sounds.

This park used to be logged: Stoltmann, *Hiking Guide*, 20.

This exhibit also allowed visitors to experience: Art Gallery of Ontario, "Anthropocene in 3-D," *AGO Insider*, October 16, 2018, ago.ca/agoinsider/anthropocene-3-d.

In response to playing the game: Lewis Gordon, "Can Virtual Nature Be a Good Substitute for the Great Outdoors? The Science Says Yes," *The Washington Post*, April 28, 2020, washingtonpost.com/video-games/2020/04/28/can-virtual-nature-be-good-substitute-great-outdoors-science-says-yes/.

Alice Chirico: Gordon, "Can Virtual Nature."

Port Renfrew: Giant Tree Hunters.

trees are "worth more standing": Ancient Forest Alliance, "Economic Valuation of Old-Growth Forests on Vancouver Island," May 3, 2021, ancientforestalliance.org/old-growth-economic-report.

In the late 1990s and early 2000s: Manuscript review by Ken Wu, August 2022.

we are running out of prime trees: Ben Parfitt, "The Looming Crash Facing Down BC's Forest Industry," *The Tyee*, April 14, 2022, thetyee.ca/Analysis/2022/04/14/Looming-Crisis-Facing-BC-Forest-Industry.

Ben Parfitt: Parfitt, "The Looming Crash." As Ken Wu told me, "The 'high-grade overcutting' of the biggest and best old-growth trees that are most accessible in the valley bottoms and lower elevations [result] in diminishing returns as the trees get smaller, harder to reach, and [yield] lower returns." Wu review, August 2022.

"an arbitrary scale used to compare the gnarliness of trees": Van Pelt, *Forest Giants*, 195.

We started by visiting Jurassic Grove: "Jurassic Grove," Ancient Forest Alliance, ancientforestalliance.org/photos/jurassic-grove.

Jurassic Grove and Eden Grove: TJ Watt named Eden Grove. Before then, it was Christy Clark Grove, after the premier of BC; the feeling was that she wouldn't cut a forest named after her (Ken Wu conversation; Rustad, *Big Lonely Doug*, 145). Ken Wu told me that he nicknamed this forest Jurassic Grove so that if it is protected one day by being added to the adjacent Juan de Fuca Provincial Park, it may become Jurassic Park. Wu review, August 2022.

Big spruce were extensively logged: For more on spruce logging, see Richard A. Rajala, *Up-Coast: Forests and Industry on British Columbia's North Coast, 1870–2005* (Victoria: Royal BC Museum, 2006).

Huu-ay-aht First Nations in partnership with Western Forest Products: TFL 44 Limited Partnership, "TFL 44 Limited Partnership Holds First Board of Directors Meeting Advancing Vision of Stronger Forest Sector in Alberni Valley," news release, May 16, 2019, huuayaht.org/wp-content/uploads/2019/05/HFN-WFP-TFL44-LP-Board-Mtg-NR_FINAL.pdf; conversations with Greg Herringer of BCTS, April 2022, and John Deal of WFP, August 2022.

Red Creek Fir: The Red Creek Fir is sometimes referred to as the biggest known Douglas-fir in the world, but as Ira Sutherland pointed out in a June 2022 email, the Doug-firs in the Washington and Oregon registries are slightly larger in terms of points (tree score). Sutherland said that it also depends on how the tree is measured.

Stoltmann's posthumous hiking guide: Stoltmann, *Hiking the Ancient Forests*, 55.

Red Creek Fir access road: I later heard the Red Creek Fir is in relatively good health, and the road not too bad.

"In the middle of the clear-cut": Rustad, *Big Lonely Doug*, 170.

People had forgotten about the name by 2014: Interview with Ken Wu, June 2022.

the loggers turned the tree into a spar: Rustad, *Big Lonely Doug*, 178–179.

Cronin estimated its value at about $50,000: Rustad, *Big Lonely Doug*, 161.

The lumber in this cutblock under TFL 46: Rustad, *Big Lonely Doug*, 155.

"Because I liked it": Rustad, *Big Lonely Doug*, 243.

"Not only were big elder trees": Simard, *Finding the Mother Tree*, 42.

"I understood the pride of claiming": Simard, *Finding the Mother Tree*, 42.

Big Lonely Doug is more susceptible to windstorms: Rustad, *Big Lonely Doug*, 184–188. More big trees are dying these days because they are not protected by buffer trees, and the storms these days are bigger than ever.

"Parks are lovely to hike through": Harley Rustad, "Big Lonely Doug Should Become Canada's Next Provincial Park," *The Globe and Mail*, September 7, 2018, theglobeandmail.com/opinion/article-big-lonely-doug-should-become-canadas-next-provincial-park.

the New Democratic Party provincial government protected: BC Ministry of Forests, Lands, Natural Resource Operations and Rural Development, "Government Takes Action on Old Growth, Protects 54 Groves With Iconic Trees," news release, July 17, 2019, news.gov.bc.ca/releases/2019FLNR0189-001452.

"Most of those trees were already unofficially protected": Bailey, "Protecting Ancient Trees."

This legislation aims to conserve: BC Ministry of Forests, Lands, Natural Resource Operations and Rural Development, "Government Embarks On New Approach to Old Forests," news release, September 11, 2020, archive.news.gov.bc.ca/releases/news_releases_2017-2021/2020FLNR0058-001711.htm. Greg Herringer and John Deal offered perspectives on the aspirational quality of the measurement, and Herringer pointed out how many trees are actually protected.

the bigger the tree, particularly in diameter: "Prior to July of 2019, the Government of British Columbia had never enacted any mandatory regulations to protect trees on Crown land in the province based on their size," unless the trees were in OGMAS or Wildlife Management Areas. Bailey, "Protecting Ancient Trees."

Timothy Morton: Morton, *Dark Ecology*, chap. "The First Thread."

true conservation: Stoltmann, *Hiking Guide*, 19.

Darius Kinsey: Van Pelt, *Forest Giants*, 31; "Kinsey Brothers Photographs of the Lumber Industry and the Pacific Northwest, ca. 1890–1945," University Libraries Digital Collections, University of Washington, content.lib .washington.edu/clarkkinseyweb/index.html.

"Vancouver Island and the upper British Columbia mainland": Van Pelt, *Forest Giants*, 31.

"My goal has been to show people": Sarah Anderson, "Breathtaking 2,000-Year-Old Cedar Found in North Vancouver," *The Daily Hive*, June 26, 2022, dailyhive.com/vancouver/giant-cedar-found-north-vancouver.

living in a 10 percent world: J. B. MacKinnon, *The Once and Future World: Nature As It Was, As It Is, As It Could Be* (Toronto: Random House Canada, 2013), chap. 3, Overdrive/Kobo. (I was one of the editors of this book.)

"Twenty percent of the earth": MacKinnon, *The Once and Future World*, chap. 3, Overdrive/Kobo.

"the same wide smiles": MacKinnon, *The Once and Future World*, chap. 2, Overdrive/Kobo.

It stands to reason that even the biggest trees: Some conservation groups, such as the Sierra Club and AFA, suggest that big trees are akin to white rhinos. "'White Rhino' Map Shows Vancouver Island's Most Endangered Old-Growth Rainforests," Sierra Club BC, March 2018, sierraclub.bc.ca/white-rhino-map-shows-vancouver-islands-most-endangered-old-growth-rainforests; "Conservationists Welcome Old-Growth Panel Report and Positive First Steps by BC Government to Address Old-Growth Crisis," Ancient Forest Alliance, news release, September 11, 2020, ancientforestalliance.org/bc-old-growth-panel-report-announcement. Thanks to Ira Sutherland for help with this idea.

Yoko Ono tweeted: Yoko Ono, "When I created CEILING PAINTING," @yokoono, Twitter post, May 10, 2017, twitter.com/yokoono/status/862344486222999552?lang=en.

she'd printed YES: "*Ceiling Painting/Yes Painting*," Wikipedia, en.wikipedia .org/wiki/Ceiling_Painting/Yes_Painting.

Louis Menand: Louis Menand shares that Lennon and Ono really connected over Ono's *Painting to Hammer a Nail In (No. 9)*—"That's when we locked eyes . . . and she got it and I got it and, as they say in all the interviews we do, the rest is history"—but the ladder piece lives on in apocrypha as the key artwork that united them through pure positivity. In fairness, Menand notes that the story of their meeting "could all be true, who knows?" Louis Menand, "Yoko Ono's Art of Defiance, *The New Yorker*, June 13, 2022, newyorker.com/magazine/2022/06/20/yoko-onos-art-of-defiance.

Nan Shepherd: Nan Shepherd, *The Living Mountain: A Celebration of the Cairngorm Mountains of Scotland* (Edinburgh: Canongate Books, 2008), 107–108.

12: The Pointed Forest

"I was on acid": Alan Jacobson, "What's *The Point?* The Legendary 1971 Animated Feature on DVD," *Bright Lights Film Journal*, April 30, 2004, brightlightsfilm.com/whats-the-point-the-legendary-1971-animated-feature-on-dvd/.

Of the forests that the BC government defines as old-growth: Karen Price, Rachel F. Holt, and Dave Daust, *BC's Old Growth: A Last Stand for Biodiversity*, Sierra Club BC, April 2020, sierraclub.bc.ca/laststand. Thanks to Ken Wu for helping me understand these stats.

"Why aren't you on the committee?": I was officially welcomed to the committee at the December 2020 AGM.

The photos went viral internationally: In his call to action on social media, TJ Watt said, "Teal Jones has clearcut over 33 hectares (more than 33 footballs fields—or 75 when you count their clearcuts close by) of highly endangered, productive old-growth forest with approval from the NDP government and has plans for further logging on the adjacent slopes," @tjwatt, Instagram post caption, November 24, 2020, instagram.com/p/CH_n123jmRz/?igshid=wjfc1t98m6pm.

Clayoquot Sound: "Clayoquot Protests," Wikipedia, en.wikipedia.org/wiki/Clayoquot_protests.

Friends of Clayoquot Sound (FOCS) Peace Camp: "About FOCS," Friends of Clayoquot Sound, focs.ca/about-us.

UNESCO biosphere reserve designation: Interview with Jens Wieting, June 2022. Interview with Ken Wu, August 2022.

about 38 percent is protected: Interview with Jens Wieting, June 2022. Interview with Ken Wu, August 2022.

In 2018, the Sierra Club BC: Daniel Pierce, "25 Years After the War in the Woods: Why B.C.'s Forests Are Still in Crisis," *The Narwhal*, May 14, 2018, thenarwhal.ca/25-years-after-clayoquot-sound-blockades-the-war-in-the-woods-never-ended-and-its-heating-back-up.

Pacheedaht Elder Bill Jones: Sarah Cox, "Inside the Pacheedaht Nation's Stand on Fairy Creek Logging Blockades," *The Narwhal*, July 1, 2021, thenarwhal.ca/pacheedaht-fairy-creek-bc-logging.

the Pacheedaht have taken back their logging rights: "Thirteen years ago, the forested area on the nation's territory—about 163,000 hectares—was allocated to third parties through licence areas and forest tenures. The Pacheedaht didn't hold any of the logging rights. Today, the nation manages or co-manages about 140,000 cubic metres of annual cut on its territory—enough trees to fill 3,500 standard-sized logging trucks." Cox, "Inside the Pacheedaht Nation's Stand."

Teal-Jones was granted a court injunction: Cox, "Inside the Pacheedaht Nation's Stand"; "Fairy Creek Blockades," *The Narwhal*, thenarwhal.ca/topics/fairy-creek-blockade.

The RCMP moved in to remove protestors: "Fairy Creek Blockades," *The Narwhal*.

Hišuk ma c̓awak Declaration: "The Hišuk ma c̓awak Declaration," huuayaht .org/wp-content/uploads/2021/06/declaration-FINAL-signedpdf.pdf.

In response to a request from the Nations: Cox, "Inside the Pacheedaht Nation's Stand."

Deferrals aren't permanent protections: The provincial government has twin commitments to supporting Indigenous sovereignty and to acting on climate change, so it has been able to stall through short-term deferrals, but not all First Nations want deferrals. In response to the 2.6 million hectares (6.4 million acres) earmarked for deferrals in November 2021, Squamish Nation Council chairperson Khelsilem said, "The BC NDP are giving a terrible choice by only offering consent for temporary deferrals but not requiring consent for logging. Deferrals are needed now to provide the opportunity for long-term planning." Jens Wieting, "When Will the B.C. Government Prove Whether It Really Intends to Save the Last Old-Growth?" *The Narwhal*, December 22, 2021, thenarwhal.ca/opinion-bc-prove-old-growth-protections.

old-growth logging can currently be the best economic alternative: Torrance Coste, "Old-Growth 2022—Facts and Fiction," webinar, June 28, 2022, copresented with Jens Wieting, Sierra Club BC; interview with Ken Wu, August 2022.

Garry Merkel and Al Gorley: Al Gorley and Garry Merkel, *A New Future for Old Forests: A Strategic Review of How British Columbia Manages for Old Forests Within Its Ancient Ecosystems*, BC Ministry of Forests, Lands, Natural Resource Operations and Rural Development, April 30, 2020, www2.gov.bc.ca/assets/gov/farming-natural-resources-and-industry/forestry/stewardship/old-growth-forests/strategic-review-20200430.pdf. Merkel and Gorley were appointed by the BC government but worked as an independent panel.

The review calls on the BC government: Wieting, "When Will the B.C. Government." The Gorley and Merkel report didn't adequately define at-risk forests, so the government formed an additional advisory panel of scientists to do so. Its 2021 report included the finding that most valuable old-growth wasn't protected (big coastal trees, for example), and that protected old-growth wasn't all that valuable (subalpine and bog areas, for example).

the three-year framework: Coste, "Old-Growth 2022"; Insights West survey results from Coste, "Old-Growth 2022."

"When comparison is rooted in separation": Selassie, *You Belong*, chap. 2, Overdrive/Kobo.

"I'm absolutely convinced": Giant Tree Hunters.

the tallest tree in the Amazon: Jill Langlois, "Researchers Discover the Tallest Known Tree in the Amazon," *Smithsonian Magazine*, September 27, 2019, smithsonianmag.com/science-nature/researchers-discover-tallest-known-tree-amazon-180973227.

As she said in an interview: Brandon Keim, "Never Underestimate the Intelligence of Trees," *Nautilus*, October 30, 2019, nautil.us/never-underestimate-the-intelligence-of-trees-8573.

Kurt Vonnegut: Kurt Vonnegut, *Hocus Pocus* (New York: Putnam, 1990), chap. 32, Overdrive/Kobo.

Pacific willow: Pacific willow is also called shining willow, which is its name in the registry.

Oliver Burkeman writes in favor: Burkeman, *Four Thousand Weeks*, 224.

a new connection to trees through firewood: Arbutus is dense and burns long, but it's hard to come by as we gather only wood from trees that have fallen. Arbutus is too revered in this landscape to cut. Fir and cedar are desirable; balsam burns quickly but is easy and cheap to obtain.

"I've found that your chances for happiness": Ondaatje, *The Conversations*, 9.

"Roots didn't thrive when they grew alone": Simard, *Finding the Mother Tree*, 161.

Richard Powers: Everett Hamner, "Here's to Unsuicide: An Interview with Richard Powers," *Los Angeles Review of Books*, April 7, 2018, lareviewofbooks .org/article/heres-to-unsuicide-an-interview-with-richard-powers. I came to this interview via Wallace-Wells, *The Uninhabitable Earth*, 215 and endnote.

capitalism weakens in the face of antiproductive goals: Thanks to writer Kathryn Kuitenbrouwer for help with this idea.

podcast Object of Sound: Hanif Abdurraqib, "Transformation Through Repetition (feat L'Rain)," *Object of Sound* (podcast), March 18, 2022, object-of-sound.simplecast.com/episodes/transformation-through-repetition-feat-lrain-7MGRM_GL.

the algorithm that skews toward extremes: This algorithm idea is influenced by Ezra Klein, "Can We Change Our Sexual Desires? Should We?" *The Ezra Klein Show* (podcast), September 7, 2021, stitcher.com/show/the-ezra-klein-show-2/ episode/can-we-change-our-sexual-desires-should-we-86609069.

"To capitalist logic": Odell, *How to Do Nothing*, xxiii.

"Often record trees are not the perfectly formed specimens": Stoltmann, *Hiking Guide*, 28.

Mick walked around the cedar: Mick Bailey last saw this cedar in spring 2017. Bailey review.

I widened my lens: I borrowed this idea from a Buddhist mindfulness teaching, inspired by Shinzen Young's book *The Science of Enlightenment: How Meditation Works.*

"My initial interest [as a big-tree tracker]": Stoltmann, *Hiking the Ancient Forests*, 9.

"When you start on a long journey": Zen teaching, quoted in David Bayles and Ted Orland, *Art & Fear: Observations on the Perils (and Rewards) of Artmaking* (Santa Cruz, CA: Image Continuum Press, 2001).

John McPhee: John McPhee, "Structure," *The New Yorker*, January 6, 2013, newyorker.com/magazine/2013/01/14/structure.